FAITH, RACE, AND THE LOST CAUSE

Faith, Race, and the Lost Cause

CONFESSIONS OF A SOUTHERN CHURCH

Christopher Alan Graham

Foreword by the Reverend Melanie Mullen

University of Virginia Press | Charlottesville and London

University of Virginia Press
© 2023 by the Rector and Visitors of the University of Virginia
All rights reserved
Printed in the United States of America on acid-free paper

First published 2023

ISBN 978-0-8139-4879-9 (hardcover)
ISBN 978-0-8139-4880-5 (paper)
ISBN 978-0-8139-4881-2 (ebook)

9 8 7 6 5 4 3 2 1

Library of Congress Cataloging-in-Publication Data is available for this title.

Cover art: St. Paul's Episcopal Church, Richmond, photograph by Theodore Clemens Wohlbrück, ca. 1905–10. (Courtesy of the American Antiquarian Society, Wohlbruck Collection)

For the people of St. Paul's, past, present, and future

Social calamities may come not from any deliberate wickedness, but from the human inability of many people, even essentially well-meaning people, to change their frame of thought. It is lack of imagination, rather than lack of decent impulse, that may keep the ruling class in a society blind to the overturnings which are bound to come....

Where there needed to be a sensitive social conscience, there was often a blind spot. It was hard for the privileged, even the most kindly ones, to conceive that the Negro might have aspirations equal to their own.

—Rev. W. Russell Bowie, 1969

CONTENTS

Foreword by the Reverend Melanie Mullen ix

Acknowledgments xiii

Introduction 1

1. The Sacred Obligation of Slavery at St. Paul's 11
2. St. Paul's in War and after Emancipation 32
3. The Social Gospel in a Lost Cause Church 70
4. St. Paul's in Reaction 94
5. Effective Witness 121

   Epilogue: Our Sacred Obligation Now 151

Notes 163

Bibliography 195

Index 207

FOREWORD

ON HOLY SATURDAY of 2016, the day before Easter Sunday, dozens of Richmond Episcopalians from St. Paul's church shivered in the cold. They had hiked along the city's Trail of Enslaved Africans, beginning at Ancarrow's Landing on the James River, where the grief-filled experience of thousands of enslaved Africans gave meaning to the American phrase "sold down the river." The congregants stopped to say the Holy Saturday liturgy prayers at the site of human bondage and sale. The morning ended under an overpass a stone's throw from the State Capitol, in a field of unmarked graves and slave execution sites.

The idea of the liturgy was unprecedented, but it became possible because St. Paul's had undertaken to explore its own gaps in knowledge in the narrative of racial justice and the church's contribution to Southern history.

This account of a Southern church doing radical historical exploration shows the ways racial reckoning and reconciliation begins as community-led discovery. *Faith, Race, and the Lost Cause* details the work of St. Paul's History and Reconciliation Initiative (HRI), and the recovery of a generative history (one that expands the theological and moral imagination) beyond a vestigial Lost Cause theology. That is the source of mythmaking on display in the parish sanctuaries like St. Paul's, and that continues to create narratives of systemic injustice and erasure in Southern communities. It is a work of historiography and an account of community ministry of truth-telling and narrative justice.

I served St. Paul's as an Associate Rector when this study began in 2015. At that time the people of St. Paul's were unaware of the church's connection to the Confederacy. They had never really noticed the many stained-glass windows and even confessed to being confused about the "sudden interest" in uncovering their meaning. Previous generations had conflated the stories of Robert E. Lee and Jefferson Davis with biblical scenes etched in stained glass. The congregation didn't understand the incongruity of the Exodus story and the biblical touchstone of the African American experience.

By the following year, on that Holy Saturday I witnessed a collective sense of narrative justice began to take shape. Many in the church began to sense the flaws in the social imagination that the stained-glass windows and memorials on the walls of this church had shaped.

To get there, parishioners—many retirees—learned the basics of Ancestry.com, and the 1860 US Census' slave schedules, logging onto tablets and laptops before graduating on to microfilm and library trips to decipher the curlycue font of wills and manuscripts. Each lay historian had a hands-on invitation to see the myths, lies, and hard truths of their history as descendants of Virginian colonists and stewards of the capital. This parish, once known as the "Cathedral of the Confederacy," had a unique narrative debt to the South's racial identity and capacity for justice.

It is important for St. Paul's and other modern churches in the American South to understand its relation to the Lost Cause and its attribution to Christian perfection of Confederate leaders. They must discern their narrative inheritance and make sense of a faith formerly "wrapped up in reverence for Confederate saints."

Storytelling is a political act. St. Paul's work of radical remembering and gathering the fragments of identity and story revealed complex history and revealed the redemptive elements buried inside. They noticed that they worshipped and existed within an architecture of loss—that they were not the progenitors of the narrative and racial problems but were still empowered to recover lost histories and point to deep psychic cuts and gashes in the social imagination of American peoples. There was a pattern of deeming racial discussions as political, not religious, in times of discomfort and challenge. That in St. Paul's case, long after people have stopped noticing the windows, the "dangerous narratives remain alive."

St. Paul's History and Reconciliation Initiative engaged a slow process of history, allowing for the deep exploration of the structural working of racism in America and seeing St. Paul's place in it. The slowness of the process, as *this book* points out, allowed for the church to identify more than just generic complicity in slavery and segregation and more than just the outrage of the veneration of Jefferson Davis. Instead, we see St. Paul's learning a way of seeing how slavery and segregation worked for the people of St. Paul's and how they, in turn, shaped the racial landscapes around them and often harmed the dignity and bodies of Black people in it.

The HRI project made space for core questions affecting the theological lens as it progressed. Questions about what we take pride in, what we imagine God loves and approves of, who we choose to honor, and what histories we ignore and why, who is good, or what happens to ancestors and forbearers who contributed to unjust systems of oppression and exploitation. Or "is my ancestor in hell?"

Faith, Race, and the Lost Cause reminds us that the story isn't over. This church, whose leaders contributed to the bail of a jailed Jefferson Davis, promoted campaigns to disenfranchise generations of Black people and supported a diocese responsible for cultivating hostility to desegregation. There is still considerable work to do. Removing the kneelers with Confederate symbols was one small gesture toward turning around a narrative, and but the first step in a longer story.

A Rabbinic query asks, "what is the beginning of the Torah," and answers that all spirituality is rooted in "God is telling us stories." That is rooted in the socially generative, theological ideal that "God created the world because He needed to tell stories." Thus biblical scriptures describe a community of faith built on storytelling as a holy activity, and in *this book,* we see the modern storytelling work of rediscovering racial and political identities in the world.

St. Paul's efforts with its History and Reconciliation Initiative represent one part of the Episcopal Church's *Becoming Beloved Community* project. This initiative calls on parishes to begin a long journey toward "responding to racial injustice" and to become communities of "reconcilers, justice-makers, and healers." Part of the initiative includes *truth-telling* and acknowledging past harms through parish racial self-audits. With the report that served as the anchor of this book, and the other HRI projects, St. Paul's has begun that journey.

The journey often evokes a fear that many forces in our community are prepared to exploit, knowing that fear drives people toward more defensive and conservative responses. Yet, St. Paul's work shows us that we can—and have to—find our way to a shared story. If reconciliation along moral narrative has a long-term goal, it must be about reimagining who we are and what history is to be.

Faith, Race, and the Lost Cause shows us how urgently a different story needs to be told, one that helps people grasp the depth and power of racial perception. The church can go boldly into this narrative justice journey in its attempts to find what is missing in our histories, to challenge the Christian social imagination, push us to think theologically about the origins of racial and cultural identities, and toward the profound and hopeful role of the church in shaping healthful ways of understanding ourselves and preserving a just and honest history. For Christians, our work is to attend to the moral narrative in our religious mission and change our imagination. And the complicated historical journey chronicled here illuminates the unexpected gifts encountered along the way.

Reverend Melanie Mullen
Director of Reconciliation,
Justice, and Creation Care
The Episcopal Church

ACKNOWLEDGMENTS

THOUGH THIS BOOK carries my name on the cover, it is the work of a congregation.

The St. Paul's vestry, with Dabney Carr as senior warden, prompted by Rev. Wallace Adams-Riley, initiated this project in 2016, and charged the History and Reconciliation Initiative with this investigation. It has received the ongoing support of the vestry under the leadership of senior wardens Jane Nelson, Lee Switz, Dr. Joseph James, and Barbara Holley. St. Paul's clergy and staff have also provided invaluable support, including Rev. Molly Bosscher, Jason Cherry, Rev. Kelli Shipley Cooper, Mike Dabney, Rev. Rainey Dankel, Rev. Dr. Charles Dupree, Rev. Susan Eaves, Sarah Foote, Alicia Hart, Rev. Rock Higgins, Carter Johann, Rev. Melanie Mullen, Rev. Bill Queen, Lynn Williams, and Rich Wolkiewicz.

Linda H. Armstrong led the HRI Steering Committee until her untimely passing. She doggedly kept this project on track and moving forward while being an effective advocate for it with the vestry and congregation. Members of the Steering Committee have been the most steadfast advocates for this work, including Susan Bland, Lynn Blankman, Rev. Molly Bosscher, Rev. Benjamin P. Campbell, Rob Corcoran, Barbara Holley, Rev. Melanie Mullen, Dr. Christopher Reynolds, Matt Stehle, Michelle Walker, and Lynn Williams.

Numerous people have read this work in part or in whole and have provided critical feedback. Linda Armstrong, Rev. Benjamin P. Campbell, Daniel Howell, Mary Kay Huss, Rev. Canon Fletcher Lowe, Adrian Luxmoore, Jane Nelson, Mitch Oxford, and Dr. Donald Switz have offered substantive critiques and corrections. Outside of St. Paul's I have had useful conversations with Edward Ayers, Marvin T. Chiles, Christy Coleman, Julian Maxwell Hayter, Nicole Myers Turner, and Corey D. B. Walker.

Dozens of St. Paul's members have made themselves available for interviews, and for that I am grateful.

Over time the research team has included Pat Archer, Linda Armstrong, Mary Hunter Ayer, Ed Dickson, Miriam Farris, Rev. Canon Fletcher Lowe, Carol Parke, Mary Anne Ready, William Spencer, Geoffrey Switz, Jeff Turner,

Jim White, and Roger Whitfield. Anne Snyder proved a persistent researcher, companion, and morale-booster. Maritza Mercado Pechin helped with technical aspects of this work. Countless others have served as sounding boards, reviewers, critics, and sources of encouragement in large and small ways.

At University of Virginia Press, I am grateful to J. Andrew Edwards, Nadine Zimmerli, and the anonymous readers who prodded me to find and incorporate some of the more interesting stories that appear in these pages.

Every single sentence in this book bears the imprint of Anne S. Hayes and Dr. Elizabeth L. O'Leary. They shared equally the research burden with me and have read and commented on innumerable drafts. Anne's tenacious research skills and ability to tie stories together has been an utter inspiration. Beth's dedicated historical professionalism, elegance in writing and storytelling, and faithful friendship are the cornerstones of this book. The late-night email threads with Anne and Beth excitedly sharing and digesting research finds have been among the most satisfactory moments of my career as a historian. Those finds continue to this day. They have worked overtime to keep me accurate; any shortcomings and mistakes in fact and interpretation you may find, therefore, are mine alone.

FAITH, RACE, AND THE LOST CAUSE

Introduction

On June 17, 2015, a young white man infatuated with Confederate history and enthralled by narratives of racial difference murdered nine Black Christians engaged in Bible study at the Emanuel AME Church in Charleston, South Carolina. Eleven days later at St. Paul's Episcopal Church in Richmond, Virginia, the Reverend Wallace Adams-Riley asked in a sermon, "What if in this last summer of the Sesquicentennial of the American Civil War, we begin a conversation at St. Paul's about Confederate symbols here in our worship space?" The rector gestured to grand, two-story, stained-glass memorial windows picturing biblical scenes and dedicated to Jefferson Davis and Robert E. Lee that graced the sanctuary, and to small Confederate flag motifs that embellished a few wall plaques and two kneelers. He asked, "What do those images say? What do they say about us to someone, in particular, a person of color, who walks in off the street?" His query took the congregation by surprise.

Why?

Yes, St. Paul's had once embraced its identity as the "Church of the Confederacy." Here, in the gleaming white Greek temple that sits in downtown Richmond, Virginia, Confederate idols had once knelt in worship, and St. Paul's never let Richmond forget it. For generations the congregation proudly pointed to the pews where Robert E. Lee and Jefferson Davis sat and told and retold the dramatic scene of Davis, sitting in his pew, receiving a telegram from Lee announcing the fall of Petersburg at the end of the Civil War. Here, also, the tragedy of war played out in the melodramatic story of John Pegram's marriage at the St. Paul's altar less than a month before his funeral from the same spot. St. Paul's installed memorial windows and plaques not just to their members, but most prominently, to Lee and Davis themselves, and honored them with birthday observances and historical tableaux to keep their memories alive. Later, a story emerged about Lee and a Black man kneeling together at the communion rail. If one pays attention, you might also hear the echo of a tale about the wartime rector's mercy for a pair of condemned Black men, or a later generation's benevolence toward a Black church employee upon that man's death. Those stories reinforced St. Paul's—and indeed, white southerners'—

conviction that they, and only they, cared for Black people *in the right ways*. Veneration of Confederate saints and demonstration of paternalistic race relations: indeed, St. Paul's had once stood comfortably, as one observer noted, as "a silent Confederate sermon."[1]

But these stories had evaporated from St. Paul's contemporary identity. The congregation in 2015 never thought of itself as a Confederate church, especially considering the racial and cultural revanchism that "Confederate" connoted in the second decade of the twenty-first century. After all, other things had happened at the church than just the Civil War and its legacies, events that did not appeal to a tourist market but that the congregation of today knows intimately. In the early 1970s St. Paul's—a historically all-white congregation—had embarked on a remarkable transformation. Its people undertook daring outreach initiatives. Its charismatic rector at the time cultivated a Christian education program that drew scores of young families with no connection to Richmond's past. This generation of St. Paul's congregants— growing ethnically more diverse and theologically and politically liberal— became intentionally attentive to the realities of race in modern America, and unintentionally forgetful of the things that had mattered to the congregation long ago. The Lee and Davis windows, after all, did not picture those men, but biblical scenes, and the pair blended well with the twenty-three other stained-glass memorials. The small flags on the bronze plaques receded into the patina, and one had to look close to find them among the larger number of plaques devoted to parishioners with no Confederate connection at all. Indeed, by 2015, quite a number of St. Paul's people simply had not noticed the Confederate imagery in the church, let alone in its history. St. Paul's, to them, was something else entirely. Hence the surprise at Adams-Riley's suggestion that this forgotten history, this forgotten identity, still mattered.

This paradox is why St. Paul's story is so important now. Untangling and understanding it is one of the key questions of this study, and in the answer lies the complicated journey of so many white people today. Unlike most neo-Confederates who receive an inordinate amount of media attention, the majority of predominantly white institutions of long duration—churches, museums, preservation societies, charities—have adapted to new racial realities over time. Many white people today are satisfied with this progress, and their histories remain dormant or unknown. Exploring this paradox—of how history indicts and obliges even the most well-meaning—helps reveal the cognitive reasons behind hesitation and hesitancy exhibited by many white people in seeking a deeper critique and understanding of their place in our racial landscape. For instance, how do we square the sins of people who we learned to admire with their avowed nobility and generosity? How do we come to understand why, and accept that, others might have good reason to see us the way they rightly see us? Can we find a germ of goodness—something to inspire—in people who had significant shortcomings? Is this history irrelevant if we are different now? Understanding and explaining these histories provide answers that enable people to move forward. Yet too many fail to do so, and so many of us liberal-minded folks possess a benign ignorance about the past that helps produce what one-time St. Paul's rector Russell Bowie—with his own critical historical hindsight in mind—called "blind spot[s]." These are the hardest to see. I know... I have had them myself all along.

It is a universal journey that many readers may share, but not be aware of. Briefly tracing its steps—for me and for St. Paul's—can be instructive.

I came up in a relatively multicultural post–World War II, upper south metropolitan suburb that had no particular connection to history. In my earliest memories my parents modeled excellent liberal post-racialism, and my father actively stifled expressions of racism that my friends snuck into our home. "We don't say that in this house," he quietly, but with deadly seriousness, intoned. I idolized him. I didn't need to hear any explanation. I never said those sorts of things in my house, or anywhere else.

At the same time, and not knowing any reason to be conflicted, in my Industrial Arts class I made a screen print of a Confederate flag. But it wasn't the Confederate flag. It was the logo for *The Dukes of Hazzard*'s famous car, the General Lee, sporting the flag on its roof. My friend from Long Island made the same thing. My growing attachment to Confederate things, I think, began shortly thereafter in elementary school when another friend a few grades ahead came home from her first lesson about the Civil War in history class and divided up her friends by North and South based on birthplace. Since I had been born in North Carolina, she placed me on the Confederate side. I knew nothing else about it, but I had been emblazoned with an identity I could carry forward with a sense of rootedness in a transient world—that of a *southerner*. St. Paul's had several versions of this benign birth into an identity. The Confederacy happened to it and only an accident of local geography drew their future saints into their pews. Unlike me, the church conscientiously embraced the Confederacy and what it meant at the time; but for the generations of St. Paul's people afterward, like Russell Bowie, St. Paul's rector in the early twentieth century who grew up in the church, it was bestowed—uncomplicated and uncontroversial.

The meaning of Confederate identity shifted over time. St. Paul's deployed it in the 1940s to hone good citizens as young adult groups learned about leadership and faith from stories about Robert E. Lee. They mobilized it to face challenges like World War II, but they did not study the primary documents of secession to cling to that particular understanding of this history. They likely never read them. My own meaning, like so many others in the early 1980s, did not come from a reading of those documents either. It came from an affinity for countercultural rednecks like sit-com characters Bo & Luke Duke and, later, to bands like Alabama and the Allman Brothers and the easy defiance to the slick 1980s of imagining oneself a *rebel,* rather than to Confederate ancestors, of which I had none, or Confederate monuments, which one couldn't find among the strip malls of Woodbridge, Virginia. Had one charged me with complicity in Alexander Stephens's racial vision articulated in his "Cornerstone Speech," I would have been too perplexed to even be in denial.

In middle school I became, thanks to Bruce Catton and Time-Life's *The Civil War* series, infatuated with the American Civil War and shortly thereafter joined the ranks of the rapidly growing circle of reenacting hobbyists. I spent a great deal of my youth enjoying the camaraderie of the campfire and learning about the minutiae of soldier life—the majority of it while wearing Confederate gray. It was also a social club that produced meaning for me outside of historical interests. On various reenacting weekends I learned to love the Grateful Dead and roots music, had my first kiss, tasted my first alcohol, and smoked my first joint. My friends and I mocked Lost Causers before I really knew what that meant (you could just tell something wasn't right). We also wrote anti-racist language into the bylaws of our organizations, and many of us genuinely sought to understand the place of slavery in the Confederate experience. I look back now and feel a connection to impressionable young St. Paul's congregants who went to window dedications or who sat through a sermon about Robert E. Lee's virtue not because they wanted to glory in Confederate history, but because they wanted to sit near a crush or pull a prank on the dour old ladies in the sanctuary. More recent generations at St. Paul's intentionally exposed themselves to serious study of southern history. Some, like beloved parishioner, Philip J. Schwarz, produced academic study of slavery in Richmond to support historical equity in the city. As I learned more from a sober study of the Civil War, I saw my own Confederate identity as less romantic, and more problematic, just as did St. Paul's in the most recent generation.

Can you see my blind spots? I couldn't. Despite my increasingly nagging conscience, I thought I "did history" the right way, didn't see how others perceived it, and certainly didn't understand how I might have perpetuated something harmful while engaging in the relationships that had such great and good meaning to me. The same hesitant relations happened at St. Paul's, too, as it continued to rent space to Confederate heritage organizations even after the church attempted to handle them with a willful ignorance.

I spent a lifetime telling myself that I was one of the good ones; that my friends and I were honest and academic—serious historical interpreters not carried away by the Lost Cause (as I eventually came to know it) and other inaccurate nonsense. To an extent, we were, but what did it put into the world? A small bit of slightly more accurate history wrapped in a terrible way of doing it; weak Rebel yells under Confederate flags on fake battlefields littered with laughing dead men and where, somehow, the Yankees were always the bad guys—and always the losers—and with no Black people in sight in period clothing or in the audience. That made a way of imagining the past that was rooted in a dangerous history that flourished as a loaded contemporary agenda no matter what I did.

I don't reenact anymore and that decision didn't happen as a single conversion experience. It came through a slow process of learning—not just through graduate school, but also in growing into a liberal-minded adult in the world—which forced me to struggle not only with realizing the historical limitations and modern racial implications of reenacting, but also with the pain of having to abandon lifelong friendships and associations in order to ease out of the hobby. I participated longer than I wanted to, only because of the bonds of love I developed for my companions. Such renunciations can be grueling—a little bit of self-murder in fact—even if you know it's the right thing to do. And I didn't even have to come out from under several generations of attachments as St. Paul's has had to. This matches the experience of so many white southerners and white institutions. St. Paul's surprise at Adams-Riley's call stemmed from the same sense of having thought of themselves as among the good ones and having actually done race relations right—if not in the past, at least now—and not knowing what had ever been wrong.

This was the same white innocence that I had harbored for so long. Even if I loved talking about Confederate deserters and dissent on the southern homefront, I still did it in environments that only saw the tragic experience of white soldiers as the only thing that mattered about the Civil War. I didn't imagine that it simultaneously produced alienation in someone like Ta-Nehisi

Coates, who said that "[n]owhere as a Black person, do I feel myself more of a problem than at these places, premised, to varying degrees, on talking around me."[2] St. Paul's people, even if they held a liberal-minded view on race in the twenty-first century, did not think too hard about worshipping within a physical envelope that included windows and plaques dedicated to Confederate leaders and their Lost Cause, or to being an avenue for perpetuating a misunderstood story about Robert E. Lee and a Black man.

Doing things right did not somehow negate the things that had formerly been wrong. Dangerous narratives remained alive in those weak rebel yells and for the tourists who came to see windows and pews—narratives that continued to possess power. I could see, when I joined this project in 2016, that St. Paul's and I were going through this together. We still are.

While I regard myself as still doing history right, if doing it differently and in a different context, and St. Paul's thinks of itself as a racially liberal and exceedingly welcoming congregation, the work that this book represents challenges us—and people like us—to keep digging deeper into our assumptions about race and to finding a morally equitable path forward—not only about what is right and what is good, but about what history obliges us to do. For that reason, tracing this journey in these pages is a worthwhile endeavor for those also undertaking this process.

That question—of what history obliges us to do—has hounded America with ever increasing urgency. The Charleston murders set off another national wave of reckoning with Confederate iconography in American public life. The National Park Service stopped selling Confederate battle flags. Universities began renaming campus buildings. Some cities, most notably New Orleans, removed statues of Confederate leaders. And the General Convention of the US Episcopal Church passed a resolution strongly urging "all persons, along with public, governmental, and religious institutions, to discontinue the display of the Confederate Battle Flag" and pronounced the emblem at odds with "the reconciling love of Jesus Christ."[3] These efforts, however, were not just isolated exercises in iconoclasm. They represented a growing and critical mass of awareness about the persistence of white supremacy in American society. The Black Lives Matter movement (since 2014) and advocates like Michelle Alexander in her book *The New Jim Crow* (2012) had been exceedingly effective in drawing national attention to the enduring systemic racial inequalities that continued to victimize people of color in post–Civil Rights America.[4] Deep historical problems required deep historical excavation to be understood and rooted out.

The Episcopal Church had, since 2006, mobilized the language of history in its anti-racism programs. In that year, it passed resolutions calling for reparations for slavery, and for its dioceses and parishes to pursue restorative justice as well as Truth and Reconciliation-style initiatives. The church would make historical self-study a cornerstone of its 2017 *Becoming Beloved Community* program.[5] Alongside this process, the St. Paul's vestry, after several weeks of prayerful conversations with the congregation, established the History and Reconciliation Initiative (HRI) in January 2016 with the intention of examining the church's historical connection to race, slavery, segregation, and persistent discrimination in Richmond, Virginia. This history is the partial result of that work. Because of the election of Donald J. Trump to the presidency and his emboldening of racial revanchists and his stoking of a racial culture war, this work has remained tragically relevant and unfortunately necessary as a representative of some white southerners testifying to the process, risks, pitfalls, and possibilities of change.

This study begins with the question: How did the people of St. Paul's, over time, understand race and racial relations from a Christian perspective? How did they act upon those beliefs in their church and in their public lives in Richmond? Some explanation for my approach is warranted. It takes as its method of inquiry the theory of "lived religion." Defined by scholars like Robert Orsi and David Hall, lived religion is the study of how faith is enacted in daily routines. Obscuring boundaries between metaphysical and the material and "elite" and "popular" religion, lived religion is a "study of how particular people, in particular places and times, live in, with, through, and against the religious idioms available to them in a culture—all the idioms, including (often enough) those not explicitly their 'own.'"[6] So, this is not a church history. It is not a history of theology or a theological inquiry. It is a history of practice—the intersection between theology and life on the ground in ways that blended a theological imperative with a social reality that created a way of understanding the world and the relationships of people living in it. But the theological context is critical. In fact, the chapters are not organized by familiar secular periodization, but by broad theological regimes from proslavery Christianity to the Social Gospel, and later, the liberal universalism of the Cold War.

Another note is required. As you read on, you will discover that this is as much a confession as it is an explication and analysis. For that reason, I have taken a position toward what I talk about and what I do not. Specifically, this is about how the white people involved thought and acted, and about that alone. I have attempted to describe the harmful impact of that action on Black people, and the way that Black people reacted or resisted in ways that my subjects saw, even if they refused to see it. But I have averred from describing harm from a Black perspective or going inside Black churches or other refuges to extract that information. I acknowledge that that harm is a part of this story, and you should be aware that it is present on every one of these pages. But I have never felt comfortable, or equipped, in describing or articulating the pain that is neither my own, nor that of the people I study here. So many others have done so more effectively than I could. You should seek them out.

In the end, this is about how institutions change—change unintentionally by swimming in the larger, slower, evolutionary currents of society, and by the sudden shoves of that society at war. But also intentional change—a willingness to conscientiously alter a behavior, think differently, and break from the past. Both of these have happened to St. Paul's. They happen to everyone, but the latter is a choice and the impact of that choice is a function of many factors, not the least being the historical imagination.

This is also about the not-so-hidden costs of good intentions. Every generation here imagined it acted on its best intentions. This study sees that those intentions produced harm. Thus, it is a warning shot of a sort for those of us who possess supreme confidence in the righteousness of our causes, no matter how morally correct they may be—to first consider the blind spots. These are not just the potential for unintended consequences—but the assumptions about morality and action that may be rooted in a historically harmful and whiteness-based understanding of obligation, responsibility, neighborliness, and even reconciliation.

The following pages cover the full 175-year history of St. Paul's in five chronological chapters and explores the racial legacy of this church in two separate, but intertwined, ways. First is how St. Paul's communicants and clergy engaged with African Americans and racial politics in slavery, segregation, and beyond—in parochial, public, and private arenas. Second is how St. Paul's embraced and cultivated its identity as "the church where Lee and Davis worshipped." The Lost Cause ideology that St. Paul's shaped, nurtured, and long embraced was never just about grief and never just about history. The church's deep affection for the Confederacy, even when framed as the admiration of the Christian qualities of eminent men, had implications for its members' understanding of race relations in their time and for generations to follow.

Indeed, narratives are key here. Narratives of racial difference born in nineteenth century proslavery Christianity found new life in twentieth-century historical storytelling, bolstering an enduring mythology about the antebellum slave regime and a separatist war fought to defend it. Stories populated with noble white masters and mistresses watching over incompetent but content Black people happy in enslavement and, later, in post-emancipation servitude gave the past, and the future, new meaning. For so many years St. Paul's imbibed in these narratives, advanced them, based public policy and power relations on them, and in the process helped shape the racial landscape of Richmond today.

Faith, Race, and the Lost Cause reveals a rich, and at times surprising, picture of St. Paul's history. As expected, the church's founding generation—composed of Virginia's white elite—enslaved people. So too, did they maintain a fealty to ideals, both Confederate and religious, that fueled narratives of racial difference long after the end of the Civil War. In the early twentieth century, St. Paul's people reinforced racial hierarchy and paternalism while at the same time becoming deeply involved in "interracial cooperation" movements that condemned racial violence and challenged particular excesses of the Jim Crow regime. They did little to advance the Civil Rights Movement after World War II, but in the last three decades of the century they burst forth with outreach programs and an outlook designed not only to alleviate the symptoms of systemic inequalities, but also to pioneer new ways for white and Black Richmonders to relate to one another at the moment the city faced its most racially acrimonious period since Reconstruction.

Today's readers may be shocked by the racial opinions that they read in these pages. They will not, however, find the virulent and violent racists of the popular imagination. In fact, the chief challenge here may be in coming to grips with the fact that St. Paul's people always considered themselves to be acting in the best material and spiritual interests of, and with the warmest regard for, Black men and women. *And they meant it.* Oftentimes St. Paul's people emerged as the racial liberals of their day among southern white people (admittedly, not a very high standard to meet). Understanding that racial damage may come from a self-defined place of love and benevolent concern just as much as from hatred and violence is an extremely sobering thought, and one worth troubling our consciences today. St. Paul's one-time rector, the Reverend Russell Bowie, recognized it late in his life, noting that "[s]ocial calamities may come not from any deliberate wickedness, but from the human inability of many people, even essentially well-meaning people, to change their frame of thought. It is lack of imagination, rather than lack of decent impulse, that may keep the ruling class in a society blind to the overturnings which are bound to come."[7]

This is not just a singular story about one unique church. This book chronicles one small place that grappled with the big historical questions that many have had to contend with over time. None of those questions have been more consistent and more consequential than how Americans—white Americans in particular—have faced the challenges of racial equity and equality in slavery, segregation, and beyond. Examining this question compels the reader to contemplate critical questions: How do we recognize white supremacy when it does not come cloaked in racist intentionality? How do we cope with the fact that many of us grew up as white liberals but in a context that perpetuated white supremacist assumptions well after the Civil Rights revolutions of the twentieth century? Our intentional, and humble, response to these broad realizations matter.

At the heart of this book are also questions about memorials, historical narratives, how they intertwine, and the tangible ways they both inspire and harm people that all Americans need to ask. As I write this, in the iconoclastic summer of 2020 as Richmond's colossal Confederate monuments are toppling, being able to articulate those connections between statues and actions is more important than ever. Too many still argue that statues are harmless; that they possess simple and innocent messages. They do not. They never did.

Faith, Race, and the Lost Cause also asks us to consider what obligation we have to a past that is simultaneously foreign and present, even if we today actively renounce the historical sins of our predecessors. Simply removing a memorial, expressing regret, and never speaking of it again is not enough. This book argues that the evolving historical stories we tell matter, in very tangible ways.

Just as St. Paul's people grounded their historical connections in the Confederacy for themselves in the nineteenth and twentieth centuries, we can now look upon St. Paul's broader history to make meaning for ourselves in the twenty-first century. Doing so is more than just about correcting the historical record. It is about doing justice.

1 | The Sacred Obligation of Slavery at St. Paul's

IN 1854, in Richmond, Virginia, Edward Bozeman, Hannah Campbell, and Milly Harris, free people of color, and Joe, Dick, and William Christian, enslaved, assembled "in a house occupied by a free woman named Martha Ann Trent." Their gathering attracted the attention of Richmond police who surrounded the Trent house, arrested the attendees, and presented them to the magistrate, charged with unlawful assembly. Officers called the scene "completely ludicrous." The *Dispatch* reporter described the accused's "shouting, singing and stamping" as a "kind of religious gathering."[1]

The reporter's sarcasm obscures the actual intent of the gathering—perhaps he mocked a routine party. But had it actually been religious, his disdain reflected the anxieties that white people had about Black people's religious lives and practices. White people worried, first, about interaction of enslaved and free Blacks away from the surveillance of masters. In fact, since 1832, state law had prohibited gatherings of Black citizens for religious purposes without the supervision of a white minister.[2] Second, the reporter's mockery of the scene as ridiculous reflected widespread belief that Black Christians could not understand proper religion. Third, that a superficial grasp at Christianity was actually a surreptitious cover for conspiracies to do mischief to white people, or to plot an escape. These anxieties were shaped by an ever-evolving set of circumstances in the pre-emancipation slaveholding states. Slavery flourished with the opening of the cotton frontier, and proslavery politicians in the 1850s flexed a remarkable influence over United States policies at home and abroad. As an economic system, slaveholders operated as ruthless labor managers, driving men, women, and children with the lash and the balance sheet. As a cultural system, slaveholders positioned themselves as loving mentors to Black people, and the actions of Black people themselves in response often produced a remarkably nuanced way of social interaction between enslavers and those they enslaved.[3] This often contradictory mix of realities and aspirations, fears and desires, produced anxieties about Black religious autonomy and shaped how Richmond's religious people practiced their faith in the antebellum years.

William Barret owned three of the men arrested at Martha Ann Trent's party. They were among the fifty-five men Barret enslaved, most of whom worked in his tobacco factory, one of the largest in Richmond in the 1850s.[4] Among them had been Henry Brown, whom Barret had inherited from his father in Louisa County. Brown had regarded Barret as a relatively lenient master, but he reconsidered as Barret—a well-known Christian—stood by as he allowed Brown's wife and child to be sold away.[5] Brown famously made his escape to Philadelphia in a box. Barret's factory produced "Negro Head" brand plug tobacco, and it was the scene of frequent violence between Black workers and white supervisors.[6] Barret contributed to the founding of St. Paul's and rented a pew there. After he died in 1871, Barret's estate gifted $50,000 to the St. Paul's Church Home for Orphans. In the 1850s, when he approached the altar rail for communion, he stood—and knelt—alongside peers like Bolling Haxall, James Dunlop, Joseph Reid Anderson, and others among Richmond's merchant and industrial elite.[7] St. Paul's Episcopal Church, founded in 1844 and consecrated in 1845 at the corner of Grace and Ninth Streets just across from the Virginia state capitol in Richmond, grew in this mix of religious-racial anxiety and ostentatious wealth and power. They could not disentangle faith from slavery. Indeed, communicants at St. Paul's and Episcopalians across Richmond and Virginia followed their church's guidance in understanding slavery and the relationship between white and Black people. That relationship—defined by masters—consisted of a mutual obligation for white people to nurture and care for the enslaved, and for Black people to happily submit to and faithfully serve white people. It rested on assumptions white people rooted both in the Bible and in day-to-day prejudice—that they were competent and benevolent, and Black people were childlike and dangerous. White Christians cast it as a sacred obligation, and it became a foundational element of the narrative of racial difference that long outlasted slavery.[8] These faithful men and women, then, weighed their souls on the scale of proslavery Christianity.

The houses, outbuildings, streets, and alleys in 1840s Richmond teemed with free and enslaved Black people, living in proximity with white people. Domestic and industrial slaves slept in attics and outbuildings of Richmond's cramped townhomes and urban estates.[9] Because most Black people living downtown in white households were domestic workers, most were women. For this reason, Allen Lyons's household in 1840 was unusual. Twenty-four people lived there: Lyons, his wife, six sons, and two daughters. Fourteen enslaved people lived there as well, including ten Black men, and four Black women. The census taker listed fourteen people as employed in "manufacturing and trade," presumably Lyons himself, the ten Black males, and at least three of his sons.[10] Lyons was not a member of St. Paul's, but a stonemason who likely utilized his enslaved laborers in laying the foundation and other stonework of St. Paul's alongside white workers under the direction of architect Thomas Stewart. Enslaved artisans working at Tredegar Iron Works, owned by the church vestryman Joseph Reid Anderson, likely crafted the ironwork used at St. Paul's as well.[11] They all stayed busy in Richmond's building boom in the 1840s.

Richmond churches experienced explosive growth alongside the city in those years as they hustled to keep up with the increasing sophistication and modern ecclesial fashions. Richmond's religious people drew on trendy neoclassical and Gothic Revival styles in a host of new church buildings radiating westward from downtown. First Baptist Church established a new building on Broad Street across the street from the State Capitol in 1841, and Second Presbyterian constructed a Gothic edifice in 1848, complete with stained-glass windows just downhill in a fancy new residential section. Richmond's growing German populations erected the German Lutheran Evangelical Church in 1843. St. James's Episcopal began, with members from Monumental Church in a slightly older but still wealthy neighborhood at Fifth and Marshall in 1838. St. Peter's Catholic Church, built in 1834, and Centenary Methodist, in 1843, dotted Grace Street, Richmond's poshest new neighborhood.

When First Baptist moved to its new building, it shed an enormous Black congregation that became First African Baptist. It remained in the old church building on the eastern slope of Navy Hill that overlooked Shockoe Valley, home to Richmond's reeking tanyards and the great slave trading houses that powered the interstate trade. First African's congregation numbered over 1,000 in 1841 and rapidly doubled becoming the *de facto* center of Richmond's African American community.[12] Beyond the Valley rose Church Hill, once wealthy but now working class, with homes for workers that served the industries and warehouses on the waterfront below. Atop Church Hill sat St. John's, Richmond's oldest Episcopal congregation.

Just up the hill from First African Baptist, the Episcopalians remained at the moldering Monumental Church. Monumental had sat at the very heart of Richmond's political and cultural life for several generations. Founded in 1811, the congregation had sometimes met in the state capitol building and included luminaries like John Marshall as members.[13] But in the 1840s, after the once-novel octagonal sanctuary had become dingy, and the center of fashionable culture had moved west, the still wealthy congregation could not resist a relocation. In 1843, the year after the death of Monumental's rector and Bishop of the Diocese of Virginia, Richard Channing Moore, the new rector, the Reverend William Norwood, most of the congregation, and all of the vestry established St. Paul's. Two years later, the gleaming white Greek Revival building with columned porticos, a soaring pointed steeple, and a large sanctuary illuminated by two-story tall clear glass windows was consecrated on the corner of Ninth and Grace Streets.[14] In 1850, a pedestrian could take in Thomas Jefferson's state capital, the towering new George Washington on the statehouse grounds, and St. Paul's all in one glance.

The growth in churches reflected a tremendous expansion of Richmond as a population and manufacturing center. In 1830, 16,060 people called Richmond home—7,755 white people 6,345 enslaved Black people, and 1,960 free Black people. That number increased by over ten thousand in two decades: in 1850, 15,273 white, 11,699 enslaved Black, and 2,576 free Black men and women crowded Richmond's streets.[15] The city's white elite thrived on grain milling, tobacco production, the downriver slave trade, slave renting, shipping, iron making, and a host of commercial, legal, financial, and professional services.

The founding generation at St. Paul's dominated that landscape. They came chiefly from the merchant class, men who owned and operated stores that sold everything from fabric and farm equipment to jewelry and grain. James Brooks's retail establishment, Brooks & Bell, was located on the bustling commercial corridor on Main Street in Shockoe Slip, while Brooks lived in the fashionable Court End neighborhood on Navy Hill.[16] Also on Main Street, Robert Gwathmey ran a grocery and commission store where he advertised a variety of services, including selling "all kinds of produce, hire out Negroes, collect money's &c, at the usual per cent."[17] James Allen partnered with co-congregants Isaac and Griffin Davenport in a commission house in Shockoe Bottom that sold or auctioned all manner of dry goods and farm produce. Though no St. Paul's members ranked among the slave trading magnates like Silas Omohundro or Robert Lumpkin, these commission and merchant houses did occasionally sell enslaved people. Davenport, Allen & Co., for instance, in the course of conducting estate auctions, regularly included Black men and women in their inventory.[18] So did Henry Wood Moncure and his kinsman James Dunlop who also operated an auction house in Shockoe Bottom.[19]

Moncure's partner Dunlop engaged in much larger businesses. He formed a different partnership with Henry Moncure and another St. Paul's member,

Thomas McCance, to mill flour at a factory in Manchester on the south side of the James River; by the 1850s they were engaged in international commerce. As the owner of the commission house, he served as a broker for slave hiring at the Midlothian coal pits in Chesterfield County, and likely had an ownership stake in that operation. Dunlop also served on the board of directors at the Farmer's Bank of Virginia along with at least four other St. Paul's members.[20]

Other men excelled at industries along the James River straight downhill from the Grace Street corridor. Bolling Haxall and his brothers owned the Haxall Flour Mills, producing flour on the river just below the James River and Kanawha Canal. The extended Haxall family diversified into railroads and insurance.[21] Abraham Warwick took ownership of the pioneering Gallego Mills, also producing flour for an international market.[22] Just up the river from the flour mills lay Joseph Reid Anderson's Tredegar Iron Works. William H. Macfarland, president of the Farmer's Bank of Virginia, also invested in industry, partnering with Bolling Haxall in the Belle Isle Iron Works.[23] Macfarland parlayed his business success into political leadership, leading Richmond's Whigs and representing the city in the General Assembly.

Not all of the first generation were grandees. Many of the merchants owned rather modest shops. Some members clerked in those shops and lived in boardinghouses. Not an insignificant number of early members were wives of professional men, like Gertrude Marshall, wife of a Gallego Mills bookkeeper, and Elizabeth Tucker, wife of a Richmond physician.[24] Yet all members from heads of industry to a non-slaveholding widow lived enmeshed with slavery in the city.

Most St. Paul's members listed as vestry and pewholders in 1845 enslaved people. Thirty-five such men and women appear in the 1850 United States Census Slave Schedule, owning from two to eighteen people and averaging about nine per household. An 1849 list of St. Paul's members reveals an average of five enslaved people per slaveholding household. Non-slaveholders in St. Paul's congregation tended to be older people, widows and widowers, members who had not yet left their parents' households, or single people who lived with other families or in boardinghouses. While lacking extant documentation of slave ownership, however, many may have hired the labor of rented workers.

St. Paul's people thoroughly engaged in the practice of slavery in Richmond in ways both mundane and terrible. In this city, thousands of Black people did not work for their enslavers, but for people who hired them from their owners. St. Paul's people both hired enslaved people and rented them out. Mary and Charles Barney, for instance, solicited for a "well recommended" dining room servant for their Main Street home.[25] Others like Miles George hired out people they owned. George advertised "a small GIRL, suitable for a NURSE" for rent.[26] Hired slaves, beyond the direct control of owners, had greater opportunity to escape bondage altogether. Another of Miles George's people, named Hubbard, "left the Tobacco Factory of Messrs. Grant and Bennett," where he had worked, and George offered $50 for his return.[27]

Hubbard was not the only captive of a St. Paul's parishioner to slip his or her bondage. Julia Mitchell's man, Stepney, ran away in 1859. Her brother-in-law Samuel P. Mitchell, also a St. Paul's member, posted the runaway ad and described Stepney as "a good looking man, but a little stooping and round shouldered." He offered a reward of $50 if captured in Virginia and $100 if captured out of state. Stepney likely stowed away on a ship at Shockoe Bottom, and he made his way to Philadelphia where he reported to William Still, a prominent conductor on the Underground Railroad. Stepney, revealing his last name as Brown, told Still that he had belonged to Julia Mitchell, who was "decidedly stingy and unkind, although a member of St. Paul's church." Brown sought his freedom because, "I believed that I had a right to be a free man." William Still directed him north, where he crossed into Canada at Niagara Falls and settled in Brantford, where he joined the First Baptist Church and turned his thoughts to marriage.[28]

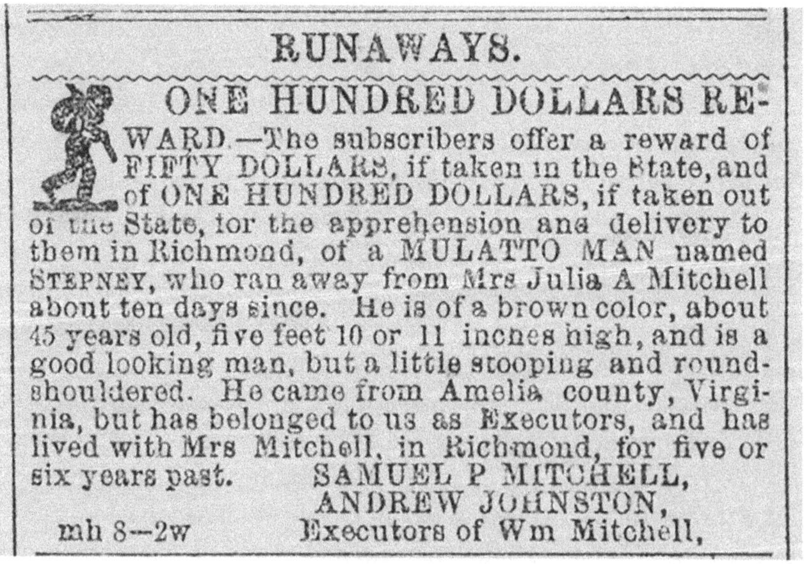
RUNAWAYS.

ONE HUNDRED DOLLARS REWARD.—The subscribers offer a reward of FIFTY DOLLARS, if taken in the State, and of ONE HUNDRED DOLLARS, if taken out of the State, for the apprehension and delivery to them in Richmond, of a MULATTO MAN named STEPNEY, who ran away from Mrs Julia A Mitchell about ten days since. He is of a brown color, about 45 years old, five feet 10 or 11 inches high, and is a good looking man, but a little stooping and round-shouldered. He came from Amelia county, Virginia, but has belonged to us as Executors, and has lived with Mrs Mitchell, in Richmond, for five or six years past.

SAMUEL P MITCHELL,
ANDREW JOHNSTON,
Executors of Wm Mitchell,

mh 8—2w

FIGURE 1. Advertisement for the return of Stepney Brown. (Library of Virginia)

The Sacred Obligation of Slavery at St. Paul's | 17

FIGURE 2. Julia Mitchell, the St. Paul's member who Stepney Brown called "decidedly stingy and unkind." (American Civil War Museum)

Bondage in slaveholding Richmond, dominated by the great industries commanded by St. Paul's members, differed from the traditional picture of rural plantation slavery. In 1840, enslaved workers comprised 43 percent of Richmond's industrial workforce; and, ten years later, that number had increased to 48 percent.[29] St. Paul's vestryman Joseph Reid Anderson pioneered the use of enslaved people in southern industry at his Tredegar Iron Works where he purchased enslaved men and trained them as iron workers. When a group of his white workers struck in protest, Anderson fired them and purchased more Black men. He set 117 enslaved people to work at his factory in 1848 and 80 in 1860.[30] Bolling Haxall owned the Haxall Flour Mill, and his brother, William Henry, worked as a manager there. Bolling also served as president of the Old Dominion Iron & Nail Works and had an interest in the Richmond & Petersburg Railroad Company. They and their wives, Anne and

Clara, attended church at St. Paul's regularly.³¹ The firm of Haxall & Brother owned eighteen men valued at $15,680 in 1856, and Bolling separately owned another eighteen for use at his home and farms.³² Pewholder James Dunlop routinely partnered with banker William Macfarland and others in the endorsement and employment of slave insurers and slave hiring brokers.³³ Dr. James B. McCaw provided services to slave insurer, Lynchburg Hose and Fire Insurance Company, as a medical examiner.³⁴ St. Paul's people were fully engaged in Richmond's slave-based economy.

White Richmonders, preoccupied with the surveillance of free and enslaved Black people, sat atop a bustling city of semi-autonomous African Americans. In the city's taverns and alleys, Black people participated in illicit activities like gambling, drinking, and having sex in racially mixed places. In 1864 one man, named Grandison and owned by St. Paul's white sexton William Irving, ran an illicit confectionery stand in the alley behind the church.³⁵ White authorities occasionally worried about the dangers of unsupervised and unruly Black people and periodically tightened municipal laws on their movement and associations.³⁶ Black people of all status, with proper papers in hand, gathered for church, social, and other activities.

City police arrested those without evidence of permission to move about and congregate. For instance, Stepney Brown's friend, John Dungee, who escaped shortly after Brown, had previously been detained as a participant alongside a man named William owned by William C. Allen of St. Paul's, in what the *Dispatch* called "The United Sons of Ham." This underground organization was a religious meeting that convened at night in John Caskie's backyard to pray and to discuss plans to run away. We do not have the words of the Sons themselves, but their action of combining expressions of faith with advocacy for freedom indicates an altogether different religious priority for Black people, and a complete rejection of proslavery Christianity's claims of beneficial spiritual nurture within bondage. In one scandalous 1852 case, about 100 free and enslaved Black people, several of whom belonged to members of St. Paul's, were seized by police for attending a dinner in the basement of the Washington Hotel directly across the street from the church. The hotel manager, W. Bowen, had permitted a dining servant to host the dinner. News of the event spread and the city fined managers for permitting the unlawful assemblage. Following negative publicity, during which Bowen denied all responsibility, the hotel's owner and St. Paul's donor Mann S. Valentine sold the business, which reopened in 1853 as the Monument Hotel.³⁷

Some white people fretted about the presence of so many free African

Americans in Richmond. Their presence complicated the strict binary that held white people as citizens and Black people as slaves. Many Virginians, including Richmond Episcopalians, joined the American Colonization Society after its 1816 founding. Advocates of colonization—or the deportation of free Black people to Africa—described the initiative as beneficial to emigrants who could proselytize both the religion and the republican government they had learned in America. Emigration also served as a test for the potential end of slavery. Mass emigration could be a solution, reasoned the Colonization Society, because in their view white and Black people could not live together in freedom.

Many Society members also regarded free Black people as a dangerous example among enslaved people in America.[38] John C. Rutherfoord, a member of St. Paul's, thought so. As a delegate in the General Assembly, Rutherfoord pressed for removal of free Black Virginians in 1853. He considered them "idle, ignorant, degraded, and immoral." They, he claimed, promoted crime and encouraged enslaved people to steal from their masters. Even worse, Rutherfoord continued, free Black people transmitted abolitionist ideas to the enslaved and encouraged a "spirit of discontent" among them. Rutherfoord felt that they, ultimately, threatened "the peace and happiness alike of the master and the slave." William Meade, bishop of the Diocese of Virginia, supported colonization, and expressed an interest in sending his own enslaved people to Liberia. The managers of the Colonization Society of Virginia met in the St. Paul's basement vestry room in 1849 with William Macfarland, John Rutherfoord, John Steger, Thomas Ellis, and J. J. Fry in attendance for a routine meeting.[39]

In Rutherfoord's appeal lay the fundamental tensions, and contradictions, of the way white people imagined slavery. First, it was absolutely race-based, and free Black people represented a cognitive dissonance. Second, slavery should operate smoothly, meaning that white and Black people should exist in harmony defined by the terms of slavery. White people who defined themselves as conscientious, enlightened, and liberal therefore worked to rid slavery of what they considered its problematic elements—violence, family separation, and worst of all, unwarranted notions of freedom. These white people imagined themselves as benevolent, patient, and loving masters.

St. Paul's people concerned themselves with fulfilling their obligations as paternalistic masters. St. Paul's register, Thomas Ellis, as well as Joseph Reid Anderson and Bolling Haxall, for instance, signed an 1852 clemency petition for Black tobacco worker Jordan Hatcher, who had killed his supervisor at the Walker and Harris tobacco factory.[40] Later, St. Paul's rector, the Reverend Charles Minnigerode extended the same advocacy to two enslaved men who had been condemned to death for burgling his house in 1865.[41] Such cases gave Christian masters the opportunity to demonstrate their capacity for mercy within a legal relationship that required none and a social order that demanded violence.

These white masters who styled themselves benevolent and slavery beneficial genuinely believed it to be so. It strains credulity that they did not more readily testify to the violence, rape, family separation, grief, and human suffering that they undoubtedly witnessed, and that many of them undoubtedly inflicted. Many of their co-religionists did, and often spoke of alleviating the *evils* of slavery, but not slavery itself.[42] Still, in their self-deceptions, they adhered to the narrative that they were good, even if in a system that was—they admitted—occasionally not. Their descendants latched onto this claim and dismissed any other account of slavery to build the lie of "the good master," and their white compatriots believed it.

Aside from legalistic and material considerations that paternalists imagined made them good masters and made slavery function efficiently, another matter concerned them. Effective slavery, the Christians among them believed, depended entirely on the evangelization of enslaved people and of the masters themselves. In fact, some argued, that was the whole point of American racial slavery.

White Southern Protestants almost unanimously agreed that the Bible and Christianity justified slavery. They developed a theology and a theory of practice for proper Christian slaveholding and declared that attempts to end slavery were attempts to subvert God's will and true religion. Virginia Episcopalians, most notably Bishop William Meade and the diocesan newspaper the *Southern Churchman,* wrote passionately about the core claim of proslavery Christianity—abolitionists were "the enemy of the Black man," because "he denies him the opportunity for religious development." Slavery, then, not freedom, was the key to evangelization of Black people, in the opinion of white Christians. They reasoned that without the formalized oversight made possible by slavery, they could not mentor Black people, nor could Black people find proper religion on their own. This germ of a thought grew to a multifaceted religious, social, and political narrative that eventually encompassed a worldview that a nation could be built on.

Bishop Meade entered early into the proslavery Christianity cause with his 1836 publication, *Sermons Addressed to Masters and Servants*, but the Diocese of Virginia did not actively engage in proslavery practice until the 1850s. (Meade's publication came to the attention of Frederick Douglass, who ferociously termed the bishop's prescription for punishment "evangelical flogging.")[43] In more prosaic arenas, the diocese expended a great deal of time in the 1850s in institution building—shoring up the Episcopal High School in Alexandria and the Women's School in Staunton. Bishops and clergy also worked to raise money for the contingent fund for retired ministers and to encourage members to subscribe to the diocesan newspaper, the *Southern Churchman*. The diocese had perhaps been distracted from pursuing the evangelization of enslaved people because it spent a great deal of intellectual energy pushing back against the Oxford Movement—an attempt by English churchmen to return to some Roman Catholic theology and practice.[44] By judging congregational interests through these initiatives, clergy often assessed the spiritual health of a church. The same was true for active religious mentoring of enslaved people.

Southern Protestants considered the compatibility of Christianity and slavery self-evident. Preachers across the South—notably Presbyterian Robert Lewis Dabney in Richmond and Episcopalian Thomas Roderick Dew at William & Mary—looked to scripture to detail a Biblical justification for slavery. In short, they believed that Black people, inherently incapable of spiritual maturity, should *willingly* subject themselves to the moral guidance and instruction of white people. In fact, evangelists considered this to be the true worth of slavery—bringing irreligious people to Christ. Black and white souls may have been equal before God, but on Earth, God ordained the dominance of one over the other. To be a good Christian meant to honor that order, and honoring that order meant that white Christians had an obligation to oversee the Christian education of Black people.[45] The *Southern Churchman* considered the matter of the moral and political rightness of slavery a settled issue but insisted that the more pressing question lie only in how "the slave and his master both be brought into subjection to Christ."[46]

With her underscored words giving emphasis, Richmond Episcopalian Sarah Benetta Valentine, a congregant at St. James's, boldly articulated her proslavery Christianity in 1860:

> God rules the soul of Southern men as well as those of others who despise them. He alone it is who tells in His own Sacred Word those duties which are only ours. God in the prolongation of time, we feel can have

but one design. It is the salvation of immortal souls. Oh if we were at this moment permitted to sum up in Heaven those souls around the Great White Throne, that from the captive body fled to thank the Providential Power that led them out from heathen lands to bask in His own "marvelous light!" God hath in a mysterious union forever united the master and slave. Man may not, *man cannot put them asunder.* Ah when the great day on which all hearts shall stand revealed arrives,—we shall not tremble at the thought that we enslaved our brother, but if we have neglected to *observe the meaning of that providence* that led us thus to act, then shall we find ourselves indeed "unprofitable servants" to the best of Masters. Irrevocable then will be our doom.[47]

It is a most difficult thing to untangle. These Christian slaveowners recoiled at the idea of inflicting physical and psychic violence on their enslaved people—the *Southern Churchman* advocated not for the end of slavery, but the "annihilation of the *evils* of slavery." And they worked to alleviate those evils. Parishioner John C. Rutherfoord struggled to maintain control of his enslaved people without being perceived as cruel. His written instructions for their management by plantation overseers includes injunctions against stripping of women, making threats, and cursing. Yet at the same time they lived comfortably within—and directed—a larger social and political world that not only countenanced control through violence and terror but demanded it as the general operating principle.[48]

That larger proslavery world sometimes misunderstood the solicitousness of white Christians toward Black people. The Reverend Adam Empie of St. James's Episcopal Church in Richmond had, earlier in his career, concluded an unhappy tenure as president of William & Mary in part because members of Bruton Parish Church had objected to his efforts to reach out to Black people in Williamsburg. Others had to assert their proslavery bona fides in no uncertain terms, as Bishop Meade discovered in 1859. In his zeal for religious instruction of slaves, he uttered words that some people mistook for the social elevation of Black people to equality with white people. Meade and his supporters shot back that, in ministry to slaves, spiritual freedom always trumped earthly liberty, and that Black people should "rejoice in the many spiritual blessings connected with" slavery.[49]

Thus, proslavery Christians had no interest in abolishing slavery. They didn't apologize for it or use it as a transparent cover for economic gain. Their theology was not a balm to a nagging conscience. The did not regard their scriptural views as a distortion, but as orthodox, grounded firmly in reasoned assessment of the Bible. They genuinely believed that God blessed racial hierarchy and slavery, that they did genuine good by practicing it, and that any attempt to force its end was an attack on God's will. They were proud of the system, even imagined themselves martyrs because the rest of the western world in general, and abolitionists in particular, condemned them for it. Proslavery Christians sought to reform slavery within the parameters of a doctrine of Christian slaveholding wherein masters treated their "servants" with charity. Their religious instruction of slaves supported a vision of slavery improved and secured, not abolished.

Proslavery Christians, Episcopalians among them, then, proudly embraced slavery, and they gladly shouldered what they considered to be a sacred obligation to guide the religious education of Black people.[50] Thus, proslavery Christians set out to conduct Sunday Schools for Black people and to concern themselves with the promulgation of sound theology for the people they enslaved.

Across the slaveholding South, since the 1830s, the Presbyterian, Methodist, and Baptist churches had developed what they called the "mission to the slaves." This consisted of efforts to create—through catechisms, hymns, and sermons—an environment in which enslaved people could encounter proper Christianity as defined by white authority. In the Georgia and South Carolina lowcountry, with its Black majorities, white Christian slaveowners proved successful in building large stand-alone Black congregations. In upcountry regions, churches made more concerted efforts to fold Black people into existing white congregations.[51]

The Diocese of Virginia did not initially expend a great deal of effort in advancing a mission to the enslaved. (The Diocese of South Carolina, reportedly, did, and Virginians envied their apparent successes.) Diocesan journals are flecked with occasional encouragements to minister to Black people and expressions of hope that efforts by clergy might cultivate their greater interest in the Episcopal Church.[52] In the early 1850s, Bishop Meade, who had long lamented the lack of Episcopal outreach, promoted the cause by commissioning an anthology of sermons designed for both Black and white people.[53]

In *Plain Sermons for Servants,* clergy from across Virginia contributed thirty-six sermons on such topics as "The Refreshing Grace of the Gospel," "God's Wondrous Love to Sinners," and "Sin a Disease—Cured by Christ." The bulk of the sermons, on conventional evangelical topics of the day, might not have been different from those delivered to any white congregation except for the presence of four sermons composed by Meade and the Reverend Thomas Castleman of Staunton. One, "To Masters and Mistresses," instructs owners on their obligations to slaves. "God hath given us an extraordinary authority over our slaves" the sermon claims. Castleman's contribution, "Servants should Obey their Masters," draws on Colossians 3:22 in its charge that "servants obey in all things your masters." Other sermons, "Duties of Servants to God" and "Duties of Servants to Masters and Fellow Servants," reinforced for both masters and enslaved people that adhering to mutual obligations of virtue and control, as well as duty and subjection, is a Christian act.[54]

In 1856, after nearly a decade of inconsistent leadership at St. Paul's, the Reverend Dr. Charles Frederick Minnigerode ascended to the rectorship and mobilized his new congregation for a rigorous program of fundraising and missionary outreach. In the 1857 parochial report to the Diocesan Convention, Minnigerode reported an increase in the Sunday School, the organization of a Children's Missionary Society, and a Ladies Sewing Society "for the support of a colporteur," the dispatch of funds to the Episcopal missions in Liberia and China, increased fundraising for the Episcopal Church's Domestic Missions (outreach work west of the Mississippi River), the "fund for disabled clergymen," and the building of new churches and missions in Richmond.[55] Though Minnigerode had a keen interest in missionary work, diocesan clergy at large fully embraced evangelism to slaves as a category of spiritual action that augured well a congregation's spiritual health.

From its founding in 1845, St. Paul's sponsored Sunday Schools. These sessions appear to have been for white children with an exception in 1847. That year, St. Paul's founding rector, the Reverend William Norwood reported to the diocese that the parish operated two Sunday Schools, "one of which is for the oral religious instruction of colored children, and has an attendance varying from 130 to 150."[56] Norwood emphasized oral instruction, of course, because of legal prohibition against teaching literacy to enslaved people. Why this Sunday School at St. Paul's appears only in 1847 is unknown, but no evidence exists to suggest that it continued. Interestingly, in the same year, Joseph Reid Anderson secured the services of the Episcopal missionary in Richmond, the Reverend William Duval, to preach "to the colored people at Tredegar Works."[57] St. James's Episcopal Church in Richmond, under the rectorship of Adam Empie and later Joshua Peterkin, nurtured a more rigorous Sunday School program for African Americans. William H. Richardson superintended the school, and Sarah Valentine—daughter of merchant and

St. Paul's donor Mann Valentine—taught there.[58] Her description of those classroom experiences is instructive.

In letters to family members, Valentine admitted feeling the weight of her obligation. She quavered before a room of twenty-six Black "scholars . . . not only children but gray-haired men and women," who looked to her "to keep [their] interest alive." But she steeled herself with the thought that she worked for God's glory, not her own, and that whatever shortcomings in her delivery of Gospel messages would be made up with "the manifest Presence."

Valentine maintained an attitude common to proslavery Christians—that Black people possessed a great piety and desire for learning but lacked the capacity to learn Christian truths on their own. Yet she was not imperious in her pedagogy. On one occasion, she wrote, "an old colored woman (sufficiently advanced in years to have been *my grandmother*) took a seat in my class." Uncertain of the woman's theology, but certain that Black people "often have peculiar notions," Valentine approached her tentatively, "fearful of coming in collision with some, which though harmless in themselves, lead on to error I would not for the whole universe have said anything that would in future keep her from coming for instruction, and yet I was resolved to compromise on no ground, which might induce in her wrong views." Valentine found great solemnity in this moment—wanting to test and instruct the woman, but not wanting to alienate her—and imagining that God waited impatiently at the outcome in order to bestow praise or scorn on his "ambassador." She continued,

> I said
> "Aunty I have just been telling these children (so that she might not think I imagined *her* a subject for instruction in a Sunday school), that the sin of *Adam,* has made *them* sinners also, from their very babyhood, and that God has declared that 'the soul that sinneth, it shall surely die;' now I asked them if this was the case, *how* were they ever to get into Heaven; and they told me that if they were born sinners, and God hated sin, that they knew they could not go there." I told her I then asked them why they went to church, or came to Sunday school but they could only laugh with perplexity. I had asked them if they had never heard in the Bible a remedy for this; One who dying for them had saved *them* from death. They then knew what I meant. I said, Aunty *you know who this was;* she immediately with a smile of real pleasure said, 'Oh yes Mistress

> I trust I know Him for many years, Oh yes marm dat I does know Him.' I found her a humble Christian, and we talked much together. I told her that I had said to my class, that God had called me *that very evening* to talk with them of Him, and that I should be called to give an account of how I had done this work. The old woman immediately gave me an idea which I had not thought of, she turned to the class and said, "Yes honey and they got to give thar account, for not 'tending as they ought, stead of trifling and playing."

Valentine considered it a spiritual triumph and a "reconciliation" that she and the old woman agreed on the point "of the fall and redemption of man."[59]

In Sarah Valentine's remarkable letter is a hint of why Black people might have attended white-sponsored Sunday Schools: a *relatively* kind solicitation of spiritual needs. But we don't know the opinion of her older pupil. Perhaps it was more akin to Frederick Douglass's observation that, "[t]he slave-holders doom the slave to ignorance first, and then take advantage of his ignorance."[60] But Valentine's self-satisfaction is far more apparent. In it lay the roots of the southern white insistence—both before and after emancipation—that white people had faithfully tended to the religious lives of the people they enslaved. It served to obscure the physical and emotional violence inflicted on bondspeople every day, and the condescending way of paternalism, too. White southerners held on to their story and never considered the alternative.

But it is still a complex missive. One striking part of Valentine's letter is the sense that white churchmen could not force Black people into churches, but instead they had to appeal to them. Indeed, many of the people owned by St. Paul's members exerted a great deal of religious autonomy within other denominations. In fact, thousands of Richmond's enslaved and free Black people worshipped at the First African Baptist Church on the next block over from Monumental Church.[61] Two other Baptist churches with predominantly Black membership emerged in this period—Second African Baptist (1846) and Ebenezer Baptist (1858). Slavery connected St. Paul's to those churches as well. Samuel P. Mitchell of St. Paul's for instance, owned Charles Matthews, the choir director at Ebenezer.[62] A number of St. Paul's members owned congregants at First African Baptist. William Macfarland, the church's senior warden, owned Mary Robinson, a First African member, and Poiteaux Robinson owned Richard Evans. The Warwick family, particularly Abraham Warwick, held ownership of at least four First African members in the late 1840s.[63]

While Black people flooded into Baptist and Methodist churches, they assiduously avoided the Episcopal Church. St. Paul's stood as a prime example. Between the first parochial report to the diocese (1846) until 1860, its rectors never reported more than six people of color as official communicants and, at that number, only once in 1856. The number of Black communicants consistently sat at three in 1852 and 1853, and one person remained on the rolls in 1857. Even before Assistant Bishop John Johns consecrated the new church in the fall of 1845, its vestry set official policy about segregated seating. They resolved on October 22 that "the West Gallery be appropriated to persons of color, to be used by them free of charge, except that if colored persons shall desire to pay rent for the privilege of having a seat, or seats."[64] Unnamed attendants who may have accompanied congregants as nursemaids or drivers occupied the gallery, and the sexton, William Irving, closely policed their behavior.[65] The handful of documented Black communicants occupying those pews were John Hilton, Margaret Tyler, and Nancy Scott (all confirmed in 1846); and John Davis and Walker Wilson (baptized in 1848).[66] Nancy Scott is the only one of these traceable in the historical record. Nineteen years old in 1848, Scott's mother, Mary, had been born a free woman who lived among the Quakers in the Fine Creek settlement in Powhatan County. A newspaper account notes that city police arrested Nancy Scott in 1857 for being about without her certificate of freedom. Another reports that she tragically died when her clothing caught fire in 1860.[67]

Black enthusiasm for First African Baptist and decided disinterest in the Protestant Episcopal Church deeply troubled the white Christian paternalists of that denomination who believed that God had demanded white supervision of Black religious life. Bishop Meade admitted in an 1847 book, *Sketches of Old Virginia Family Servants,* that Black converts associated with Episcopal families tended to choose other denominations. He concluded that "this is to be accounted for by the low state of religion in the Episcopal Church at the time of their making a religious profession."[68] This troubled Episcopalians because failure to attract enslaved people reflected poorly on their spiritual health of white Episcopalians. The impasse, by the late 1850s, prompted a number of searching and revealing discussions within Episcopal circles.

The Diocese of Virginia considered the problem in 1860.[69] In a committee report at the diocesan convention that year, clergy contemplated "the best means of securing the permanent attachment of the colored population to our Church." The committee, chaired by Bishop Johns, first discussed the results of a questionnaire they had previously circulated. Although less than "one out of six ministers of the Diocese" had responded, the committee felt comfortable drawing conclusions. They were satisfied that ample space in churches had been afforded to Black people and that ministers in the countryside had expended considerable effort to preach to them in their cabins or outdoors (though they noted that ministers in towns rarely made that effort). They were satisfied that clergy diligently pursued people of color but were concerned that lay people had not done enough to offer instruction and fellowship to the people they enslaved in their own homes.[70] The combination of clerical efforts and lay indifference resulted in what the clergy regarded as a disappointingly negligible number of Black communicants across the Diocese of Virginia—272 in 1860. Even worse than the lack of Black Episcopal communicants was the fact that indifference had resulted in "the custom [of owners] . . . to leave them to themselves, which generally amounts to surrendering them to others of their own color, no wiser nor better than themselves, for mutual delusion and debasement." This "surrender" represented an intolerable failure in the eyes of these proslavery Christians.

The committee did not stop with self-condemnation. "It is high time to inquire the cause and apply the remedy," it concluded. They pondered whether the low number of Black members could be attributed to a lack of space afforded in churches. No, they answered. The questionnaire had proven that to not be the case. They then wondered if Episcopal sermons were plain enough for Black people to understand. The committee asserted that Episcopal sermons were the most intellectually accessible and coherent of all Protestant denominations. That could not be the reason. The same held with the liturgical services and the Book of Common Prayer—features that other denominations lacked. Those, too, they decided, were self-evidently not the cause of Black reluctance. They wondered if Black people had a strong theological preference for full-immersion baptism and concluded that could not be the cause because Methodists did not offer such baptism yet were just as successful in attracting Black members as were the Baptists. And besides, they lamented, Episcopal clergy would perform immersive baptisms, if asked; but no one asked.

The committee then made a remarkable observation: "The inquiry in which we are engaged will not be truly answered till we find something of interest and value which the colored people enjoy among both Baptists and Methodists, but which is not adequately afforded them in their Church relations with us, and this we believe to be *the blessed privilege of Christian fellowship*." They determined that social relationships of worshippers lay at the heart of pious commitment. Lacking such connections, "the child of God will not, if he can help it, abide long in any ecclesiastical organization." Reviewing Episcopal practice, the committee wondered, "what provision is made, so far as colored persons are concerned? Very little, indeed," they concluded.

> Once a month, it may be, after the Sacrament of the Lord's Supper has been administered to other communicants, some indication is given to them, as they wait in some part of the gallery, that they may approach to receive the consecrated symbol of salvation and of Christian union—and then they retire as they came, unknowing and unknown, not only in reference to the White members, but to each other.... There is nothing to make them feel that they have any relationship to the Christian people where they worship beyond that of a hearer—any hearer who may happen to be present. There is little in the proceeding to identify them with the Church, still less to gratify their instinctive craving for Christian fellowship.

This committee, then, had very accurately diagnosed the unspoken Black critique expressed by indifference as a problem white people had to solve. It was a problem rooted in the very way white Episcopalians had constructed religious race relations. The social distance created by their paternalism had created impassable gulfs in Christian fellowship. "To provide this for them among ourselves, then, is the problem. How can it be done?," they wondered.

In this moment of clarity, these clergymen faltered. They wanted to draw Black people into fellowship, but they could not bring themselves to fellowship with Black people. "Certainly not," they wrote, could change happen "by any innovation on the existing usages in our congregational worship and administration of our sacraments." This was a disingenuous claim—that the liturgy and sacraments themselves stood in the way. They then pointed to the true obstacle: "These [conditions] have grown out of the obvious proprieties of the case, and may not be changed." Though an opaque reference, "proprieties of the case" evidently refers to the necessity of upholding the social etiquette of racial inequality by avoiding any suggestion of social equality. White and Black parishioners approaching the communion rail together might engender Black loyalty to the church, but it would be an intolerable concession to social equality. Earthly priorities trumped spiritual ones.

The committee decided that the best way to secure Black membership in the Episcopal Church was that "we must give them their own stated and separate service." They looked to the Diocese of South Carolina, where plantations with large Black populations had made separate services, and even churches, more logical, and noted the high number of Black communicants. Success there alleviated some of the committee members' anxiety about distancing Black members from the patriarchal surveillance of white parishes. With that, the committee recommended that separate Black parishes be established, with white trustees holding property and white ministers performing liturgical and pastoral services.

At the same time that the diocesan committee collected responses to its questionnaire, a committee of Richmond Episcopalians anticipated that body's conclusions and met in the basement of St. Paul's to discuss how to proceed with the establishment of a separate Black congregation in Richmond. Minnigerode opened with a prayer then turned the meeting over to George Woodbridge, rector at Monumental. The group's minutes record that St. Paul's member Thomas Ellis was appointed secretary while congregants John Steger and Samuel P. Mitchell participated. The Reverend Richard Wilmer of Emmanuel Church at Brook Hill spoke first and expressed grief that separate congregations were necessary. "Divisions between the classes, among Christians, [was] a contravention of the gospel." He thought it distasteful and regrettable but bowed to the same reality that would impress the diocesan committee: "the establishment of the separate Church will not *produce* the *distinction:* it *exists.*" John Steger of St. Paul's arose to speak and made a passionate appeal for lay participation in the effort to raise a church, recognizing that religious instruction of servants must be shouldered by lay masters and not just clergy. Steger's vision of that religious instruction was steeped in the patriarchal language of the Victorian household: "[T]hey should be controlled as with parental authority, and taught even as our children are taught, to set their hope in God, and not forego the works of God, but keep His commandments." Despite the appeal to religion in the home, Steger endorsed the establishment of a separate church. The Richmonders resolved "that a committee, consisting of the Rector and one Lay member of each congregation, be appointed to devise and procure means for the erection and organization of an Episcopal African Church in Richmond."[71]

That Episcopal African Church later became St. Philip's, but the immediate effort to build and support its congregation stalled as public events took priority. While Richmond Episcopalians fretted over the implications of separating "children of God" by race, they could not countenance the external political force that attacked the foundations of their sacred relationship and challenged their narratives of racial difference. Elite Richmonders had long articulated and advocated a southern nationalism. The rise of the Republican Party in the late 1850s nudged them toward southern separatism. Thomas McCance, a St. Paul's member, chaired a public meeting that called for a convention to consider secession just after Republican Abraham Lincoln's election to the presidency in November 1860. Parishioners R.B. Haxall, James Dunlop, William Palmer, Ambrose Carlton, Joseph Reid Anderson, Thomas Ellis, William Macfarland, and Bolling Haxall all sat in the audience as speakers decried "the aggressions of the abolition party" and the "anti-slavery sentiments of the North, which denies to the Southern States their rights."[72] Denied white Christians their ability to fulfill God's will, they might have added. Macfarland, a staunch Unionist took the speakers' lessons to heart. As a delegate to Virginia's secession convention, he proclaimed that if Northern hostility to slavery did not cease, he "would not consent to remain in the Union with the people of that section."[73] Sarah Valentine believed that "God hath ... forever united the master and slave," but now Republicans threatened that sacred bond. Religious people took to arms to protect it.

2 | St. Paul's in War and after Emancipation

AT AN 1863 meeting in Richmond, ninety-six clergy from nine of the eleven Confederate States affirmed their core commitment to Confederate nationhood by reasserting the divinely ordered relationship between white masters and Black slaves. Though no clergy from St. Paul's attended, Reverend Joshua Peterkin of St. James did. They began their "Address to Christians throughout the World" by insisting that Republicans did not intend to honorably restore the Union, but to cruelly subjugate the South. The wartime violence employed to do so served to prove Confederates right in their charges of bloody-minded abolitionism. The chief exhibit in their appeal was "the recent proclamation of the President of the United States, seeking the emancipation of the slaves of the South." Aside from lip service to the brutality of military campaigns, the clergy presented no other evidence.

These southern clergy scorned as "philanthropists" those who claimed to act in the moral cause of abolishing slavery. "What shall sound Christianity say to that one-idea philosophy which, in the name of an *imaginary* good, in blind fury rushes upon a thousand *unquestionable* evils?" Southerners, religious or not, had long held that Black people could not govern their passions and, that without the benevolent control of white masters, would either instigate a "servile insurrection" or slowly die off without the aid of the master race. In 1863, Confederate clergy predicted—and shuddered—that the former might happen because of the Emancipation Proclamation: "Christian sensibilities recoil from the vision of a struggle that would inevitably lead to the slaughter of tens of thousands of poor deluded insurrectionists! Suppose their owners suffered; in the nature of things the slaves would suffer infinitely more." White people loved to claim that they doted on the welfare of the enslaved—by insisting that Black people could only survive in slavery—and marked this concern as a sign of genuine, if persecuted and misunderstood, love. The clergy stood on this vision of a bloody and sinful result of Republican rule, claimed moral righteousness, and assured the Christians throughout the world that "men in deadly contention wrestle in fields of blood, protesting against the crimes that, in the name of liberty and philanthropy, are attempted!"[1] In the middle of the war, Confederate clergy declared that the course of events had only proved them right about race and about abolitionist's vicious and heretical intent. Bishop William Meade concurred, claiming from his deathbed that the "war against us is iniquitous."[2]

The following month, the Missionary Society of the Diocese of Virginia, chaired by St. Paul's rector Charles Minnigerode, struck a similar, if slightly less apocalyptical appeal. The committee that had overseen the religious instruction of slaves before the war now warned that the war itself might interrupt their sacred duty. "God forbid," the committee wrote, "that the dangers which surround us, should make us forget our duty." That duty, of course, was "work among our colored population." It continued, "For years we have labored, to prove ourselves the true—alas! the only true friend of that race, which would be so happy if the wicked [i.e.—abolitionists] had left them to their natural and normal position in this country, but who are made so wretched by the false teachings and allurements and practices of our enemies."

"We stand between them and extermination," Minnigerode's committee concluded, "let us prove our right, defend our position, if need be die in the performance of our duty toward those whom God has signally committed to our care, whether as individuals or as a church."[3] Indeed, many would die attempting to uphold the sacred relationship between master and slave.

On the eve of the war, Episcopal clergy had craved a religious and familial bond with African Americans. During the war, scattered reports suggest that the few Black adherents they had managed to attract quickly abandoned the segregated Episcopal congregation that the Richmonders had established as St. Philip's in 1859. In 1864 the new missionary in charge at that outpost, D.F. Sprigg, reported six communicants, down from the "thirty or forty" the year before.[4] At St. Paul's, the already negligible number of Black communicants shrank to one unnamed individual, and the parochial report suggests that no "colored" baptisms, confirmations, and only three marriages took place over the course of the war. The vestry noted in 1863 that the gallery, officially designated for Black people, now contained only white people.[5] White southern Christians' insistence that Black people remained faithful servants and loyal Christians made them blind to a different reality: that enslaved people craved freedom and took any opportunity to seize it for themselves. It proved proslavery Christianity wrong, but its authors didn't even see it.

St. Paul's people, like all Episcopalians, had assessed their own faith by measuring their adherence to ordered and orthodox theology, missionary work in Richmond and beyond, and their ability to maintain a divinely ordained mastery of slaves. They never achieved the organic interpersonal, if unequal, relationships of faith with Black people that clergy coveted before the war. Even that aspiration faltered as Black people slipped away from Episcopalian desires while emancipating themselves from their owners. The war shifted white Episcopalians' theological ground, but they barely noticed. But after emancipation, as Black and white southerners across the former Confederacy began to negotiate a new relationship based on free labor, they set out to reassert a new form of dominance.[6]

In April 1862, as the United States' Army of the Potomac stalked up the Virginia Peninsula, Richmond's women huddled together sewing sandbags for the defenses at Yorktown. "We are intensely anxious," wrote Judith McGuire, "our conversation, while busily sewing at St. Paul's Lecture-Room, is only of war."[7] Years before, Episcopal women had organized themselves into sewing circles to teach and fundraise. They taught catechism and dressmaking to poor girls and made garments of their own to raise funds for missionary stations and Sunday Schools. In Spring 1861, St. Paul's sewing circles convened at the church to make military uniforms[8] and, as mangled bodies piled up before Richmond the following year, they turned to producing beds and bed clothes for hospitals.[9] Nancy Macfarland, along with the vestry, likely directed these efforts. The wife of the senior warden, she and several other Richmond women organized the Soldiers' Aid Society of Virginia which assisted in medical care in Richmond and eventually coordinated a Confederacy-wide network to bring hospital supplies to Virginia's capital.[10] The vestry complemented the women's work with a donation of its own: the pew cushions for hospitals. Dr. James McCaw, a St. Paul's member and future senior warden, directed the largest hospital in the Confederate States at Chimborazo on the city's eastern edge. To keep the hospital running, he relied upon enslaved cooks, laundresses, laborers, and even nurses.[11] Tens of thousands of sick and wounded men crowded hospitals in the city, including, at times, a makeshift ward in St. Paul's undercroft.[12]

Church members also pursued their missionary zeal in a more direct support of the war effort, following Reverend Charles Minnigerode in the Diocesan Missionary Society. The Society had previously funded missionary work in western and northern Virginia, and in foreign countries. When war restricted access to those places, the Society shifted its efforts to the Confederate army and to Richmond hospitals. In 1863, the Society, with its treasurer John L. Bacon, a former St. Paul's congregant, undertook the distribution of religious tracts for soldiers and rented a room in "the most desirable part of town" to headquarter its mission to the military.¹³ Minnigerode himself, joined by other Episcopal clergy, traveled to the Army of Northern Virginia's winter quarters in Orange Court House to preach to soldiers. "I held five services in three days," he reported, "two in the open air to the soldiers of Mahone's and of H.H. Walker's Brigades." St. Paul's congregants contributed $13,474.30 "in behalf of the army and the benevolent institutions of the town" in 1863. The influx of refugees, laborers, and soldiers to Richmond had strained the town's charitable networks, and St. Paul's undertook some of that burden when its recently established Church Home for Orphans accepted twelve girls displaced from the Fredericksburg Charity School in 1863.¹⁴

During the war years, St. Paul's received a surge of new attendees (if not communicants). Because of the church's proximity to the state capitol building and Richmond's most luxurious homes, quite a few regular visitors were highly placed in the Confederate government, including Adjutant General Samuel Cooper, Secretary of the Treasury George Trenholm, and Chief of Ordnance Josiah Gorgas alongside a parade of generals, politicians, and their fashionable wives, including memoirist Mary Chesnut.¹⁵ None were more prominent, of course, than General Robert E. Lee and President Jefferson Davis. Minnigerode befriended and spiritually mentored Davis, and Bishop John Johns baptized the Confederate leader at home and, the same day, confirmed him at St. Paul's. Certainly, the people at St. Paul's found comfort and familiarity in what Judith McGuire called "starred officers of all grades ... and civilians of every degree ... all bending together before high Heaven."¹⁶

But war encroached on that comfort, and the patriotic energy that women channeled into sewing uniforms and sandbags gave way to pervasive anxiety and gloominess. Minnigerode reported forty funerals in 1862, eighty in 1863, and forty-one in 1864. By comparison, no year before 1861 saw more than twenty funerals.¹⁷ The people of St. Paul's did not come through unscathed. Later church records identified over thirty members as fatalities. Most notably, John Pegram, long a congregant, died in battle just weeks after his society wedding at the church. His brother, William, was killed soon after. Others bore the physical reminders of combat for the rest of their lives, like future vestryman E.C. Minor, whose empty right sleeve signaled an amputated arm.¹⁸

Confederate celebrities crowded the pews, yet the emotional trauma of death and looming disaster preoccupied the people at St. Paul's. Minnigerode preached to his congregation's anxieties and bolstered the fundamentals of their faith. In a November 1864 sermon on "power," he offered a framework for understanding God's incarnation in man, including how man might exercise Godly power among his fellows. Minnigerode obliquely but unmistakably referred to the white Christian obligation to Black people when he inquired about power over others. "Have we won them over by precept and example, by a Christ-like walk and purity, by love and devotion and unselfishness? ... Do we lead their souls with ours to heaven?" That the rector in both his missionary and pastoral work, continued to count the sacred obligation as essential for faith late in the war, even when the Confederate cause appeared more hopeless than ever, testifies to its centrality for white Christians.[19]

While Minnigerode encouraged his people to adhere to foundational spiritual and racial dynamics, the war, and Black people themselves, eroded slavery from the inside. The social stresses of a besieged city created opportunities for enslaved people to test the boundaries of their autonomy. City officials responded by increasing punishment of Black men and women for ever-smaller transgressions. The Richmond Mayor's Court ordered five lashes for "Moses, slave of J.R. Anderson," for "smoking a cigar in the street."[20] The city fined parishioner James Macmurdo $20 for "permitting his servant Taff to go at large."[21] And, for some offenses, officials levied more extreme sentences. In 1865, the Hustings Court sentenced two Black men accused of stealing foodstuffs from Minnigerode's house to be executed by hanging. Minnigerode himself appealed the sentence and, having been pardoned by the governor, the two men went into Confederate service instead.[22] Heightened security could not quell the restlessness of Richmond's enslaved people. At least eight men ran away from Anderson's Tredegar Iron Works.[23] Bolling Haxall's enslaved man, Abraham, escaped in the summer of 1863, "to the Yankees I believe," he noted.[24]

In January 1865, Minnigerode returned to the pulpit to comfort his congregation as their nation crumbled around them. He noted that the year "that has passed has brought us untold sorrows and trials as a people." He encouraged the congregation to be patient with military setbacks and material shortages and instead resolve to strengthen faith, the true source of victory. "*And shall we lack the faith to bear us out in our struggle?*" he inquired. "In our struggle for liberty and honour, and wealth and independence, and a glorious future? For wife and children and home, and all we hold dear and sacred? For truth and our altars? For our lives and very existence?"[25]

To proslavery Christians, safety of family and home, of faith and truth, always remained enmeshed in both a faith in Jesus and a constellation of social strictures—including the maintenance of the sacred obligation of slavery.

Slavery's destruction would, according to them, loose a race of uncontrollable brutes upon civilized people and challenge God's prescriptions for the relation between races. When Richard Chiles, a Black messenger from the War Department carried the news of Robert E. Lee's evacuation of the Petersburg defenses down the center aisle of the church to a seated Jefferson Davis on April 2, 1865, proslavery Christians faced their worst fears.[26]

Would the end of slavery mean the destruction of white families and homes as so many predicted? More importantly—for a community of faithful Christians who had maintained that God himself ordained human bondage as the best relation between Black and white people and had given a sacred obligation for white people to fulfill their Christian duty—was another question. Could they even recognize that which they hadn't previously noticed—the actual racial theories that motivated them had been proven so inaccurate? It would take an entire generation to work through these questions, and the results would shape Richmond's racial landscape for the twentieth century.

In the meantime, amid the ashes of a burned-out city and as St. Paul's people awoke to new racial realities, they also found themselves with a new burden and preoccupation—that of their wartime experiences. Since the funeral of former US President John Tyler in 1862, the presence of the Confederate high command alongside the many scenes of grief and hope, St. Paul's had become a *de facto* state church for the slaveholding republic—the Church of the Confederacy. The next generation found itself needing to chart a course for an unexpected future. To do so, it looked to the past.

Emancipation and Confederate defeat had given lie to southern clergymen's predictions of the orgy of violence followed by the inevitable slaughter of Black people in the event of freedom. In Richmond, free people reunited families, sought education, organized for politics, and installed Black clergy to lead Black congregations.[27] Despite such evidence that the transition to freedom might prove smooth, Bishop John Johns of the Diocese's Annual Council in 1866, while acknowledging the reality of Black freedom, reestablished the claim on the sacred obligation. "[T]heir [freedpeople] influence must be determined by their own character, which, under God," Johns suggested, "depends on their moral and religious education, for which a large measure of responsibility must rest upon us." He further condemned Black people's "extravagant notions of liberty." When Johns spoke, prior to the Fourteenth and Fifteenth Amendments, the status of Black people as citizens with voting rights remained an open question. Though they accepted the end of slavery, ex-Confederates like Johns considered any aspiration to citizenship and social personhood a dangerous proposition. Though ex-slaves had never risen up to commit mass murder nor had they died out from incompetence, old proslavery Christians couldn't shake themselves of the notion that freed people would.

Freedom remained a danger for Black people, even when free, Johns maintained. He called for white forbearance. "If we of the South, who best understand these people, and who ought to direct and control this work, neglect it, other and mischievous hands will take it up to our great annoyance, and the serious perversion and ruin of many whom they assume to enlighten." A sacred obligation remained: competent white people must mentor incompetent Black people. The risk lay in *too much* Black freedom and those northerners and liberals who encouraged it. Only southern whites, this view held, possessed the capacity and goodwill to teach African Americans how to behave in their freedom. Thus, slavery may have ended, but not much had changed.

The bishop did not oppose education for freed people. He did, however, have firm opinions on who should preside over it. Johns had been alarmed by the collaboration between the federally sponsored Freedmen's Bureau, northern religious organizations, and Richmond's Black churches to start schools. He certainly had in mind the national church's 1865 establishment of the Protestant Episcopal Freedman's Commission. The church intended the new program to shape the education of freed people while attracting them to the denomination. Yet despite the northern-born Commission's paternalism, southern clergy feared it would be staffed with the alleged "philanthropists" they still scorned and feared would promote the "extravagant notions" that Bishop Johns condemned. To blunt southern fears, the Protestant Episcopal Church changed the name from "Freedman's Commission" to "Commission of Home Missions to Colored People" in 1868, but that was not enough to please white southern clergy.[28]

Virginia's clergy responded to the national Freedmen's Commission by creating a home-grown Committee on the Religious Instruction of the Colored People. In 1866 the Committee endorsed three resolutions. Two had been undertaken during slavery: the teaching of Sunday School to Black pupils and the encouragement of lay engagement in giving "particular attention to their moral as well as religious instruction." The third resolution, in acknowledgment of the transition from slavery to freedom, called for the establishment of parochial schools for Black students.[29] The following year, the diocese established a Standing Committee on Colored Congregations to review and encourage the organization of Black churches. Nevertheless, St. Philip's in Richmond continued the decline that commenced during the war. This deterioration was hastened when the Diocesan Missionary Society, chaired by Minnigerode, channeled interest and resources to a fledgling Black congregation developing at St. Stephen's in Petersburg at the expense of St. Philip's. At the same time, the Society urged the transfer of St. Philip's white rector, T. Grayson Dashiell, who, aided by the Freedmen's Bureau, had made some promising postwar gains at the struggling Black church. But Dashiell's reassignment to St. Mark's, a white working-class mission, rendered his former flock dormant—a circumstance worsened when the diocese decided to give to St. Mark's St. Philip's building as well. By 1869, St. Stephen's had advanced enough in Petersburg that the diocese officially admitted it into the fold but pointedly denied the Black church independent parish status or Council voting privileges. A struggling St. Philip's submitted no parochial report in 1868.[30]

In the immediate postwar years, Black Christians across denominations fled white churches and established congregations of their own. (Stepney Brown's friend, John Dungee noted about the Shenandoah Valley that "the spirit of the white Christians in these regions is greatly embittered against the colored people, owing to the abolition of Slavery; and they do not invite them to either church or school.")[31] The diocese's Committee on Colored Congregations noted that the "Diocese has progressed slowly indeed . . . since the change in their condition," and observed that growth was particularly slow in Richmond, where "the ground is almost wholly preoccupied by other denominations, the political excitements of the day are more keenly felt there than elsewhere, and the separation from the influences of our Church are more complete."[32] Sunday Schools—as before emancipation—and parochial schools became the chief means of contact between the Episcopal Church and Black Virginians.[33]

By the middle of the 1870s, as white conservatives reasserted political control in Virginia, diocesan reports on its mission to Black Virginians had been reduced to routine observations that work proceeded slowly, but no major initiative had been undertaken. Indeed, in 1875, the Committee on the State of the Church indicated that Virginia Episcopalians had not made any effort whatsoever: "one large and highly important sphere of missionary enterprise, our Church in Virginia can be scarcely said to have entered—we mean the colored population of the State."[34] The great interest the diocese had found in 1865 in continuing a paternalistic relationship with freedpeople had simply evaporated within ten years. With the exception of a few schools, white Episcopalians moved forward in utter ignorance of the Black Christians among them. The sacred obligation remained, but unused, atrophied and receded as a religious imperative.

While the parishioners at St. Paul's no doubt fretted about the status of freedpeople in 1866, they left little evidence—besides the votes of Reverend Minnigerode and lay representative Joseph Reid Anderson in the Annual Council—that they thought about the evolving relationship between their church, their Christian selves, and African Americans. Anderson had signed his name to a letter written by Robert E. Lee that claimed a southern paternalistic affection for African Americans but insisted that its authors—speaking for the South—were "opposed to any system of laws which place the political power of the country in the hands of the negro race. But this opposition springs from no feelings of enmity, but from a deep-seated conviction that at present the negroes have neither the intelligence nor the qualifications which are necessary to make them safe depositories of political power. They would inevitably become the victims of demagogues, who for selfish purposes would mislead them, to the serious injury of the public."[35] Minnigerode nurtured his connection to the now-imprisoned Jefferson Davis with occasional visits to the ex-president's cell in Fort Monroe in 1866.[36] Through this connection, St. Paul's people felt intimately attached to the fate of the jailed Davis. In fact, senior warden Macfarland and half a dozen of the church's vestrymen stepped forward in May 1867 to post $500 each in support of Davis's bail bond.[37]

While they remained silent and indifferent to race relations in church, several St. Paul's members made plain their opinions on race relations in an altered secular world. William Macfarland and William C. Allen represented Richmond's former Confederates in a public meeting of citizens five months after Appomattox. The representatives resolved to accept the results of the war, including "the abolition of slavery," and therefore expected a quick restoration of their equal rights as a state within the federal union. The delegates continued, however, that full equality of states meant the power to "regulate the right of suffrage for itself, as distinguished from the reckless and pernicious theories of the so-called *Radical* [Republican] party, which propose to the Southern States the alternative of negro suffrage or an indefinite exclusion from the benefits of a common and equal Union." The political status of freedpeople remained unresolved, and Macfarland and Allen made clear that they would happily return to the United States as long as the government did not insist on Black political enfranchisement. Macfarland himself carried the resolutions to President Andrew Johnson the following week.[38]

Macfarland exuded a sense of equanimity and goodwill when he and other prominent businessmen addressed a meeting of Black Richmonders the following spring. "My feelings toward you are, indeed, kind, just I hope," he said, "and full of good wishes for your progress and welfare in your new civil and political condition." But, he warned his audience, "Emancipation has not been a blessing invariably to those on whom it has been bestowed." Success, he admonished, could be found if freedpeople would be industrious, pursue education, submit to religion, and follow laws. "If, however," Macfarland threatened, "you shall be idle, profligate, seditious, and yield to wicked counsels, your last condition will be worse than the first." In regard to voting in the upcoming elections, mandated by the Reconstruction Act of 1867, Macfarland advised his listeners to cast ballots for honest and moderate men. He offered, for example, "the citizens of the white race whom you have long known" and not "strangers," meaning northerners, Republicans, and Black outsiders.[39] The local paper reported that Macfarland had been well-received, but a reporter for a Pennsylvania paper noted that "the discourse of the speakers was anything but conciliatory," and that the audience was "not going to vote as the speakers wanted them to; but for their rights."[40]

Black voters did indeed turn out in registration drives in 1868, securing a majority of registered voters in Richmond in preparation for a new constitutional convention. To push back against that majority, St. Paul's member and chairman of Richmond's Conservative Party, Thomas McCance, encouraged "every man" to scrupulously police Black voter registration for any credible reason to disqualify registrants. Of the purge, McCance noted, "it is now evident to everyone that the whites have it in their power to control this city."[41] Black people, by their political participation and insistence on voting for Republicans demonstrated in public for the first time an unwillingness to align themselves with white supremacists and their narratives of interracial harmony.

The passage of the Fourteenth and Fifteenth Amendments that enforced Black political equality compelled white southerners to begin articulating new justifications for inequality. Physician, minister, and St. Paul's pew holder Dr. James Bolton avidly read the newly emerging sciences of evolution and anthropology and in 1867 informed a public audience in Richmond of his conclusions. All men are formed from the same matter, he said, and thus constituted a unified humanity. But, each branch of mankind had been fitted for certain geographies and certain positions in life. "Man is readily gathered into groups, which consist of regular gradations, from the lowest type of humanity, which are closely assimilated to the orangoutang [sic], up to the highest types of man," Bolton proclaimed. He quickly reached his point: geography or social context "had never changed one race into another; that the negro is in his perfect state of development, never reaches the level of the Causassian [sic], but, in a state perfection, is on level with a Causassian child. Therefore," Bolton concluded, "he should be kept in a state of subjection, and deprived of the right of franchise and other rights of Causassian adults. The African has never reached a high state of civilization; that if raised to a higher standard than that of his native land, and if left to himself, he soon falls back into barbarism." Bolton could cite current pseudo-scientific observation to prove his point that "now in the southern States he is relapsing into a state of barbarism."[42] Tellingly, this churchgoer did not mention any Biblical justification for his beliefs, only scientific innovations. His observations marked a key turning point in white racialist thinking that would culminate much later. Bolton's argument previewed the next generation's search for a place to root their narratives of racial difference now that slavery had been swept away.

In the meantime, the women of St. Paul's were actively readjusting to postwar realities. Taking the lead in white public commemoration of the war dead, they simultaneously reaffirmed their place as moral and cultural elites in Richmond alongside the men who did so on the political front. In May 1866, the *Richmond Examiner* complained about Congress's neglect of Confederate dead as it organized national cemeteries for the United States soldiers, and it called upon Richmond churchwomen to assume responsibility for tending southern graves. In response, Thomas Ellis, St. Paul's register, vestryman, and president of the existing Hollywood Cemetery, invited a cross-denominational group to the St. Paul's Lecture Rooms to discuss care for the Confederate graves at Hollywood.[43] An account of the meeting noted that Reverend Minnigerode offered his blessing and "spoke feelingly of the sacredness of the movement & offered up an earnest petition that success might attend the holy enterprise."[44] The nascent Ladies Hollywood Memorial Association elected Nancy Macfarland their president, and she published a fundraising appeal in late May. The Confederate dead had not just bequeathed sorrow, she wrote, but also an obligation for survivors to be grateful for their "noble deeds." Association members led a massive procession to Hollywood Cemetery on May 31, 1866, and spent the summer clearing graves and planting flowers. They subsequently supervised the reinternment of thousands of bodies from Virginia and Pennsylvania battlefields. These efforts, led by St. Paul's women, established the commemorative agenda of Confederate memory in gender-appropriate displays of mourning and reverence. They did so, first, no doubt, from a state of grief. But their efforts also carried political implications. As women, they escaped the scrutiny of United States authorities that had deemed as treasonous men's political activity in the immediate postwar years. By insisting that the Confederate dead deserved equal treatment from the United States government, and failing to get it, the women claimed an equal part in the national story of the Civil War, insisting on the righteousness of the Confederate cause while nurturing a sense of bitter grievance as a result. These elements remained a basic understanding of the white southern memory of the Civil War.[45] The experience of war had yielded to the memory of war, and in the ritual of that memory, they made a historical narrative that combined with the men's political justification for racial inequality.

As the diocese lost interest in cultivating Black Episcopalians, the Conservative Party dominated Virginia's political arena with its reaffirmation of racial hierarchy. In the late 1870s, a shaky coalition of Black and white Republicans alongside some disaffected Conservatives formed a political organization known as the Readjusters. They coalesced around the issue of repudiation of a part of Virginia's antebellum debt and advocacy for the funding for public schools. In contrast, Conservatives advocated full funding of debt necessitating crippling cuts to nascent public education. Readjusters united behind former Confederate General William Mahone. From 1879 to 1883, the new party captured Virginia's General Assembly, the governor's office, and the Commonwealth's representation in the United States Congress. The partisan struggles, however, were exacerbated by the existence of the biracial coalition that allowed for the political advancement of Black men. Conservatives condemned the alliance and effectively mounted a campaign in 1882 that raised the specter of "negro domination" by "insolent" Black people in order to detach white voters from the Readjuster bloc.[46]

Just two days before the 1883 elections, an incident in Danville provided Conservatives an opportunity to weaponize long-festering racial fears and resentment. A melee in the streets resulted in five men dead (four of them Black and reported unarmed). Conservatives—now reconstituted as the Conservative Democratic Party—seized control of the story, describing an unruly mob of Black people and blaming their agitation on Danville's Readjuster leadership. St. Paul's vestry member Archer Anderson (son of Joseph Reid Anderson) sat on the Democratic committee that crafted a lengthy published response that justified the use of retributive violence. Anderson and his colleagues admitted that "a revolution in government" against "the corrupting chains of corrupt and corrupting tyranny" of Readjuster rule had occurred, but they denied that Conservatives had contributed to the violence. Instead, echoing William Macfarland's earlier warnings, Anderson's Conservatives claimed that "the colored race, inflamed by ambitious demagogues, with unreasoning prejudice against their white fellow-citizens," was responsible. For example, in Danville, which had "been under negro government, with negro policemen," Black people believed that they would be protected by that government, and thus "had become rude and insulting to the whites"—a charge frequently leveled at African Americans who failed to show humble deference. In the Danville incident, Anderson assessed, "what seems certain is that if the ten or fifteen brave white men, standing there and facing that angry crowd enormously outnumbering them had flinched for an instant or retreated . . . they themselves would have been butchered." After Anderson carefully attributed violence to gullible Black people under the sway of Readjuster influence, he methodically laid out statistical data about voting patterns and tax collection to claim for Conservatives popular Readjuster successes on public schools and public debt.[47] The much-reported violence in Danville—described in the northern press as a "massacre" and as a "riot" in the South—had a chilling effect on the election. Across the state, hundreds of Black voters stayed away from the polls, and the Democratic Party gained firm control of Virginia politics for decades to come.

In crafting his party's response to the Danville incident, Anderson and his colleagues reaffirmed the narrative of racial difference that undergirded slavery, but for a new age. Macfarland and McCance had signaled white Virginian's acceptance of emancipation and a genuine hope that Black people would follow their former masters' lead in electoral politics. The Readjuster movement had demonstrated that African Americans would make their own political choices. In reaction, Conservatives redoubled their efforts to delegitimize Black people's standing as equal citizens but also began to think about ways to reverse the political gains of Reconstruction. They marshaled religion and history in their cause.

After suppressing the Readjuster movement in 1883, Democrats began a slow but deliberate process of purging the Black presence from Virginia's political life. At the same time, the diocese began the same process within its own body. Evidently interested in being racial paternalists only when the political potential of Black people had been suppressed, Virginia Episcopalians in the early 1880s expressed a renewed desire to work among Black people and attract them to the church. Simultaneously, they incorporated new political and scientific theories to bolster racial inequality. Charles Minnigerode, as chair of the Diocesan Missionary Society, noted in 1881 that "colored people ... are much more the wards of the Church, and in a more blessed sense than they ever can be claimed to be wards of the nation." Subservient in the church, but invisible in the nation.[48]

Renewed diocesan interest in evangelizing Black people began when the Zion Union Association, a cluster of Black churches formerly associated with the Methodists in Brunswick and Greensville Counties southwest of Petersburg, approached the diocese for assistance and guidance in 1881.[49] The diocese dispatched Richmond clergyman Alexander Weddell (the father of St. Paul's later historian Elizabeth W. Weddell) to work among the Zion Unionists. They also assigned the Reverend Robb White from St. Andrews in Lawrenceville to shepherd them.[50] Though the Zion Unionists never formalized ties with the Episcopal Church, one of their members, James Solomon Russell, eventually became an Episcopal priest and then president of St. Paul's Normal and Industrial College (an Episcopal school, but no relation to St. Paul's in Richmond). The relationship with the Zion Unionists spurred the diocese to develop the Bishop Payne School, a seminary for Black postulants that started as the St. Stephen's Normal and Theological School in Petersburg.[51] The seminary enrolled at least six postulants in 1886, including George Freeman Bragg Jr., grandson of Caroline Bragg, previously enslaved by St. Paul's founding rector, William Norwood, and herself a cornerstone of St. Stephen's.[52] The diocese looked forward to an influx of Black Episcopalians, and the anticipation ignited the desires of the diocese's most fervent racial paternalists, who considered the church's inadequate engagement with Black Virginians in the 1870s and early 1880s a failure of its missionary obligation. In particular, Assistant Bishop Alfred Randolph, a former rector from Fredericksburg and occasional Confederate chaplain, took notice.[53] Randolph articulated a new approach to justifying racial inequality—not as God's plan, but, reflecting a stance similar to Dr. James Bolton, as a demonstrable fact according to the recent interpretations of evolution, anthropology, and history. Fully separated from a theological justification for racial inequality, Bishop Randolph's statement on Episcopalian race relations more easily fitted the new multiracial political and capitalist environments of Gilded Age Virginia.

Randolph's expressions of Christian regard for and solicitations to Virginia's Black people were disarmingly paternalistic and couched in grace. In 1884, he noted "The question of infinite importance is to win these souls to Christ, and to train them by the power of regenerating grace into moral and spiritual obedience to the ten commandments of God."[54] He condemned those who maintained "the proposition that [a Black individual was] incapable of education out of a religion of physical excitation and antinomianism and superstitious emotionalism," because that was the "equivalent to the proposition that he is incapable of salvation by the gospel."[55] The Assistant Bishop thought otherwise, that Black people had the capacity to understand liturgical religion and true pathways to salvation. In this way, Randolph shared the antebellum assumptions about the errancy of Baptist and Methodist theology—especially in the hands of Black people.

Randolph's stale theological commentary ended there. Emancipation and citizenship had allowed Black people to exist in political and economic realms alongside white people. Theology could not account for that, and Randolph, therefore, embraced theories of the political and economic worlds to inform his understanding of race relations in the church.

Employing prevailing stereotypes of African Americans, he advocated for the secular and material benefits of Black Christian education in the Episcopal Church:

> If I were a politician I would advocate the Christian education of the colored population, as the strongest ground for the stability of our political institutions. . . . As a political economist I would advocate the evangelizing of the race, as contributing to national wealth and material prosperity. To have a nation, a vast population with thriftless habits, living from hand to mouth, with no instincts to accumulate property, clothed with the right of suffrage but with no interest in the laws for the protection of property, must always be an element of danger and a barrier to material progress. Christianity and Christianity alone will teach them the divine authority of marriage, the sacredness of property, purity in the control of their bodies, honesty in their relations with their fellow-men, industry in their common toil, and all the virtues that contribute to the wealth of nations. If I were engaged in a trade I would advocate their Christian education, for as they are elevated by the power of the gospel all the conditions of their temporal life would be progressively improved. They would live in better houses, they would wear better clothes, they would accumulate property which would advance the resources of the State and diminish taxation. They would be better customers of the merchants in our cities and towns, as their wants would

increase through the refining influences of a Christian civilization, and thus contribute to the prosperity of the whole community.

Of course, for Randolph, the goal was salvation, with material prosperity and political stability as a happy side-effect. The assistant bishop rooted his convictions in a distinction between religion and morality: the former being truth revealed by the gospel and accessible to any man, Black or white. He saw no inequality in the ability of Black and white people to access religious truths. Morality, however, stemmed from Christian education, and it nurtured cultural sensibilities of people to "spend time in religious thought and meditation . . . be truthful and honest and just and temperate and pure and self-controlled and kindly and loving toward his fellow man." To him, morality, more than religion, served as a foundation for inclusion in American politics and public life, but morality was the very quality that Randolph—and racial theorists of his day—found lacking in people of African descent.

> The negro, and indeed all the races in the lower stages of civilization, tend toward a divorce of religion from morality. That tendency exists in various forms among all classes of the White race, modified and controlled by long ages of discipline by Christian law and public sentiment, by the churches and the Bible. The superstition belongs not only to the negro race, but it is the inveterate tendency of all the races. With the negro it is the inheritance of generations of pragmatism from the dawn of his history.[56]

Randolph's thesis was informed by current evolutionary theory: science, not theology. Only through the investment in white-controlled Christian education of Black people could the latter move along the evolutionary spectrum toward moral attainment. That goal, of course, was the precondition set by the white gatekeepers of American democracy, and that spectrum never seemed to have an end.

Randolph's advocacy was spurred by his own dim assessment of Black people and his entrenched biases:

> Stand face to face with an average man of this race dwelling among us. He has lovable qualities, and you and your children have loved him for generations, and love him today. He is kind and shrewd, he is polite and

genial, he is fluent, and often eloquent in speech. What is the difference between you and him? At first you are puzzled to define it. But place him in conditions where he is called to exercise faculties for duties which belong to what you call civilization, the forms, the meaning, the complex relations of the government of society, then you see his lack, then you begin to see the gap between you and him; he is bewildered; he loses his head; he is inaccessible to ideas, and government is instinct with ideas. He is without fixed purpose, steadiness of aim, self-control. You cannot depend on him; he is moved by unruly impulses, and of these he is unconscious. There is a deep content with himself, that keeps his life down to the same dead level. Those faculties of steady purpose and will and openness to ideas, which have trained us to deal with the formal and complex relations of government through centuries of discipline, he has had no opportunity to develop.[57]

While the people of St. Paul's said nothing overtly significant on race during the 1880s, Bishop Randolph's thinking represented the most forward-looking racial ideology of white Virginia Episcopalians. To an extent, Randolph's theology represented a critical break from proslavery religion. It was, in fact, no longer a theology. Mainline white clergy in the late nineteenth century did not even try to justify racial inequality using scripture and an understanding of God's providence.[58] Critical vestiges of the proslavery narrative of racial difference remained. White people still burdened themselves with a paternalistic obligation to mentor Black people through church institutions. White people still held Black people in place on an evolutionary spectrum. They still maintained a remarkable inability to see African Americans as anything but an abstraction, even when Black men and women stood before them in their homes and workplaces. But gone was the imperative for lay people to mentor subordinate Blacks toward salvation. Gone was the ecclesial desire for Blacks to come to white churches. Randolph's theological imagination allowed for the growth of Black social capacity toward a purely theoretical inclusivity. Theoretical, certainly in the way that he and Episcopalians formulated and acted, but it represented a critical adaption to a new reality of Black presence in public life that no slaveholder could have imagined.

Within the diocese, clergy shaped the institutional structure to reflect new aspirations and new realities. This included working relationships with a handful of Black clergy. Episcopal clergy argued that the post-emancipation movement of Black people away from the church had little to do with the actions of the church, but with the inexplicable and erroneous choices of Black people themselves. And, as articulated earlier in the diocesan councils in 1859 and 1860, they regretted the separation, accepted its reality, and even clearly noted, but overlooked, the real reasons for Black removal. Virginia's Annual Council in 1888 obliquely referred to "causes of animosity and suspicion which would inevitably arise" should Black and white laypeople and clergy commune together.[59] Those causes were likely the segregation white people imposed on everything.

George Freeman Bragg, a former Readjuster, editor of the *Afro-American Churchman* in Petersburg, and future priest, disagreed with the Council's conclusion.[60] Bragg frequently denied that overt discrimination by Virginia clergy existed. He claimed that Bishop Randolph was "as true a friend to the colored work, as is anyone" and dismissed the lack of Black clergy on the Commission on Colored Work was "an oversight only."[61] But the African American seminarian was clear eyed that Black invisibility in the church hierarchy damaged Episcopal reputation in the Black community. "It is rather uphill work," Bragg told his readers, "in attracting the attention of the masses" without Black representation in diocesan councils.[62] Bragg recognized his own difficult position siding with racial paternalists, but he agreed with Bishop Randolph's preference for the Episcopal style of worship to "the noise of some Bible beaters and the clamor and disorder common to quite a large number of denominations."[63] But in Bragg's critique is a charge that white Episcopalians refused to recognize that their inability to imagine a larger social context of racial equality drove Black people from their church and further separated Black Episcopalians and their congregations from the mainstream structure of the denomination. Bragg's self-positioning presaged the ways that several generations of Black leaders had to approach public engagement with white people who had purposefully stripped them of all political power. In the near future, Black leaders had to publicly praise the most gracious of racial paternalists in order to have a seat at the table, and in hopes of aligning with them against the more virulent racists in society. The stance of having to agree with white paternalists' harmonious assessments of race relations often obscured the critique embedded in statements like Bragg's. White people ignored the critique, reveled in the praise, and their descendants remembered that alone.

In 1885, the same year that Conservatives finally defeated the Readjusters in the streets and at the polls, the Diocese of Virginia moved to relegate Black Episcopal congregations to a Colored Missionary Jurisdiction and limit the participation of Black clergy in the Annual Council. This maneuver replicated an 1883 attempt by southern bishops—termed the Sewanee Plan—to move Black congregations from diocesan missionary boards to a separate, national, missionary jurisdiction, thus moving them even further from their neighboring white churches and the local levers of institutional power. The anticipated consequence would be that segregated white congregations would have no obligation to cooperate with, share resources with, or consider the opinions of Black congregations in diocesan work. On a national level, the General Convention's House of Deputies rejected the Sewanee Plan, but the Diocese of Virginia took up its 1885 version later that decade with the creation of the Colored Missionary Jurisdiction that consigned Black churches to a separate office in the diocese.[64]

A number of Black clergy sat in Virginia's Annual Council. Among them was George Freeman Bragg, recently ordained as a deacon. Regarding the proposed changes to the church constitution, he protested, "It is not necessary to change the formularies and laws of our Church in order to successfully operate among our people; it is not necessary to proscribe the colored student and refuse him admission to the priesthood, as seems to be the purpose . . . it is not necessary to set the colored people off in a little side show of their own."[65] Bragg spoke eloquently at the Diocesan Council in 1888 against ecclesial separation and earned the applause of the white clergy, but knowing the likely outcome, he announced his capitulation to whatever decision the Council made. Bragg's protest represented a call to an equitable faith and earthly brotherhood to which white Episcopalians politely listened but chose not to hear. In that year, the Diocese of Virginia shunted Black Episcopalians into a Colored Missionary Jurisdiction and, in 1889, limited the number of Black priests on the Diocesan Council.[66]

St. Paul's vestry performed a similar segregation in microcosm when it reaffirmed in April 1887 that "the Western Gallery is set apart for the use of colored persons attending St. Paul's Church and that they are not permitted to seats in the body of the church on any occasion."[67]

The diocesan decision represented the end of an era. No longer did it feverishly consider it a fulfillment of Christian obligation to evangelize Black people or press its parishes and lay members to a full engagement with them. That initiative survived emancipation, briefly. Now, two decades later, the diocese signaled a new order; Paternalism remained, including white people's ability to deploy it to obscure the realities of racial discrimination. But it changed in its venues: formerly in the home as a spiritual bond white people called family, now in public and economic spaces, in the homes of Black people, and in employer-employee relations that white people still called family. Paternalism remained, but the sacred obligation was no longer sacred, nor an obligation to be fulfilled, except in the barest points of contact in church schools. Lay people were released from caring about the souls of Black people.[68] This is not to say that the narrative of racial difference disappeared. As the women memorialists of St. Paul's, the scientific musings of Dr. Bolton and Bishop Randolph, and the political polemics of Archer Anderson indicated, the constructed narrative of mutual obligation found new footing in the political and cultural worlds. The people of St. Paul's embraced these secular racialist views within their church; and with an even greater fervency than they had ever approached proslavery Christianity, they wrapped their updated faith in reverence for Confederate saints.

In a city crowded with historic and grand churches, St. Paul's became a tourist draw because of its connections to Jefferson Davis. As early as 1870, Richmond booster Carlton McCarthy published a story for boys in which one young man proudly displayed St. Paul's to another, noting, "you know President Davis used to attend service there regularly during the winter."[69] Tourist guidebooks published by railroad and steamboat companies directed their customers to St. Paul's on their jaunts. The Virginia Steamboat Company in 1879 described the church's importance as the place where "President Davis was worshipping Sunday, April 2d, 1865 when notified by Gen. R.E. Lee of the breaking of the lines near Petersburg."[70] Two years later, *Richmond Virginia, A Guide to and Description of its Principal Places* elaborated on that scene: "It was here that Mr. Davis was appraised of the fact that the worst had come, when on Sunday, the 2nd of April, 1865, the sexton handed him a telegram from General Lee that succumbed to the overpowering strength of the Union troops, and that Richmond must consequently be evacuated."[71]

That second version contributed a bit more melodrama—the succumbing to the overpowering strength of Union troops—to St. Paul's foundational story and reflected several elements of growing Lost Cause historical narratives. In its narrowest sense, the Lost Cause ideology represented the ex-Confederate explanation of their part in the Civil War. In many ways, the Lost Cause adopted antebellum worldviews, like the insistence that race relations had been harmonious in slavery. It also transformed the grief of loss through sacred events like processions to Hollywood Cemetery into cultural performances. But what had been acts of mourning and recovery in the immediate aftermath of war had, by the 1880s, become a cultural institution that produced civic celebrations, books and magazines, reunions, veteran organizations, women's clubs, and a memorial landscape that worked not only to justify, but also to celebrate the Confederate experiment.[72]

A handful of historical claims lay at the heart of the Lost Cause. One pernicious example is the insistence that slavery had been beneficial to Black people as proslavery Christians had always said. The slaveholding states had seceded not simply to protect slavery, but rather, because abolitionists had unfairly attacked the constitutional legitimacy of slavery. The Confederacy only lost, the Lost Cause held, because it had been overwhelmed by the population and industrial might of the United States. Confederate soldiers were perfectly brave, and Confederate leaders like Davis and Lee were militarily unsurpassed and saintly in character. Confederate women had been selfless in their sacrifice. Finally, Reconstruction had been a disastrous experiment in racial democracy, the failure of which had vindicated white southern views on race relations.[73] Military defeat almost didn't matter to the Lost Cause because history, they claimed, had proved southerners morally victorious.

More importantly, the Lost Cause was not just about historical claims. Those historical claims represented the legitimizing historical imagination that served as a bulwark for a cultural and political worldview in the present and the future. The Lost Cause celebrated agrarianism and rural life in opposition to the industrial order and mass immigration into urban areas in the Gilded Age United States. It promoted bonds of family and community over the chains of capitalism. (The two claims might have confounded wealthy industrialists and bankers like Joseph Reid Anderson or William Macfarland. It also might have provided them a new way to understand their place in the prewar world.) The Lost Cause stereotype of the natural leadership abilities of elite white people and the stereotyped incompetence of Black people perfectly mirrored the late nineteenth-century conservative movements to marshal white political power while disfranchising and marginalizing Black people.[74]

Public expressions of the Lost Cause through memorials and parades in Richmond began as early as 1870 when, upon the death of R.E. Lee, veterans of the Army of Northern Virginia proposed a memorial for their beloved commander. Partisan squabbles between veteran organizations, and men's groups and women's groups, compounded by municipal interests, slow fundraising, and economic depression meant that twenty years passed before the Lee Memorial went up in 1890. The monumental equestrian statue was erected on land west of downtown donated by St. Paul's member Otway Allen, and

Reverend Minnigerode gave its dedicatory invocation. The 1890s saw an explosion of monuments large and small, from the statue of Williams Wickham in Monroe Park (1891) to the towering memorial to Confederate Soldiers and Sailors on Libby Hill (1894). It also saw the founding of key institutions of Lost Cause memory, the United Daughters of the Confederacy (1894) and the Confederate Museum (1894), the latter just blocks from St. Paul's. These two organizations worked tirelessly to ensure that the general public, North and South, accepted the tenets of Lost Cause history.[75]

1889 proved a year of fateful convergences for St. Paul's. In the spring, Charles Minnigerode retired from his 33-year rectorship. The vestry took the opportunity to act. Significant structural problems with the sanctuary had accumulated over time, including dingy walls and peeling paint. Worse, some complained, the white walls had become "bare and cold." Minnigerode had apparently hesitated to rectify the problems, so when the Reverend Hartley Carmichael arrived, the fashion conscious vestry in a first order of business presented him with plans for a major renovation that included a deepened chancel, new interior paint, and the installation of stained-glass windows behind the altar. For the bare walls that so irked the congregation, the design committee "proposed to decorate them handsomely."[76]

The church reopened after its renovation on December 20, 1889, just sixteen days after the second important event of 1889—the death of Jefferson Davis. His passing stung St. Paul's. The vestry confirmed that

> Profound gloom rests like a pall on our southern land, and the hearts of all are filled with sorrow at the death of their great leader, Jefferson Davis. We the vestry of St. Paul's church, unite with mourners, bound as we are to the deceased by the closest ties of Christian fellowship. Mr. Davis was confirmed and received the Holy Communion at its altar, and as during the most trying years of his life he was indeed one with us, we learned to love him not as the soldier and statesman, but as the simple and humble Christian gentleman.

They resolved that St. Paul's observe funeral services simultaneous to Davis's actual funeral in New Orleans, that the church be "draped in mourning," and that "a committee of the vestry shall select two conspicuous windows of the church to be dedicated as memorials to perpetuate the names of Robert E. Lee and Jefferson Davis."[77]

News of St. Paul's resolutions reached the Stewart family of Brook Hill on the outskirts of Richmond. During the Civil War, John Stewart—a founding member of the church—offered up a Richmond townhome to Lee as a private residence, and Lee returned the favor by inviting the family to shelter there when fighting neared their country estate.[78] In 1889, sisters Annie Carter, Lucy Norma, and Elizabeth Hope Stewart quickly offered to pay for a pair of memorial windows to Lee.[79] Having initially determined that all windows should be made in London or Munich, Carmichael and the design committee worked with the Stewart sisters to negotiate an appropriate design from English artisan Henry Holiday.[80]

St. Paul's unveiled the windows during a simple All Saints' Day service on November 1, 1892. Hartley Carmichael delivered the sermon, comparing Lee to Judas Maccabeus. "War is terrible," intoned Carmichael, "but as long as men are what they are there will be war. Sometimes there ought to be and should be war, as when the sword is drawn in defense of hearths and homes, and rights, the belief in which was matter of deep and earnest conviction." Here the rector alluded to Lee's resignation from the United States Army, wherein the Virginian declared "save in defense of my native State, I never desire again to draw my sword." Carmichael ended on a conciliatory note, "sure that in time the animosities and passions of the late conflict would entirely pass away, and this great man would be acknowledged North as he is South for the great general and humble Christian that he was."[81]

The pair of Jefferson Davis windows had a different path to existence. Joseph Reid Anderson wrote to Davis's widow, Varina, the news of St. Paul's memorial resolutions in 1889. She replied with gratitude, recalling that it was at St. Paul's, "my husband first knew the consolations of religion." She also remembered that she had buried three young sons from St. Paul's and requested of Anderson permission to install a window to their memory as well.[82] That proposed window eventually became a bronze tablet to the Davis sons. Perhaps the Great Depression of 1893 slowed the effort to raise funds for the Davis windows—it had hobbled other Confederate memorial efforts. After several false starts, and after "repeated inquiries and expressions of surprise from disappointed strangers," Rev. Carmichael constituted a Davis Memorial Window Committee to raise money and move the project forward. Chaired by Anne Ross and seven women from St. Paul's, the committee advertised the fundraising drive in newspapers across the nation and issued a flyer through the extensive network of Confederate veterans and women's organizations. It read,

It was in this church that [Davis] was confirmed, and it was here, while attending Morning Service, April 3 [sic], 1865, that the telegram was handed him from General LEE announcing the retreat of the army from Petersburg and the virtual ending of the war. It is meet and proper, therefore, that a Memorial should be erected in this historic church to the memory of the first and only President of the Southern Confederacy. More imposing monuments will bear testimony to Mr. DAVIS' great qualities as a statesman and a soldier; be it ours to hand down to posterity those graces of his Christian character which for four long years were devoutly renewed in this church, and where strength was given him to exemplify that faith which supported him in all the fierce conflicts of war and government, and that resignation which at the solemn end was not found wanting in him, enabling him to suffer vicariously for his people long after the conflict was over.

Donations arrived from scores of individuals: most in Virginia, many from across the South, and a few from as far away as Los Angeles, California, and Portland, Oregon. The Committee received donations from 104 United Daughters of the Confederacy chapters and 40 United Confederate Veterans camps. Even the Sunday School at St. James's across town contributed a small sum.[83]

Unlike the unassuming reveal of the Lee window, St. Paul's unveiled the pair of windows dedicated to Jefferson Davis in sensational fashion. A parade of veterans, their wives, representatives from Confederate organizations, elected officials from Virginia and other states all preceded the guest of honor, the widowed Varina Davis. But Fitzhugh Lee—nephew of Robert E. Lee, Confederate general, and a former Virginia governor—stole the show. Lee had been the American Consul in Cuba when the *USS Maine* exploded in Havana harbor two months before. Dropping in on the unveiling service on his return tour of the United States, Lee was in demand as the most prominent American with an eyewitness view of the impending conflict with Spain. Congress would declare war just three days later. In Richmond, Lee's entourage included his wife and "his pretty Cuban protégé Senorita Cisneros." Crowds "arose to catch a glimpse of the man who had made so fearless a stand for 'Cuba Libre'" and who would soon take command of a United States Army Corps bound for the Caribbean. They raised such a commotion outside the church that Carmichael "called the attention of the assemblage to the fact that this was a religious ceremony" and requested that people not clamor or leave immediately after the mid-service unveiling.

The Reverend William Meade Dame, himself a Confederate veteran and memoirist, preached the sermon. He, like Anne Ross's fundraising committee, eschewed praising Davis as a soldier, statesman, or leader. "What warrant," he challenged his listeners, "have you for your deed in placing this memorial here," in a temple of God? Dame answered himself by claiming that Davis "deserves the honor of the world and of the human race as one of its noblest servants and representatives," and he enumerated the reasons for viewing Davis in a Christian light. First, Davis had been called to lead a heroic nation. Then, after the war Davis stood as "representative of his people in suffering." There was Davis's stoic and unapologetic stance during Reconstruction (Dame noted "the fight from 61–65 was child's play compared to 65–72"). Finally, he noted, Davis had given Robert E. Lee to the world by elevating the Virginian to command of the Confederate army. Dame summarized that Davis deserved a memorial in a church because "in the devout conviction of devout men this man is worthy to be numbered with God's saints." Upon the unveiling, and during the offertory anthem that followed, the crowd promptly forgot Carmichael's plea, and "there was a general withdraw."[84]

Despite the resemblances that occasional viewers claimed to see in the Biblical figures represented in the memorial windows, the Lee and Davis windows are not meant to depict the physical likenesses of the Confederate leaders. The negotiations between St. Paul's and the artisans who made the windows contain no explicit or implicit instructions to produce such likenesses. And when referring to the windows' imagery, contemporaries accurately referred to Moses and St. Paul. However, incidents represented from the lives of Biblical figures were indeed chosen to amplify stories that the Lost Cause told them about Lee and Davis.

Drawn not from Exodus, but from the New Testament Book of Hebrews 11:24 describing Moses departing Pharaoh's house, the inscription on the Lee window reads: "By Faith Moses refused to be called the Son of Pharaoh's Daughter; Choosing rather to suffer affliction with the Children of God. For he Endured as seeing Him who is invisible."[85] A cornerstone of Robert E. Lee hagiography is the fact that the incoming Lincoln administration had offered Lee a significant command in the United States Army to suppress the rebellion in 1861. Lee refused and instead sided with the Confederate States. The image, then, conflates Moses refusing Pharaoh's riches and favor to go with his benighted, but righteous, people with Lee's rejecting the honor of

FIGURE 3. Lower part of the Robert E. Lee memorial window, with dedication obscured. (Brian Palmer/brianpalmer.photos)

command to go with *his* righteous people. The dynamics of the story are telling. Few white southerners in 1861 would have described the northern states as a tempting, glittering seat of wealth and civilization. In fact, they claimed that the southern United States were only held back from recognition of their world-historical importance by a grasping, hostile, chaotic, and dangerous democracy in the North. The picture of the northerners as wealthy and the southerners as humble, righteous victims, could only have emerged from a postwar world that had proven out those disparities. Further, there is little evidence to suggest that St. Paul's people were aware of the centrality of Moses to African American theology as God's chosen leader who led his people out of slavery. And certainly, there is no reason to think they would have recognized the irony of explicating the life of Lee through Moses, even if public speakers regularly invoked the parallel to the Black experience. That same year, a Black speaker at Richmond's Emancipation Day celebration, "drew strong comparisons between the colored people and the children of Israel," and "the same God who brought the Negro out of American bondage would carry him on until he shone before the world a perfect man."[86] As the Lost Cause proved over and over again, the actual realities of Black lives and history usually escaped its authors.

The theme of righteous victimhood continued in the lower Davis memorial window, depicting the passage from Acts 26 where the Apostle Paul, in chains prior to his transportation to Rome for trial, appears before Herod Agrippa in Caesarea. Upon hearing the Apostle's pleas, the king remarked, "This man doeth nothing worth of death or of bonds." The upper window, showing the Angels of Goodness and Mercy, bears the inscription from Job 31:6, "Let me be weighed in an even balance so that God may know my integrity."[87]

These scenes reflect two themes common to the Lost Cause. As Anne Ross's fundraisers and Rev. Dame had noted, Davis represented "his people in suffering." White southerners found the fact that Davis had been clapped in chains while in prison to have been execrable and humiliating. Yet the Apostle, too, wore chains while compellingly pleading the cause of Christ to Agrippa, in the same way that Davis insisted throughout the rest of his life that he had done nothing for which to be punished or humiliated. The upper window's inscription also repeated a common ex-Confederate appeal—that they had faithfully defended their cause, and it was up to the world to fairly judge their integrity. Ex-Confederates had no doubts the world would vindicate them.

White southerners appreciated the fact that Davis never, for a moment, hesitated to defend the righteousness of the Confederate cause. After the war he did not pollute himself with politics and never lost himself in the business of business (despite a disappointing turn as an insurance executive). Instead, he retired to Mississippi and patiently composed a two-volume legal defense of secession and history of the Confederate nation. When Davis evacuated Richmond in 1865, he left a controversial and unpopular president. The narrative of Davis in chains, honorably pleading the South's case to the world, underscored and blessed metaphorically by St. Paul's allegorical endorsement,

St. Paul's in War and after Emancipation | 59

FIGURE 4. Lower part of the Jefferson Davis memorial window. (Brian Palmer/brianpalmer.photos)

successfully transformed him into the Confederate saint that the Richmond church venerated.

In the years between the church's 1889 renovation and the 1898 installation of the Davis windows, congregants installed six other stained-glass windows, including memorials to St. Paul's founders or early vestrymen including Adolphus Blair, Griffin Davenport, Bolling Haxall, and Joseph Reid Anderson.

Because of the generation being memorialized, many wall plaques, installed in subsequent years, noted service in the Confederate army or navy. Mention of individual military service did not necessarily promulgate the larger narratives at the core of the Lost Cause—meaning the righteousness and purity of the Confederate nation—in the way that the Lee and Davis windows did. However, one additional plaque did: that memorializing Varina Anne "Winnie" Davis. Jefferson Davis's daughter, who had been born in Richmond during the war and baptized at St. Paul's, had emerged in the 1880s as a favorite of old veterans who saw in her an unsullied and pure example of southern white womanhood. As her biographers have shown, she endured the adoration out of a sense of duty to her father but would rather have lived her life as an art critic and "new woman" in New York City.[88] Upon Winnie's untimely death in September 1898, her mother, Varina, requested permission to install a bronze tablet to her memory next to her father's window. Emblazoned with two Confederate flags, the tablet proclaimed Winnie "The Daughter of the Confederacy."

Another family that installed memorial windows in 1896 had extensive links to Confederate memorial institutions across the South. Dr. Charles Macgill, originally from Hagerstown, Maryland, arrived as a refugee in Richmond in 1863. He and his four sons served in the Confederate army, and while his family dispersed all over the South after the war, Macgill remained in Richmond and a member of St. Paul's until his death in 1881.[89] Macgill's daughter, Mollie Ragan, married Swiss-born commercial shipping magnate Henry Rosenberg of Galveston, Texas; and, upon his death, she dedicated his considerable fortune to bolstering the Confederate memorial landscape across the South. In addition to providing a memorial plaque to several of her siblings at St. Paul's, she endowed churches in Maryland and Texas, created and led the Galveston United Daughters of the Confederacy chapter, paid for the Confederate monument in that city, and served as the Texas representative on the board of regents for Richmond's Confederate Museum. The *Richmond Times-Dispatch* remarked that she "might be called the patron Saint of the Confederacy."[90]

Even during the Civil War, people sought out St. Paul's because so many famous Confederates attended. It became a tourist destination after the war, even as the dingy interior dissatisfied its members. The 1889 renovation and decision to modernize with stained-glass windows brought the sanctuary into line with the congregation's Gilded Age aesthetics. The embrace of Confederate memory in the four memorial windows, however, elevated and sealed St. Paul's public identity and reputation as "the Church of the Confederacy." The

Richmond Dispatch called St. Paul's "the historic temple."[91] The *Times* called it "The Westminster Abbey of the South."[92] The *Parish Register* noted that "St. Paul's [is] invested with a sacred significance to hundreds who rarely, if ever, enter its walls."[93] Joseph Reid Anderson desired that "the memories of the Confederacy might ever cling 'round'" St. Paul's.[94] The public agreed, with the *Dispatch* claiming that the Davis windows endowed the sanctuary with "the devotion of the Confederates to the Lost Cause and many a heart will be thrilled with reverent joy to see the soft light streaming through the pictured panes in that famous old place."[95] Elsewhere, the paper called St. Paul's "a silent Confederate sermon."[96] Before the century ended, small commemorative plaques marked the pews once occupied by Lee and Davis—markers that would remain for more than a century to come.

The people of St. Paul's had been adherents to proslavery Christianity, but they never particularly led or pioneered in that movement. But the church stood second to no other religious institution in contributing to the larger Lost Cause ideology. Key to understanding the Lost Cause is its attribution of Christian perfection to Confederate leaders who, in their own times, had reputations for inflexible sectarian dogmatism (Stonewall Jackson) or those with no Christian reputation at all (Davis). The religious blessing of southern churches transformed the genuine rectitude of men like Lee into the highest model of Christian manhood for generations of white southern boys and men. The religious blessing of southern churches caused Jefferson Davis's brief incarceration and postwar defense of the Confederacy to transform the once-controversial president into a Christlike sufferer universally acclaimed among white southerners. Lee had always been popular, but the Lost Cause—with no small assistance from St. Paul's—*resurrected* Davis.[97]

Jefferson Davis's baptism and confirmation, his receipt of the fateful 1865 note while at Sunday worship, John Pegram's marriage and funeral, and Robert E. Lee's very presence: St. Paul's excelled at telling stories. Davis's sacrifice and Lee's faith fed a larger historical narrative that bolstered the claim of the moral superiority of white southerners and their view of the world, while eliding, at best, historical reality. For instance, vestryman and veteran Robert Stiles, who had earned a name for himself as an orator at reunions and memorial unveilings, equated military service in the war with sanctification. He later published a sanitized version of his own service as the memoir *Four Years Under Marse Robert*.[98]

The religious aspects of the Lost Cause entwined with a larger spectrum of values that defined the white southern worldview at the turn of the twentieth century. The Lost Cause and its extended cultural critiques had something to say about military prowess (Carmichael on Lee), about political rectitude (Dame on Davis), about gender relations (Confederate veterans on Winnie Davis), and not least, about race in modern America. St. Paul's people contributed those stories as well.

When commenting on race relations in the Old South and in contemporary times, Lost Cause advocates often blurred chronology and the bounds of history and fiction to demonstrate what they claimed to be essential character traits of Black and white people. They expressed some constancy over time regarding the truths they had identified. Ex-Confederates excavated their resentment about their allegedly misunderstood love for their slaves while insisting that Black people had been content and loyal in bondage. Their view of Black people as happily enthralled in slavery perpetuated their contemporary notion that Black people had been overwhelmed by freedom and looked wistfully to old times. The "happy slave" and "happy servant" tropes appeared in all manner of cultural media from advertising to pulp literature.[99]

Sallie May Dooley, a prominent St. Paul's congregant, published her novel, *Dem Good Ole Times,* in 1906. In it, she featured an aged ex-slave, Old Ben, who in thick dialect lamented his freedom. In slavery, he explained to his grandchild, "we had plenty to eat, a plenty to war, un mighty little wuck to do, case day was so many to do it." He also fondly recalled his mistress who comforted his mother with Bible readings. "Whar you ever hear in dem times," he concluded, "uv a crazy nigger? Now de country is full on um; pears to me like dey all crazy." Ben—or, to be precise, Dooley speaking through her fictional character—condemned the behavior of Black people who enjoyed their freedom too much. They "strut bout wid an empty stummuck." Black children in freedom, Ben—again, Dooley—claimed, grew up sassy, not knowing their place. He sighed that with old days lost, "my ole heart is empty is de aig shell de little checken jes lef."[100]

Dooley clearly imitated the literature of the prolific writer Thomas Nelson Page, a Virginian whose plantation romances celebrated dashing young cavaliers and loyal slaves who supposedly flourished before emancipation. Such sentimentalized historical commentary had implications for contemporary expectations of race relations, as explicitly revealed when Page took to the pages of a national magazine to defend the lynching of out-of-control Black people. He turned to history to explain why Black men had suddenly, allegedly, begun to rape white women. "Then came the period and process of Reconstruction, with its teachings," he said. "Among these was the teaching that the negro was the equal of the white, that the white was his enemy. The growth of the idea was a gradual one in the negro's mind." Of course, Page firmly believed that this false problem had not existed in slavery.[101]

Beverley Bland Munford, a lawyer, former state delegate and senator, St. Paul's member, and fixture in the cohort that constructed Richmond's Confederate memorial landscape, echoed Dooley's and Page's fictional perspectives with dispassionate historical analysis. His deeply influential 1909 book, *Virginia's Attitudes Toward Slavery and Secession,* claimed that Virginians had long desired to end slavery but could not because of abolitionist affronts to slaveholder honor. Secession happened, he reasoned, not to protect slavery, but to fight federal coercion and insult. For decades after its publication, the United Daughters of the Confederacy ensured that Munford's book found its way into classrooms to shape the history curriculum of generations of Virginia schoolchildren.[102]

The women who managed Richmond's Confederate Museum—among them St. Paul's communicants Kate Pleasants Minor and Sally Archer Anderson—also used history to affirm the contemporary racial order. One pamphlet produced by the institution claimed that in "Old Virginia," the "little darkeys" were "anxious to serve." The Museum demonstrated the benevolent care of white masters by displaying documents, including the "Address on Religious Instruction of Negroes" and the sheet music from the minstrel tune "Old Black Joe." Museum staff exhibited not only historical artifacts, but they also collected books and articles that revealed an intense interest in the status of Black people in the post-emancipation South. Such materials, like Page's essay, also cast lynching as a justifiable act.[103] These all perpetuated narratives of honorable white people and loyal Black servants that were not only what they regarded as history, but also was prescriptions for the future.

The double effect of the Lost Cause's racial expectations and projections of stoic and noble white people facing adversity and incapable Black people dangerously emboldened by freedom converged in one enduring story about St. Paul's that first appeared in 1905. On April 16, the *Times-Dispatch* reported an interview with Thomas L. Broun, a Confederate veteran visiting from Charleston, West Virginia. Broun stated:

> Two months after the evacuation of Richmond, business called me to Richmond for a few days, and on Sunday morning in June, 1866 [sic], I attended St. Paul's Church. Dr. Minnegerode [sic] preached to a con-

gregation fairly good. It was communion day. When the minister was ready to administer the Holy Communion, amongst those who first arose and advanced to the communion table was a tall, well dressed negro man; very black. He walked with an air of military authority. This was a great surprise and shock to the communicants and others present, who frequented that most noted of the Episcopal Churches in Virginia. Its effect upon the communicants was startling, and for several moments they retained their seats in solemn silence, and did not move, being deeply chagrined at this attempt of the Federal authorities, to offensively humiliate them during their most devoted Church services. Dr. Minnegerode [sic] looked embarrassed.

General Robert E. Lee was present, and he, ignoring the action and very presence of the negro, immediately arose, in his usual dignified and self-possessed manner, walked up the aisle of the church to the chancel rail, and reverently knelt down to partake of the communion, and not far from where the negro was. This lofty conception of duty by General Lee under such provoking and irritating circumstances, had a magic effect upon the other communicants, who immediately went forward to the communion table. I, being one of the number, did likewise.

By this action of Gen. Lee, the services were concluded, as if the negro had not been present. It was a grand exhibition of superiority shown by a true Christian and great soldier under the most trying offensive circumstances.[104]

Later generations would interpret this story as Lee demonstrating a particularly liberal racial largesse — modeling tolerance to an intolerant audience — and therefore exhibiting his own exemplary character. Broun's description of the act, however, clearly reveals the opposite agenda at work, with characterizations that fit perfectly into Lost Cause racial dynamics. The unidentified Black man is described as "well dressed" and one "who walked with an air of military authority." Those observations were not admiration, but accusation. Sallie May Dooley and her literary-historical cohort had praised Black people who humbled themselves in their demeanor and appearance around white people, while condemning confident and assertive Black people as strutting about, offensively brandishing their autonomy. In Broun's account, then, the Black man's approach was a serious affront. Broun called it so, stating that it "deeply chagrined" the congregation as through some form of federally

FIGURE 5. St. Paul's sanctuary after 1898, with memorial windows and the pews of Jefferson Davis and Robert E. Lee clearly marked. (Cook Collection, The Valentine)

imposed humiliation. The Lost Cause, after all, held that Reconstruction was the vicious federal imposition of a dangerous racial order on a blameless and undeserving South. To the congregation, Broun's story relates, the man's assertiveness had been "provoking and irritating." Did Lee use his example to teach his church a lesson in interracial civility for a new age? He arose, embodying the stoic, duty-bound poise that Lost Cause advocates attributed to all Confederate soldiers, an attitude he used to pointedly ignore the Black man. No solicitation of regard, no warm welcome, but an act of negation and erasure. Communion continued not as if St. Paul's had an unexpected but ultimately accepted guest, but as if the man hadn't been there. Lee, in Broun's narrative, had not offered a lesson in reconciliation and tolerance. Reflecting his reputation as unflappable in the face of battlefield crisis, Broun's Lee modeled white response to such affronts with stoic and dignified self-possession. Popular writer Myrta Lockett Avary cited and amplified Broun's narrative. In her 1906 book, *Dixie after the War,* Avary wrote that the Black man's approach to the altar was "sinister, a challenge, not an expression of piety." After Lee's silent rebuke, "the people followed and the service proceeded as if no innovation had been attempted."[105]

Richmond Episcopalians had explicitly rejected equality at the communion rail just five years before this alleged event and emancipation had done nothing to alter their views of the proper relationship between white and Black people. In the years to come, St. Paul's, the Diocese of Virginia, and the Protestant Episcopal Church all reaffirmed and deepened segregation within the church. Aside from Broun's story, the alleged incident cannot be independently verified. But had it taken place, and had Lee intended to demonstrate racial reconciliation, the lesson was lost on St. Paul's and on Broun's audience. Only later generations in different contexts took up that specific lesson.

Ex-Confederates constructed a new history and imprinted it upon the sacred and secular landscape. That history was rooted in the experience of defeat—a sense of righteous martyrdom mixed with real grief. While they based some tenets of the Lost Cause in a few historical realities, the unity that white people claimed on behalf of the Confederacy, the saintly Christianity of its leaders, and most importantly, the distance they placed between themselves and slavery contributed to a way of understanding the Civil War that was significantly detached from historical reality. When delivering the keynote address at the 1890 unveiling of the Lee Memorial on Monument Avenue, prominent St. Paul's member Archer Anderson remarked that "a people carves its own image in the monument of its great men."[106] That image promoted by white Virginians in the 1890s, was not only of noble men and women, but also of hapless or degenerate African Americans. Those same white Virginians moved to enshrine that entrenched dichotomy not only in monuments and memorials, but also into Virginia's law and customs.

Virginia's Democratic leaders, since the suppression of the Readjuster movement, had sought to control politics through the restriction of voting rights of Black men and even poor whites. They had been shaped by rhetoric like Archer Anderson's description of undeferential and violent Black people in Danville, and by Bishop Alfred Randolph's conception of African Americans as generationally incapable of political competency. The General Assembly restricted some voting with the 1894 Walton Act. The Constitutional Convention called in 1901 included among its delegates Otway Allen, a St. Paul's communicant. William A. Anderson, a Lexington lawyer, nephew of Joseph Reid Anderson, and future St. Paul's congregant, served as the convention's President Pro Tempore. The convention President, John Goode, summarized its motivation to draft protocols for disfranchisement—that the Fifteenth Amendment guaranteeing African American suffrage had been "a stupendous blunder . . . a crime against civilization and Christianity." Concluding deliberations in 1902, the convention delegates crafted legislation that essentially repealed Black suffrage through a combination of a poll tax, a grandfather clause, and an "understanding clause" designed to test voters' knowledge. The new constitution worked well toward its intended goal— the near complete purge of eligible Black voters in the Commonwealth and the entrenchment of a conservative Democratic political regime that would govern unchallenged for nearly a century. Few white Richmonders opposed the constitution. Among them was John S. Wise, a son of former St. Paul's member Henry A. Wise Sr., and brother of one-time assistant rector, Henry A. Wise Jr. But Wise was not a St. Paul's member and was then an outsider to Richmond. Instead, representing mainstream orthodox racial paternalism, William A. Anderson, the new Attorney General and St. Paul's congregant, struck down Wise's lawsuit and oversaw the constitution's implementation.[107] Alfred Randolph, then Bishop of the new Diocese of Southern Virginia and ever the advocate for "the evangelization of the negro," approved, saying that "the Southern States which had limited negro suffrage had acted wisely, and that such action had removed obstacles to the spiritual, moral and intellectual development of the race."[108] In his view, and the view of all like him, the right relation of the mutual obligation of the races that they prescribed could only be approached if Black people did not aspire to political equality. The 1902 Constitution solved that problem.

In 1907, the Protestant Episcopal Church enacted what turned out to be a rather symbolic, but important, act of racial segregation. Upon the motion of George Freeman Bragg, by then an Episcopal priest in Baltimore and leader in the Protestant Episcopal Church's Commission on Colored Work, the Church studied a resolution to dissolve diocesan colored missionary jurisdictions and organize a separate national jurisdiction under the supervision of the more liberal General Convention. At the 1907 national gathering, held at St. Paul's (and the adjacent State Capitol) southern bishops—citing the authority of bishops within their own dioceses—opposed the move. As racial paternalists, they firmly believed that Blacks still required the close supervision of whites, and southern whites at that. After much discussion and a flurry of counterproposals, the Convention voted to activate special suffragan bishops—assistant bishops designated to oversee Black congregations within individual dioceses. However, these suffragans—intended to be Black men—would not be eligible to join the House of Bishops and had to report to diocesan bishops instead. Therefore, the national church offered some slight autonomy to Black churches; but with the affirmation of diocesan control (rather than more benevolent General Convention oversight). By rejecting a larger voice for Black clergy, it completed the marginalization of Black people within the church.

The institution of Black suffragan bishops was symbolic, however, because outside of North Carolina, no southern diocese actually enacted the new program, leaving Black churches in limbo for a generation. Nevertheless, at its conception, Richmonders looked upon the moment with evident approval. The *Times-Dispatch* noted that the 1907 General Convention set about "bettering the missionary influences put about the negro race in America." While many disagreed about the proper course, "it is fully believed that the time has come when the negro can be discussed without heat and unnecessary bitterness." Black people, white commenters reasoned, could be approached with affinity so long as they represented no real threat of political, social, or ecclesial equality.[109]

St. Paul's left little evidence that its clergy, vestry, or communicants engaged in outreach to Black communities or cooperation with Black Episcopalians, which would have aligned with the long-held concept of racial obligation from the nineteenth century. The mutual obligation had simply ceased as a religious imperative while it survived and thrived as a social and political ethic. St. Paul's people may have attempted to enact it outside of their church, as always, but they made no effort from within. Instead, St. Paul's played no small part in perpetuating the narrative of racial difference and hierarchy through its embrace of the Lost Cause. The church's version of the ideology—a southern civil religion—prioritized the saintly character of Lee, Davis, and those who fought for the Confederacy and the righteous victimhood of the white Confederate South. Indeed, the people of St. Paul's, more than most white southerners, adopted the sentimentality of the Lost Cause. Elizabeth Wright Weddell's history of St. Paul's, published in 1931, focused primarily on the church's antebellum and wartime years, with particular nods to Davis's and Lee's attendance, Minnigerode's leadership, and the drumbeat of funerals. Her second volume, which opened with a mere skimming of the years between 1865 and 1907 and then touched briefly on events in subsequent decades, devotes itself to a lengthy annotated listing of church monuments to date. She considered her volumes a chronicle to "the historic years," focusing primarily on "the names of noble men and women," rather than the more prosaic years between the war and the books' publication.[110] The war and Confederate connections mattered in the church's own telling, but not much else.

Yet the larger Lost Cause that St. Paul's helped build had an unmistakable conception of Blackness that stood in clear contrast and connection to that of whiteness embodied by Lee and Davis. It defined a historical narrative bolstered by the science of the day that prescribed action in the present and the future. The theological and providential assumptions of the sacred obligation at the heart of proslavery Christianity had been obliterated. Instead, white supremacy leaned on a narrative of racial difference in the secular world that motivated people to act. And as the twentieth century unfolded, St. Paul's deployed its newly burnished historical identity in unexpected causes.

3 | The Social Gospel in a Lost Cause Church

MARY-COOKE BRANCH Munford rallied elite white people to support the expansion of Richmond's Memorial Hospital to serve African Americans in 1916. Before a fundraising banquet at the Jefferson Hotel she proclaimed, "Nothing in the past has occurred to make us see the solidarity of the human race more than movements of this kind. They show us that 'we are our brother's keeper.' It is indeed the call of 'Old Black Joe—I'm coming.'"[1]

Munford referred to the minstrel song, "Old Black Joe," in which an aged slave looked to the angels in heaven for relief of his infirmities. She may have encountered it in the Confederate Museum, which had the sheet music on display. Condescending words to our ears today, in 1916 they reflected one part of the activating impulse for the most liberal-minded of Richmond's racial paternalists. Inspired by Lost Cause tales of benevolent masters, these white women and men used their social standing and wealth on behalf of the city's Black population. Munford was the daughter of a Confederate veteran and postwar Conservative Democrat who attempted to reach out to Black voters during Reconstruction, and she was the widow of Beverley Bland Munford, Virginia's premier historian of slavery. In the early decades of the twentieth century, she stood as the state's leading practitioner of white paternalistic liberalism during the Jim Crow era. Not a stereotypical southern belle, Munford was a tireless social reformer. She took a keen interest in women's higher education and suffrage, quality public schools, the care of orphans, and a scientific approach to the problems of public health and poverty. She served on the boards of numerous organizations dedicated to African American social improvement, including the Community House for Negro People, the Virginia Industrial School for Colored Girls, and Janie Porter Barret's reform school. Drawing on a latent sense that Black Americans had to evolve into full civic participation combined with a heavy dose of racial obligation, Munford reportedly said that "White people here know what is best for our Negroes and when we feel that they're ready for it, we're going to give it to them without them asking or fighting for it." White liberals actively pursued a proactive benevolence precisely—according to them—to avoid "fighting" or other forms of racial friction. Proslavery Christians had anticipated that God would end slavery in time. Now, their children claimed that benevolent duty for themselves when contemplating the future of segregation. Despite the seeming foreclosure on any Black political and social aspirations as a result of turn-of-the-century southern state constitutional revisions, the newly oppressed generation across the south engaged in daily struggles and negotiations with segregationist regimes over the terms of the marginalization. Indeed, events like protests against segregation on public streetcars that marked many southern cities, were often countered by a tightening of racial ordnances. Race relations, then, remained volatile and negotiable even at the depths of the public disfranchisement of Black people. White liberal paternalists like Mary-Cooke Munford, then, found it necessary to continuously act to maintain their version of paternalism.[2] In pursuit of those goals, Munford entered relationships and used methods that her father and his generation could hardly have imagined.[3]

W. Russell Bowie, Munford's nephew, became St. Paul's rector in 1911. He adored his aunt and recognized the faith convictions behind her actions. "Religion," he later wrote, "had never been associated for her with rest."[4] A native Richmonder, who grew up attending St. Paul's himself, Bowie frequently invoked Lost Cause imagery about benevolent masters and a sainted Robert E. Lee. In 1915, Bowie drew directly on the Lee Memorial window to tell local college students that "the revered chieftain of the Confederacy, in leaving the high position in the Union to serve his own people in the South, made a great personal sacrifice like unto that of Moses, who left his station of ease, wealth and glory in the palace of Egyptian nobility to lead his chosen people out of bondage and into a fair and free land." So he worked well alongside Munford in the same social causes. In fact, he likely saw little difference between himself and his aunt in his understanding of the racial order.[5]

Yet Bowie arrived at activist solutions for social problems with a remarkably different theological agenda. A Harvard graduate who enrolled at the theologically conservative Virginia Theological Seminary, Bowie spent a year attending classes at Union Theological Seminary in New York City. There, he worked in lower-east-side settlement houses and imbibed the progressive theology known as the Social Gospel.[6] The Social Gospel drove its practitioners to combine Christian ethics with social sciences to solve the problems of modern industrial America, including poverty, alcoholism, crime, and labor strife. Critically, the Social Gospel saw racial inequality, like a broad spectrum of societal problems, not as God ordained, and not determined by history and evolution, but rather as a man-made sin deeply rooted in secular social systems.[7]

Bowie expressed his Social Gospel bona fides in the lyrics he composed for the hymn, "Holy City Seen of John":

Oh Shame to us who rest content
While lust and greed for gain
In street and shop and tenement
Wring gold from human pain,
And bitter lips in deep despair
Cry, "Christ has died in vain!"[8]

When St. Paul's vestry called Russell Bowie to its rectorship in 1911, the twenty-eight-year-old priest sat its members down before him and extracted a commitment. "Did they want [St. Paul's] to represent a real welcome and concern for human beings, whatever their backgrounds may have been?" he asked. "Did it want to begin to move conspicuously beyond parochial involvement? Would it try to be a dynamo of power for all the church's missionary service everywhere?" These were less questions than a set of demands. The vestry conceded.[9]

Munford and Bowie seemed locked into the same course. But the respective foundations for their activism—Munford's Lost Cause-based racial paternalism versus Bowie's Social Gospel—constitute the central struggle within St. Paul's identity in the early twentieth century. Between the two movements and the years 1911 and 1939, St. Paul's stepped to the forefront of social activism and white liberal racial advocacy in Richmond. In their time, this generation at St. Paul's continued their transformation—in how they understood the sacred obligation—but also about race and theology and the structure of white supremacy. But when that change challenged their historical imagination, they arrived at an impasse.

The Lost Cause civic culture at the turn of the twentieth century was utterly conservative. Its genteel authors—chiefly women, and many from St. Paul's—insisted on propriety in the handling of Confederate flags, artifacts, and memory in near-sacred anniversary and religious observances.[10] St. Paul's, then, was a popular venue. The Lee and Davis windows served as a draw for gatherings of Confederate memorialists, and the church became the religious annex to Richmond's frequent reunions, monument unveilings, anniversaries, and funerals.

In 1907, St. Paul's threw open its doors for the throngs who crowded Richmond for the unveiling of the Jefferson Davis statue on Monument Avenue. The George E. Pickett and R.E. Lee Camps of Confederate Veterans, along with members of the Hollywood Memorial Association and the United Daughters of the Confederacy, listened as rector Robert Forsyth "made a gallant defense of the memory of President Davis from the charges of personal cowardice, that his enemies have so freely made."[11] The rector's defense reinforced St. Paul's attachment to the Davis family evidenced by the Davis memorial windows, as had the funerals there of Winnie Davis (1898) and Varina Howell Davis (1906), highlights of Richmond's increasingly routine Confederate burial scene.[12] Funerals for Mrs. W.H.F. "Rooney" Lee, Fitzhugh Lee, and the church's own Confederate luminaries like Eppa Hunton, a Confederate general and US Senator from Virginia, and Joseph Reid Anderson, all drew overflow crowds. Hundreds of Black Tredegar workers attended Anderson's funeral at St. Paul's, where they sat in the segregated western gallery. The *Richmond Planet* eulogized him as "particularly the friend of the coloured people."[13] The United Daughters of the Confederacy (UDC) held annual services in the sanctuary, and in 1926 its ladies crowned their relationship with St. Paul's when they presented a Confederate battle flag to be flown from the portico on various anniversaries.[14] On the occasion of the large national Confederate veterans reunion in 1915, during which rector Bowie preached on the Lost Cause, the *Parish Register* coyly called St. Paul's an "interesting Mecca."[15]

In light of St. Paul's heightened profile as a center of sacred social activity for the elite in an increasingly expanding industrial city, the vestry recognized that maintenance of the church structure required greater financing than could be had from the Sunday collection plate and pew rentals. The Endowment Fund, chartered in 1905, raised money for the "preservation, insurance, [and] improvement" of the sanctuary, its memorials, its charitable outreach, and the St. Paul's Church Home for Orphans on Leigh Street. The authors of the initial Endowment Fund report—Beverley Munford and Archer Anderson—remarked on the church's history and noted that "On account of the pious and patriotic interest with which the church and its memorials is invested, it is necessary to keep its doors always open, thus entailing the expense of the daily presence of a sexton and the constant heating of the church during the winter months." The first contributions to the fund came from the estates of

Frank B. Davenport ($1,000) and Richard L. Maury ($1,000 in state bonds).[16] While some Richmond churches had begun a migration to the placid western suburbs, St. Paul's history—and now its endowment—permanently fixed it to its downtown location.

By the end of the century's first decade, while the congregants on ordinary Sundays still enjoyed the Episcopal liturgy and socializing after the service, St. Paul's had fully embraced its public ministry of extolling the virtues of Confederate saints. St. Paul's sat at the center of a memorial landscape in Richmond, and Virginia that marked every identifiable instance of Confederate history and excluded nearly everything else. The Lost Cause, for white Richmonders, was more than just their explanation of the Civil War; it was an integral part of a larger cultural ethos and social ordering of their world that included a reverence for history, an insistence on elite rule, a celebration of genteel values, and white supremacy. The history that they revered was not simply an account of former times, but a prescription for the future—a usable past—created to support the white supremacist power structure made manifest in the Commonwealth's 1902 Constitution.[17] The guardians of that history often made plain their opinion of where African Americans fit in. In 1932 the city proposed a playground for Black children at Clark Springs, nestled into an enclave of Hollywood Cemetery. A female spokeswoman from the Hollywood Memorial Association declared that "our Confederate dead [are] more important than any living person. We do not want a Negro playground within a mile of that cemetery," thus establishing clear delineations of who was welcome in the city's civic culture, and who was not.[18]

Russell Bowie—grandson of a Confederate officer—easily wove Lost Cause tropes into his sermons. At the 1915 veteran's reunion, he preached on the "the dauntless courage that dares to fight hard battles against tremendous odds, and the unflinching faithfulness displayed by the men and women who fought and bled and gave up their loved ones that the principles for which they stood might triumph." It was a lesson drawn from the windows—principle proved right by honor and courage—particularly in defeat. Bowie didn't just praise past heroics of Confederate veterans. He continued, "The qualities which are needed today in the life of Richmond and of the whole South . . . are those which made the 'Lost Cause' not lost, and which can take the seemingly forlorn hopes of moral warfare and turn them into glorious victory." Lost Cause speakers after the 1890s frequently claimed that the principles for which the Confederate States struggled had not actually been lost. The return to power of the conservative white regime and re-imposition of a firm racial hierarchy had proven them right after all. Restoration of a conservative racial order, in their view, allowed them to turn from political struggles toward battles in a "moral warfare" against sin and social decay.

But this "moral warfare" was much more than simply the duty of white supremacy. In the Lost Cause's faulty historical imagination of the Old South as a genteel, organic, society where noblesse oblige and not material pursuits drove its adherents to promote a sensibility of honesty, courtesy, decency, and respect for every person regardless of social class or race. The stories that people like Bowie wove about moral righteousness of the Confederate past and the southern present crowded out any other story and vindicated the ruling class. But when Bowie concluded that "we are not sorry for this to-day," he meant more than just the racial legacy of 1902, but the larger ethos of genteel society, and the expectation that everyone would play their race-defined part in it, and struggle for moral causes no matter the odds.[19] The sacred obligation had been resurrected not as theology, but as civil religion.

The stories about the Lost Cause—particularly descriptions of slavery—shaped the way that white Virginians chose to understand race relations in the early twentieth century. St. Paul's—through its dedicated windows, its embrace of a Confederate identity, and the public actions of its members—participated in creating a dominant historical narrative that had serious consequences for their lives and the lives of those around them.

White southerners, including St. Paul's people such as Mary Wingfield Scott, Russell Bowie, and Ellen Glasgow, stocked their memoirs with glowing descriptions of intimate relations with Black nurses, cooks, chauffeurs, and other domestic servants.[20] An emphasis on gratitude and loving attachment to such household staff became central to the identity of southern white elites alongside the fact that their dependence remained a central reality. The historic framing of benevolent masters and loyal slaves locked in an organic relationship could not be distinguished from the way twentieth century white people talked about familial relationships with domestic employees.

Despite the gauzy white nostalgia, however, some St. Paul's women updated the terms of the servant-employer relationship for a modern era, shaken by a massive migration of southern African Americans to the North, racial tension, and industrial dislocations sparked by the Great War. Members of the Richmond Board of the National Housewives League discerned in 1919 a "servant problem." They presumably intuited a discomfort among Black women to perform or maintain not only loyalty, but to also adhere to a one-sided term of employment. The Housewives League, which included Rosalie Archer among its leaders, proposed an employment bureau for servants, where housewives could be matched with maids, cooks, and nurses that the bureau would deem to appropriately professional. Whether that meant an up-to-date knowledge of the amount of starch for a collar, or a suitable attitude of deference was unstated. But should a bureau not work, the Housewives League proposed an alternative: attempt to import white servants from the North. The organization embodied the temperament of the white ruling class: ready to be genteel and gracious in its approach to Black employees, but just as prepared to leave Black people behind if they did not come along. This concern about the instability in the domestic servant labor pool continued into the Great Depression, when St. Paul's member Lawrence Moore, regional manager of a federal employment agency, noted in 1940 the need to provide professional training to domestic servants, in order to justify generous wages.[21] Employer and employee friction ensued in varying degrees. On one tragic occasion, it spilled over into violence. In 1937, chauffeur Joe Deas killed his employer, St. Paul's vestryman E. Mulford Crutchfield, in a dispute over pay. The Richmond newspapers gave front-page accounts of the murder, and afterward, when the fugitive was gunned down by city police when discovered hiding in the tenement of a friend.[22]

St. Paul's pinnacle of faithful-servant rhetoric came in 1925. In April of that year, a streetcar struck and killed Robert Damell at the corner of Brook Road and Broad Street. Damell, an African American man, had been employed as St. Paul's sexton since 1907, and his genial presence warmed the hearts of St. Paul's congregants. The vestry, in their sense of obligation to Damell, paid for his funeral and insisted that it be held at St. Paul's, volunteered as honorary pallbearers, and made the dramatic decision to allow Damell's family and friends to occupy the off-limits lower pews while the white folks retreated to the upper galleries.[23]

This inversion of the traditional order delighted the local white press. The *Richmond News-Leader* noted the "praise for his unfailing courtesy, his faithfulness, and his life for St. Paul's was heard on all sides at the church." The *Times-Dispatch* counted 1,500 attendees for the "faithful old sexton" at the "religious shrine of the Confederacy." In a separate editorial, the same paper reveled in the irony of so many Black people sitting in the historic church, and made its point:

> They say the War Between the States was fought to preserve slavery; they say the South hates and is cruel to the negroes; they say the true

freedom and true kindliness are to be found by the negro only outside the South. Without bitterness and without spleen, it is asked: Can there be hatred and cruelty and oppression here, when in the capital of the Confederacy, in the church which was its chief temple, an old negro man who has died in service draws together at his death the very flower of the South to join in sorrow in hope to do him honor.[24]

For its white readers, the editorial framed the Damell funeral as a refutation of charges of racism and as a true picture of race relations in the South.

Damell's funeral in 1925 came at the peak of a national rage for romanticized notions of faithful slaves and beloved "mammies" of the antebellum South. In addition to literary descriptions in novels and memoirs, the United Daughters of the Confederacy proposed a monument to "mammies" in Washington, DC, in 1923. Ultimately, it wasn't built, but faithful slave and servant memorials proliferated across the South.[25] In Richmond, numerous St. Paul's women joined in fundraisers for St. Monica's Mission, a nondenominational charity dedicated to the care of elderly Black women and the provision of a nursery for working Black mothers. One 1912 notice for a fundraiser chronicled booths staffed by "women who remembered ... their old 'mammies' ... and who were thus endeavouring to help them."[26] Beyond Richmond, the Episcopal Diocese of Virginia in 1916 consecrated a mission church in Berryville for a Black congregation and raised money for it by appealing to white people who fondly recalled their "mammies" from their youths. "All the money to build this church of concrete and to furnish it," noted the Episcopal Church's mission magazine, "was sent by white women and men as a token of grateful love for those dear souls who were faithful unto death to their white charges and to the service of women and men who owned their bodies."[27]

Damell's funeral in 1925 also came at a particular moment of white racial hysteria in Virginia that revealed the hard edge that white Virginians could take when challenged on their racial assumptions. Fueled by eugenic theories of racial purity and obsessed with the specter of white racial decline through interracial sex, the General Assembly passed the Racial Integrity Act in 1924. It strictly delineated the definition of whiteness and strictly prohibited interracial marriage. The Act's passage, however, did not calm eugenicist fears. The Damell funeral took place simultaneously to white agitation over an incident at Hampton Institute, the Black college near Norfolk, in which ushers seated the wife of a Newport News editor next to Black attendees in a mixed audience for a student dance recital. Her outrage fueled advocacy for the Public

Assemblages Act, also known as the Massenburg Bill, that passed in 1926 and strictly enforced segregation in all public events and venues. The Newport News editor compared the Damell funeral and the Hampton Institute incident, noting the appropriateness of the separation of races at St. Paul's compared to the "mixed audiences" at Hampton. He added that, of course, "no well-bred Virginian could hate the negro." He went on, "the funeral of the colored sexton in St. Paul's was a special occasion and the tribute to him was understood by both negroes and whites. . . . It was quite in accordance with our time-honored customs." Those who approved of Hampton Institute's mixed audiences clearly, he declared, "have not the Virginian instinct."[28]

No doubt, the congregants, staff, and clergy at St. Paul's, all of whom presumably shared the "Virginia instinct," held genuine affection for Robert Damell. But the news coverage of the Damell funeral revealed that the lives of those employed as servants would not only be defined by their subservient relationships to white people, but also used to justify larger systems that kept accomplished men like Damell as low-wage laborers. What went unsaid in the *Times-Dispatch* editorial was anything about him other than his status as a "faithful old negro."[29]

Born enslaved in Northumberland County, Virginia in 1852, Robert Damell served aboard watercraft as a sailor until he enlisted in the United States Army's 10th Cavalry in 1876. He served in Indian Wars campaigns in Texas and, upon reenlisting in 1878, served in the 9th US Cavalry—the other all-Black regiment popularly known as "Buffalo Soldiers"—until his discharge in 1883. Damell worked as a day laborer in Richmond in 1900 and lived with his wife, Fannie, and daughter, Charlotte, in Jackson Ward. He worshipped at Ebenezer Baptist Church. St. Paul's hired him as its sexton in 1907 (employment perhaps enabled by the newly established endowment fund) and though he worked there for seventeen years, the church rarely referred to him in staff rosters by his full name, but simply as Robert. In long-held linguistic differentiation, the Black man was also denied an honorific title, although white staff members were carefully listed as Dr., Mr., Mrs., and Miss. Even when the editors of the *Parish Register* did list his last name, they spelled it wrong just as often as they spelled it right.[30]

St. Paul's paid for Robert Damell's headstone in Evergreen Cemetery. The stone describes him not as a family man, nor as a United States Army veteran, but rather as "faithful servant." St. Paul's dominant story about itself and the larger white fantasy of Black lives intruded on Damell, even in death, and eclipsed a fuller accounting of his life. Damell wasn't the only Black person subject to this treatment from St. Paul's people. George and Anne Ross of St. Paul's installed a headstone for their "faithful servant," Agnes Weeden, at her grave in Evergreen Cemetery and Otway Allen marked the grave of Lucy Taylor with "Mammy Nurse in the Family of Wm C. Allen, Faithful Unto Death," in the Shockoe Hill Cemetery. These same men and women who orchestrated Robert Damell's funeral also wrote the history of slavery and the Civil War for twentieth-century Virginia.[31]

The narrative of faithful slave/waged servant and benevolent master/employer served its purpose. It justified white supremacy, erased the realities of African American experience, and maintained Black people in a limited economic and social positions. It had also long served as a foundation for a continued, self-defined, white obligation to work for the improvement of Black lives. Yet where the generation of Mary-Cooke Munford and Russell Bowie differed fundamentally from that of Alfred Randolph was not only in the casting of racism as a human sin, but also in the Social Gospel theology and in its use of social-scientific underpinnings.

St. Paul's member John Kerr Branch, chairman of the campaign for the 1916 Memorial Hospital fundraiser, boasted that in the matter of "taking care of our colored people . . . is as good as settled now." Branch meant it: he pledged a stunning $30,000 of his own money toward the African American hospital.[32] But the channels of this historical imagination could be expanded. Some St. Paul's people, including Richard Carrington, and successive rectors Bowie and Beverley D. Tucker Jr., who otherwise adhered to the Lost Cause historical imagination, sustained an ardent, if futile, opposition to eugenicists, the Racial Integrity Act, the Massenburg Bill, and local segregation ordnances. Not that they were opposed to segregation, or a narrative or racial difference, but because they imagined a genteel relationship between races that was more defined by a now well-articulated framework of "separate but equal," that allowed for more dignity than enforcement of a performative deference in all cases. This generation never fully broke free of their historical imagination, but in its actions, it made new space.

In 1919, racial politics intwined with gender politics as the question of woman suffrage roiled the Commonwealth—and St. Paul's members representing opposing factions. In previous years, Mary-Cooke Munford, Kate Pleasants Minor, and sisters Fontaine and Lou Belle Jones worked tirelessly in the Virginia Equal Suffrage League. Rector Bowie gave public support to the votes-for-women effort, as did other churchmen. Prominent opponents also numbered among congregants, including Mary Mason Anderson Williams, Annie Rose Walker, and Sallie May Dooley, who sat on the board of the Virginia Association Opposed to Woman Suffrage. As that organization's president, Williams (daughter of Archer Anderson) published an open letter in the *Times-Dispatch* addressed to state legislators regarding the pending vote on the ratification of a federal amendment. In it she raised the Association's most virulent—and ultimately effective—argument that if women gained the vote, then Black women could potentially double the size of the Black electorate in many parts of the state. To that end, Williams warned the lawmakers against "forcing upon the whites negro political supremacy" and "racial social equality and intermarriage of Blacks and whites." She concluded with "a call upon whites for the supremacy of the white race." Pro-suffrage advocates, who excluded Black members from their League for "expediency," countered that the same laws that kept Black men from the polls would undoubtedly deter Black women as well. The opposition arguments prevailed; the following year, the General Assembly voted against ratifying the Nineteenth Amendment.[33]

While still rector at St. Paul's, Bowie had previously joined St. Philips' rector the Reverend Junius Taylor, at a biracial gathering at the Black Leigh Street Methodist Episcopal Church in 1921. Rev. Bowie spoke on "The Colored Citizens and the Community" and began by praising the "loyalty of the colored people in the days past." Because of that loyalty, Bowie urged white support for "better housing and schooling" for Black children and "justice in courts and equal opportunity for employment."[34] Bowie's nostalgia for an imaginary past was routine; however, his stance—*alongside* Black people—marked a significant transition for a religious body that, just a decade before, could not countenance or imagine white people and Black people communing together. Bowie's sermons, while still invoking southern history and elevating values of gentlemanliness, pushed past that former relationship to forge new ones based on his terms of mutual courtesy in an attempt to attack systemic problems. Even though such positioning repeatedly failed to identify racial hierarchy and segregation as the actual sources of those systemic problems, it still represented an important revolution in St. Paul's theology of race. The Social Gospel catalyzed that theology.

Developed in the late nineteenth century, the Social Gospel combined innovative theology with social sciences to address the problems of poverty in industrialized societies. Social Gospel theology, articulated by northern Protestant ministers like Washington Gladden and Walter Rauschenbusch, described a single humanity devoid of hierarchy but divided by sin. (Compare this to the ordained racial divisions described by proslavery theologians.) In the urban North, Social Gospel practitioners saw poverty, poor public health, bad education, and hostile labor relations as the result of human sin. They included racism in this panoply of problems that needed addressing. Though Social Gospellers stopped short of demanding racial egalitarianism, they did position racial inequality as a man-made sin to be overcome. Its practitioners' motto, "the fatherhood of God; the brotherhood of man," worked to demolish biblically inspired boundaries between races. The new theology, in the hands of white people, still recognized the existence of racial differences that they attributed to evolution and history and used to justify segregation, but they did not automatically assume that those differences represented insurmountable inferiority or obstacles to full interracial harmony.

In the realm of applied Christian ethics, the Social Gospel conceived of church outreach in even more revolutionary fashion. Christians had long practiced an outreach infused with a conviction that sin and individual moral failings produced poverty and its attendant symptoms, and they approached those social problems with evangelism and charity. In this new age, however, Social Gospellers attacked the systemic problems of poverty, illness, alcoholism, and economic inequality with scientific study and political advocacy.[35]

Russell Bowie returned to Virginia from his year in New York City energized by the Social Gospel, but he was hardly its first clergy practitioner among Richmond's mainline white churches. Hugh Maclachlan, pastor of the Seventh Street Christian Church, had already earned a reputation for activism and advocacy for change within the juvenile justice system and public health education. And as the example of Mary-Cooke Munford illustrates, by 1911 many white and Black Richmonders were already mobilizing behind public health and education causes, and against mandated segregation.[36] When he arrived at St. Paul's, Bowie immediately joined fellow parishioners A. H. Christian Jr., Andrew D. Christian, E. Randolph Williams, and Mary-Cooke Munford on the Society for the Betterment of Housing and Living Conditions in Richmond. The Society had formed in the wake of the 1911 city residential segregation ordinances, and it conducted a major study of housing conditions for Richmond's working-class white and Black neighborhoods meant to justify new city services.[37] Bowie also placed St. Paul's in a prominent position as an advocate for the closure of saloons in predominantly Black Jackson Ward in the interest of public health during a heated prohibition campaign in 1914.[38] These campaigns responded to the paranoia about the spread of contagious diseases. That concern had a racial angle, as white people tended to associate diseases with poor communities—most specifically from Black neighborhoods. John Kerr Branch, chairman of the 1916 Memorial Hospital campaign to construct a separate medical facility for Black patients, noted that "all of us know the grave danger resulting from the close contact between the two races, of the peril to our children who may be nursed by an infected woman."[39] Bowie had found a home, and his arrival affirmed St. Paul's new profile as a central actor in Richmond's reform scene.

Bowie's hand-picked successor, the Reverend Beverley D. Tucker Jr., continued the Social Gospel approach to racial activism. In a 1929 sermon in which he condemned yet another city segregation ordinance, Tucker affirmed that while a "natural segregation" might exist, the principles of "justice and mercy" demanded that white Richmonders provide truly equal city services to Black neighborhoods. He concluded by citing the Apostle Paul's dictum that in Christ Jesus "there was neither bond nor free." That passage had long been a staple of abolitionist theology, but now a southern-born cleric in a slavery-apologist church employed it from the pulpit to champion a mild racial justice.[40]

Richmond churches were a bit more progressive on racial matters than the Diocese as a whole. For example, the annual State of the Church address in 1912 still held on to resentment about "a time when flattering promises were held out to them [Black people] of freedom and plenty." The authors focused less on "justice and mercy" and more on the "distinct and alien" characteristics of the "race so widely separated from us," and the "obligation of strength and weakness" that "we owe them."[41]

The Social Gospel theology, tinged with southern racial paternalism, drove white liberals toward new relations with Black men and women through the interracial cooperation movement. Southern white racial liberals were few and concentrated almost exclusively in the region's major cities and among their business, education, and religious elites. These white men and women supported racial cooperation and racial uplift—efforts to work *with* Black leaders to provide equal provision of government services and equal opportunities for advancement. To be sure, these progressives never opposed segregation itself. In fact, they largely believed in what newsman and Robert E. Lee biographer Douglas Southall Freeman called "separation by consent," or what rector Beverley Tucker called "natural segregation."[42] Such voluntary separation promised—in their minds—to produce the most harmonious race relations possible. To that end—of harmonious race relations—they not only vigorously opposed Ku Klux Klan activity and racial violence, but also any legislation that might insult Black leaders by codifying segregation without corresponding improvement of Black social and living conditions.[43]

The presence of racial liberalism in a virulently racist society created tensions—even in the enclaves of that liberalism. Many of St. Paul's most prominent clergy and members in the 1920s and 1930s pursued an active racial cooperative agenda, while other congregants, as members of local and state governments, found themselves required to enforce segregation measures with which they may not have agreed with. All were limited by a narrow historical imagination that they themselves had created.

Russell Bowie and Mary-Cooke Munford were joined by other St. Paul's members in the racial cooperation movement. White southern liberals created the Commission on Interracial Cooperation (CIC) in Atlanta in 1919. Organizers anticipated heightened tensions between southern white people and African American soldiers returning from the Great War and sought ways to work with Black leaders to find solutions to racial inequities. The CIC prioritized harmony and justice over violence and oppression, and it marshaled social science methods to identify and alleviate problems in public health, education, and municipal services. Yet the white members of the CIC remained firmly rooted in the socially conservative elite and not only failed to identify segregation and racism as *the cause* of material inequality, they—like the proslavery Christians before them—remained committed to making racial segregation work.[44]

The Richmond branch of the CIC opened in 1921, first led by a group of prominent women, including St. Paul's Mary-Cooke Munford, Kate Pleasants Minor, and Rosalie Archer. They declared: "We deplore any conditions in our midst that tend to widen the breach between peoples whom circumstances have thrown together and whose destinies are inevitably interwoven in our own and coming generations. We believe righteousness, justice, peace and good will can be established between races of different colors."[45] In making this statement, the women invoked the Golden Rule in another example, like Beverley Tucker's, of the adoption of key abolitionist rhetoric for a socially minded faith in the twentieth century.

Having successfully removed most Black men from political life with the passage of the Commonwealth's 1902 Constitution, white Virginians moved battles over the Black presence in civic life into public spaces and residential arenas. Since *Plessy v. Ferguson* in 1894 had affirmed the constitutionality of racial segregation, with a mere pretense of equality, Virginia and Richmond lawmakers moved forward with a segregationist agenda. A state law mandating separate railroad cars for Black and white passengers in 1900 was followed by similar legislation on municipal streetcars. In Richmond, the Virginia Passenger and Power Company announced enforcement of segregation statutes in its cars in 1904, a move promptly met by an unexpectedly rigorous boycott organized by the city's Black leaders John Mitchell Jr. and Maggie L. Walker.[46] The boycott ultimately failed to forestall an agenda of racial restrictions on residences and the co-mingling of races in public spaces that tightened over the next two decades.

White participation in the cooperation movement touched on the usual spectrum of progressive causes at the beginning of the twentieth century. The Richmond CIC carried out its mission with a study of how the Virginia Electric Power franchise over transportation negatively impacted Black Richmonders. The organization opposed the Ku Klux Klan and supported anti-lynching initiatives. Its most consistent area of study and advocacy was in Richmond's inequitable housing, about which it conducted major studies in 1925 and 1927.

Richmond's population exploded in the 1910s, and residential overcrowding and substandard housing became the biggest problem facing city planners, particularly in Black neighborhoods. The most desperate communities that drew the attention of reformers lay in Shockoe Valley and Jackson Ward. Mary-Cooke Munford reported to the City Council in 1912 the results of a survey of Black neighborhoods, where "whole blocks of houses, in which hundreds of people live, from three to eight in a room, and in whose behalf neither the city nor the property owner has raised a hand in years."[47] The city strategy for easing overcrowding was the annexation of new land and expansion of city services to new enclaves. Yet annexed land tended to be reserved for white families, and Munford and her allies pleaded for annexation for Black families as well.

Until new land became available, African American families sought better houses and services in traditionally white neighborhoods, and local white leaders regarded the block-by-block migration as a crisis. Richmond passed the state's first residential segregation ordinance in 1911—the year Russell Bowie arrived at St. Paul's. The law prevented Black home purchases and rentals on predominantly white blocks.[48] Meant to keep out Black families, white promoters of the ordinance cited the need to protect property values and the respectability of white neighborhoods. In supporters' minds, a Black presence automatically meant the introduction of poverty, crime, and other alleged dangers. One key point of conflict in 1914 tangentially involved St. Paul's. In that year the trustees of the white Immanuel Baptist Church at the corner of Fifth and Leigh Streets attempted to sell their building to a Black Methodist congregation. Disaffected white congregants took their trustees to court, and in a case overseen by St. Paul's Treasurer, Judge R. Carter Scott, claimed that "citizens in the neighborhood protest against the sale on the grounds that the church is near St. Paul's Church Home and an orphanage for white girls." They could not understand why "there should be such a special effort made to so injure the interest of the white property owners and practically to ruin a district which is now exceedingly desirable on account of its proximity to business, shopping, churches, and schools."[49]

St. Paul's members, including Mayor David Richardson and Alderman Graham Hobson, defended and enforced the 1911 segregation ordinance. Mary-Cooke Munford opposed it, claiming that "it would work a hardship on the negroes in forcing them to live in great congestion in a narrow and constricted area."[50] George Wayne Anderson, Assistant City Attorney and St. Paul's member, defended it in court in 1914 but ultimately recommended that the city cease enforcement when the United States Supreme Court overturned racial residential segregation in the 1917 *Buchanan* v. *Warley* decision.[51]

Some St. Paul's members became involved in the Richmond branch of the Commission on Interracial Cooperation, including rector Beverley Tucker. The racially mixed meetings of the CIC regularly convened in the St. Paul's Parish House, prompting much less fanfare than the 1925 biracial funeral of Robert Damell in the church. Richard Carrington, superintendent of the St. Paul's Sunday School and president of the church's Men's Association as well as an attorney and General Assemblyman, became chairman of the Richmond chapter of the CIC.[52] As chairman, Carrington led opposition to a renewed residential segregation ordinance in 1929. He went to the Interdenominational Ministerial Alliance of Richmond and Vicinity conference at Hood Temple AME Zion Church. There he told an audience that the proposed law would not succeed in separating the races, that "it will involve large financial loss to holders of so-called 'colored property,'" and that it would have "injurious effect" on Richmond's Black people, while not touching its white people. He told the same thing to both the Richmond Chamber of Commerce and the City Council.[53]

Beverley Tucker also campaigned against the ordinance. Where segregation proponents insisted that Richmond's Black people were well provided for, Tucker drew upon CIC studies to claim the opposite, and that "one has only to make a casual visit to the sections of the city where most of the colored population is naturally segregated to reach the conclusion that we do not make an equal provision in the way of streets and sidewalks, or sewerage and lighting." Tucker, again insisting that a "natural segregation" existed, demanded that the best way to safeguard it would be "to do plain justice by the Negroes—clean up districts in which they live at present by providing decent streets and sewerage, and then plan for their expansion into some new suburban district where the same public facilities are afforded to the Negro population that are given to whites under similar conditions."[54]

Carrington embodied the white paternalist acting to alleviate inequality while failing to question its sources. In fact, he confessed to the biracial Interdenominational Ministerial Alliance that "he had been trained to believe in white supremacy," and that training demanded that he "treat the colored people fairly." He told the same thing to the City Council and cajoled them that because of "the political dominance of the white race ... the white citizen must assume the obligation to treat the colored man justly." Carrington claimed that "the Negroes naturally desire to live together. They do so in other cities because of better housing conditions." Carrington's point was that Richmond's substandard housing fostered racial friction because Black people looked to white neighborhoods for better housing.[55] Nevertheless, for all the efforts of the biracial coalition against the new law, it passed the City Council unanimously.

In addition to advocacy for equitable housing, the national CIC consistently campaigned against lynching, promoted anti-lynching laws, and also regularly condemned the Ku Klux Klan. The Richmond CIC chapter with its St. Paul's members followed suit. Russell Bowie denounced the Klan from the pulpit when it marched in Richmond in 1920, and again in 1921. In his 1920 sermon, printed in both the *Richmond Times-Dispatch* and the African American newspaper, the *Richmond Planet*, he warned that "There is danger in the South that these influences should embitter the relationship between the white and colored peoples and that short cuts of lawlessness should take the place of a patient search for Christian cooperation which is the only way by which a solution of any human problem can be found." One Bowie sermon in which he contrasted the genteel restraint of Robert E. Lee with the lawlessness of the Klan, drew the favorable attention of the Fisk University newspaper.[56] His successor Beverley Tucker preached an anti-Klan sermon in 1925 in the presence of a visiting "spokesman for the Klan," who ran out of the church shouting his disapproval. Parishioner Andrew D. Christian stormed after the Klansman and "knocked him down twice on the portico of the edifice."[57]

For a number of reasons, the Klan never prospered in Richmond. Aggressive white supremacists, however, channeled their energies into Anglo-Saxon Clubs that stood in contrast to the type of race relations that Munford and Carrington advocated. Anglo-Saxon Clubs were premised on the idea of racial integrity—that ethnicities and races possessed certain characteristics, or traits, that could be diluted in contact with "inferior" ethnic groups. The vector of that threat was sexual relations made possible by social and residential proximities. Anglo-Saxon Club leaders like Richmond pianist John Powell argued that interracial sex would undermine American and western civilization. Powell and the clubs had interactions with St. Paul's. As organist for Monumental Church, Powell befriended St. Paul's organist, Jacob Reinhardt, and wrote a forward for Reinhardt's "Etudes for Piano." In 1923, St. Paul's rector Beverley Tucker delivered the welcoming address at the Anglo-Saxon Club's inaugural national convention in Richmond. However, Tucker subsequently opposed the Anglo-Saxon Club's legislative agenda.[58] So while Munford and Carrington sat down in interracial dialogue, the Anglo-Saxon Clubs put their energies into passing laws like the 1924 Racial Integrity Act and the 1926 Massenburg Bill.[59] The former prohibited interracial marriage and codified the "one-drop rule," that only people with "no trace whatsoever of any blood other than Caucasian" could be considered white. The later required all public meetings to be strictly segregated. Both laws marked the peak of pseudo-scientific white supremacy and racial eugenics.[60] Their chief advocate, State Register of Vital Statistics Walter Plecker, argued the necessity to guard against miscegenation by citing the biblical injunction against marrying "foreign wives," a remarkable reference to proslavery gospel that most Protestant ministers had abandoned decades before.[61] At least one prominent St. Paul's member, E. Randolph Williams, found Plecker's case compelling and signed onto a petition supporting the Racial Integrity Act. Another, vestryman Dabney Lancaster, the State Supervisor of Agricultural Education, sat on the executive committee of the national Anglo-Saxon Club, formed in 1924.[62] More likely agreed. Mary-Cooke Munford opposed this legislation, and in doing so, incurred the ire of John Powell, who threatened her in a letter, warning that "the defeat of this bill may bring tragedy and horror upon the oldest English-speaking community in America."[63] Unfazed, Munford approached Supreme Court Chief Justice (and former US President) William Howard Taft in an effort to convince Governor Harry F. Byrd to veto the 1926 bill.[64] Byrd did not. These laws passed, but not without the continued objections of Beverley Tucker and Richard Carrington, who testified against them to the General

FIGURE 6. Richard W. Carrington. (*Virginia Biography Volume 4: History of Virginia*)

Assembly.⁶⁵ Carrington claimed, again, that the laws would hurt Black people more than they would help white people. He was right; both were critical in codifying the state's harshest Jim Crow laws.

Though Carrington, Munford, and the clergy didn't recognize it, the continued enactment of ever more restrictive segregation laws in the 1920s began to undermine any faith Black participants in the CIC harbored in the ability of interracial cooperation to effect meaningful change. One Black member, Virginia Union University sociology professor and local pastor Dr. Gordon Blaine Hancock noted the tension and expressed his frustrations. Hancock firmly believed in the interracial cooperation movement, so long as it addressed substantive issues and did not simply use biracial gatherings as a platform for white satisfaction. He recognized in 1933 that "the segregation movement . . . is gaining momentum," and that "however clumsy may be the methods of these committees . . . they are at least a step in the right direction." In light of advancing Jim Crow legislation, he grudgingly proclaimed, "consider what might be without them." Hancock's pragmatism was fueled by a clear view of the limitations of white members. He frequently complained of the evident discomfort white members displayed in biracial meetings, and particularly noted that "the white man's religion does not make him throw down the color bars and treat us like brethren . . . It is true that for two thousand years race prejudice is still rampant and the white man refuses to live the Christ way with his Negro brethren." Richmond's white racial liberals disregarded Hancock's diagnoses—if they even noticed it—and continued to advance the interracial cooperation movement as a model for racial harmony.[66]

At the twelfth annual conference of the Virginia Commission on Interracial Cooperation, held at St. Paul's in 1932, the president of the University of North Carolina, Frank Porter Graham, told the attendees, "Here, where slavery made its last stand, industrialism makes its beginning. We have the power to begin here a beautiful civilization. white people, Black people and Brown people—as we do a day's work and dream our dreams, we will all join in teaching each other." The day-long conference endorsed resolutions crafted by Gordon Blaine Hancock calling for greater Black employment in public works, greater spending on public health for Black people, and state matching funds for Rosenwald Fund spending on Black education. The call for African American employment in government jobs had greater urgency in Richmond, whose incumbent mayor at that moment, J. Fulmer Bright, maintained a strict policy of not hiring Black people for any city job.[67] At the 1930 meeting, also at St. Paul's, "topic[s] from the morning session were illiteracy, vocation and industrial trends, employment and occupational opportunities for Virginia negroes."[68] In the depths of the Great Depression, the 1934 Virginia CIC annual conference, convened again in St. Paul's Parish House considered "National Recovery and the Negro in Virginia," featuring "Representatives of Federal emergency, relief and readjustment agencies." The panel saw Dr. W. E. Garnett of Virginia Tech speaking on "'The Underprivileged Man and His Family in Virginia' from the standpoint of the whites," followed by Dr. J.M. Ellison of the Virginia State College for Negroes addressing the "same theme from the Negro standpoint." The meeting culminated with keynote speeches from the head of the American Church Institute and Charles Houston, the dean of the Howard University Law School. Virginia Union University's Sabbath Glee Club and Octet provided the entertainment.[69] The Virginia State College Choir performed at the 1933 annual conference, also held at St. Paul's.[70]

St. Paul's members of the CIC went to other churches to speak. For the 1929 "Race Relations Sunday," Beverley Tucker and Richard Carrington accompanied the St. Paul's choir to Leigh Street Methodist Episcopal Church, where they joined Black clergy and laymen to speak on the topic, "What should be my attitude to a brother of another race?" Tucker insisted that "the promotion of amity and good will between the races should be approached not through theory, but through facts, and ... the Negroes may help the movement by making clear their belief in racial integrity." In other words, even for racial liberals like Tucker, the abiding issue of miscegenation always loomed as inviolable in their thinking, and he still demanded that Black people confirm acceptance of voluntary segregation. Nonetheless, Leigh Street's pastor, Robert Williams, praised Tucker as "one of the liberal, Christian and broadminded white people who are doing most for the Negro."[71] On the spectrum of white people and their racial activism, he probably was.

As Tucker's remarks demonstrate, the simultaneously radical and conservative nature of the racial cooperation movement was on display in these gatherings. Certainly, few white people would claim *earthly* brotherhood with Black people in previous generations, and in that, conceptual boundaries continued

FIGURE 7. The Executive Committee of the Virginia Commission for Interracial Cooperation on St. Paul's portico, 1939. (The Valentine)

to fall. Yet the white CIC members from St. Paul's remained committed to "natural segregation" and mandated it in their own sanctuary at a significant function. In 1930, St. Paul's hosted its largest Race Relations Day, featuring the Virginia CIC leadership, two bishops, the governor, and a biracial audience. Robert Russa Moton, a Virginian and successor to Booker T. Washington at the Tuskegee Institute, was the keynote speaker. Moton praised Virginia for comparatively good race relations but claimed that much more needed to be done, including equity in transportation and other public facilities. The St. Paul's vestry had heartily approved the event, but only on the condition that "the Church be divided, the different races being seated on either side of the center aisle." Richmonders noticed. The *Richmond Planet* marveled at the scene. "One finds it difficult to picture Jefferson Davis," it wondered, "sitting on the same platform with Frederick Douglass and introducing [him] in terms of appreciation and respect. Yet that was just the spectacle which was presented the other night in St. Paul's" when Virginia Governor John Pollard introduced Moton.[72] At the Robert Damell funeral, Black and white mourners did not occupy the same level of the church. Four years later, at this event, they did. Some progress, even if their continued division obviously proved Moton's point.[73]

Black intellectuals like Moton continued to push against the genteel segregation, and even reinterpreted a venerable story from St. Paul's to make their point. Educator Benjamin G. Brawley first repurposed the story of Robert E. Lee kneeling at the communion rail in 1921. In his book, *A Social History of the American Negro,* Brawley, lamenting segregation after slavery, suggested an "example of how the South *might* have met the situation [of emancipation]" in "no less a man that Robert E. Lee, about whose unselfishness and standard of conduct as a gentleman could be no question." Brawley proceeded to convey the story, but in his context, Lee did not silence a Black man's political attempt and restore racial order with the force of his dignity. Instead, Lee relied on his noted character to offer a semblance of equality. Similarly, in 1938, historian Carter G. Woodson looked upon Lee's example in the same revised fashion in a brief article in the *Negro History Bulletin* that collected instances of interracial cooperation in the Reconstruction period as evidence of what could have been.[74]

The question of segregation in higher education came to the forefront five years later when the Board of Visitors at the University of Virginia deliberated over the admission of Alice B. Jackson. Frederic W. Scott, prominent St. Paul's member and former vestryman, presided as the board's Rector as it considered the application of the Black Virginian who requested transfer as a graduate student from Smith College. Jackson had the backing of the state chapter of the National Association for the Advancement of Colored People (NAACP) in this open test of segregation law and practice. In a statement carried by the national press, Scott announced the board's decision to "refuse respectfully" her enrollment as "the education of white and colored persons in the same schools is contrary to the long established and fixed policy of the commonwealth." The following year, the General Assembly passed legislation to shield itself from similar suits by instituting the state's first graduate programs for Black students at Virginia State College and enacting the 1936 Dovell Act, which, for the next thirty years, provided stipends for qualified African American applicants to enroll in graduate programs outside of Virginia.[75]

In Beverley Tucker's final sermon as rector at St. Paul's in 1939, he encouraged his congregation to "be true to its patron saint and be ever missionary in spirit and in action." He counted the best example of such work as making "our parish house a hospitable atmosphere for the work of the Virginia Commission on Interracial Cooperation—to make St. Paul's a constructive leader in cultivating understanding and friendship between our two races that live side by side in the city."[76] An earlier program for the state CIC convention in 1933 reflected this same optimism, noting that "this problem is gradually being solved by a very simple, homely program of practicing goodwill and fairness and cooperation. The method employed by the Commission is almost too simple to put into words, but it *works*."[77] For Black participants, cooperating with optimistic white people provided a greater potential avenue for improvement than they might have had at the hands of arch segregationists like Walter Plecker and Richmond Mayor Fulmer Bright. But they began to realize that the endeavor did *not* actually produce results.

Charles Houston, Dean of the Howard University Law School noticed, and even claimed to see retrograde motion on race relations. At the 1934 CIC gathering at St. Paul's, Houston attributed this, first, to the Great Depression that impacted Black people harder than white folks. He excoriated the National Recovery Act for compounding inequities (he called it the "Negro Robbed Again"). St. Paul's genteel and conservative efforts at race relations could hardly be effective in the face of shifting power as the federal government began to influence local politics and did so with a determined segregationist agenda. No wonder, then, as Houston noted, that Black people had become "imbued with the doctrine of despair," and liable to "lend and ear to the mouthings of radicals and Communists."[78]

Despite the CIC's efforts, the same overcrowded and substandard housing plaguing Black Richmonders, against which Mary-Cooke Munford had fought against in the early 1910s still remained in the late 1930s, and certainly Houston's "doctrine of despair" prevailed in Black neighborhoods. The City Council always justified little to no spending on city services for Black neighborhoods in order to preserve a low tax rate and an air of fiscal responsibility.[79] The availability of new residential areas for white Richmonders—particularly as annexation expanded into the West End—remained abundant. All the CIC aspirations for improving an equitable distribution of resources and increasing city services had failed.

By the outbreak of World War II, Black leaders who had joined the co-operationist project as a promising option abandoned it in favor of direct action against segregation itself. They also expressed their frustrations with working alongside well-meaning progressive paternalists. In 1939 Wiley Hall of the Richmond Urban League, of which Mary-Cooke Munford had been a board member, vented about her, noting that she was a "liberal willing to work for Negroes but not to work with Negroes."[80] White liberals, having lost control of the pace and agenda of racial change retreated from interracial cooperation and took a skeptical stance toward the new emerging Civil Rights Movement.[81]

The New Deal, when it opened federal coffers for local projects, created new possibilities for improved housing. In 1934 and 1935, E. Randolph Williams, a St. Paul's vestryman, sat on the mayor's steering committee that planned how to use that money. The committee began to lay the groundwork for "slum clearance" and the construction of new, city-owned housing to be a new enclave for Black Richmonders.[82] Yet, previewing Wiley Hall's critique of Munford and reflecting Houston's frustrations, citizens of Jackson Ward became daringly oppositional to the efforts when the refusal of a dozen property owners threatened to stymie a $1,200,000 federal housing grant to Richmond.[83] The city, on the eve of World War II, faced an increasingly restless Black community and a postwar environment that portended frightening new traditions for a people that venerated the past.

4 | St. Paul's in Reaction

"Sacred shrine of the Confederacy Rounding Out Century of Life," a headline in the *Richmond Times-Dispatch* announced when St. Paul's celebrated the 100th anniversary of the laying of its cornerstone in 1943. The accompanying article offered a fairly comprehensive history of the church, but the headline and the two images of the Davis and Lee memorial windows drew attention to the cultural value of St. Paul's to Richmond.[1] Elsewhere, in notices regarding times of services that St. Paul's published in the newspaper, the copy announced the church as "A Shrine of the South."[2] Routine newspaper announcements attached the clause *the church where Lee and Davis worshipped* so often when mentioning St. Paul's that it became almost a subtitle to the church's name and the chief marker of its identity as the Confederate church in twentieth-century Richmond.[3]

The Reverend Doctor Vincent Franks, also pictured in the centennial article, did much to cultivate that image. A Canadian, Franks "was intensely interested in the history of the Church."[4] The rector composed a sermon entitled "Our Great Triumvirate," about the religious lives of three Confederate military and naval figures whose statues lined Monument Avenue: Robert E. Lee, Thomas Jonathan "Stonewall" Jackson, and Commodore Matthew Fontaine Maury. In the great Lost Cause manner of sanctifying Confederate leaders, Franks described the Bible in their lives: "Maury always had his well-thumbed Bible with him; General Stonewall Jackson was noted for his piety and church attendance, and General Lee for nobleness of soul that characterized all his action."[5] Franks also preached a sermon titled "Noblesse Oblige! An Encomium to General Robert E. Lee."[6] His successor, the Reverend Robert Brown, later published an entire book on the religious life of Lee.[7]

Confederate stories of the type told from and about St. Paul's dominated the mainstream history of midcentury Richmond. Yet the white historical consensus that a generation before had a pragmatic Black participation was fast losing its ability to force the same acquiescence. In 1945 the Norfolk *New Journal and Guide* columnist Arthur Davis reported on the case of Dr. James A. Chiles, a Black dentist in Richmond. Chiles's grandfather had been the free

Black man who delivered the April 2, 1865, message to Jefferson Davis in St. Paul's most famous historical scene. Dr. Chiles's father had agreed to portray his own father in a historical tableau sponsored by "an organization of Confederate ladies" (though the light-skinned Chiles refused the ladies' request to blacken his face to fit their fantasy). When Dr. Chiles's father died in 1935, the ladies turned to Dr. Chiles to reprise his father's (and grandfather's) role. Dr. Chiles refused. Columnist Davis reported that Chiles "politely, but firmly, he said NO." Davis continued: "He told them that he had no interest in glorifying Jefferson Davis. When they reminded him that James's father had gladly taken part, he told them that things which his father considered appropriate were not necessarily fitting for him." Davis noted that a white person had been engaged, and he surmised that he performed the role in blackface. Like the enslaved people who self-emancipated during the antebellum years, and the Black faithful who studiously avoided the Episcopal church after emancipation, Black activism in the mid-twentieth century forced a change in the cultural assumptions that underpinned white Episcopalians' sense of themselves.

The pageant may or may not have occurred at St. Paul's. No record of it is found in the church archives. But Arthur Davis finished his column with a critique of the very type of historical imagination that St. Paul's actively cultivated at the middle of the twentieth century. "[S]uch participation [as the ladies desired of Dr. Chiles] tacitly condones a tradition which is still actively used against us as a group." He turned to the matter of "mammy" memorials and said that it would be an honor except that it is never just an honor. "It immediately becomes a symbol of the 'right' place for the Negro..." Davis tackled the complication of the historical landscape for Black people. "[T]here is nothing in America—tradition or anything else—that the Negro can accept straight. There are always racial overtones to be considered." For Black men like Arthur Davis and Dr. Chiles, the impulse to publicly puncture the dominant historical imagination of white people represented just one of many ways that Black activism provoked a generation of crisis within the white community.[8]

The 1954 Supreme Court decision in the *Brown v. Board of Education* decision overturned segregation and forced white southerners to face a reality and a future that most did not want. A small few—and no known St. Paul's members—openly embraced integration of public schools as an immediate response to the decision (though some did, later). The Commonwealth of Virginia first formulated a plan that allowed for some integration but also opened the door for private segregated academies. The state then changed course to oppose all integration. Massive Resistance, as official opposition was labeled, was a crisis and a watershed moment for Richmond's segregationists.

Beyond the city, the *Staunton News-Leader* published an editorial in 1955 titled, "Who Has God's Word on Integration?" The editors wondered why some Christians insisted that "integration is the word of God" and why others "have received no word from the Throne of Grace that public school integration is God's wish." They chided integrationists for claiming a divine message when equally fervent Christian segregationists prayed hard but had received none. The segregationists, the editors believed, lacked racial hatred and animosity. Their list of estimable Virginians "who have taken the lead in advocating avoidance of public school integration who are friends of the Negro and have aided his advancement . . . and whose Christian citizenship is beyond challenge" included St. Paul's vestrymen Dabney Lancaster and Thomas C. Boushall.[9] Both Lancaster and Boushall took what was for prominent white Virginians moderate courses in the integration crisis—opposing the state's Massive Resistance tactics but favoring private school workarounds to avoid integration.

These types of "estimable Virginians" had dominated state politics from the beginning. They congratulated themselves for governing in a style known as "the Virginia Way": civility over contention, peace over conflict, integrity over corruption, order over protest, and a willingness to embrace anyone who played by those rules, white or Black. The sensibility of white people and their view of race relations in "the Virginia Way" was deeply rooted in their historical imagination of benevolent white people and loyal Black people. Its practitioners knew how to be expansive and liberal within it. Its practitioners did not know how to respond when Black people like Dr. Chiles began to refuse to play by the rules. At the tail end of the 1930s, and gaining momentum in the 1940s, Black activists abandoned interracial cooperation efforts and demanded political equality on their own terms. White leaders, like Lancaster and Boushall, desperately wanted to control the pace of progress as the Civil Rights Movement unfolded and made their historical imagination ever more untenable. But unable to, they professed a cautious moderation. But cautious moderation set against the accelerating demands—and results—of the Civil Rights Movement appeared to be stasis even when it was not actual resistance.

During World War II, in 1942, the church first opened the Episcopal Service Center in its parish house, which provided meals and leisure activities for white active-duty military. The influx of soldiers and their families into Richmond on sightseeing trips also prompted the church to form a tour-guide corps and increase its rounds in the sanctuary. The new guide staff, consisting of female volunteers, allowed the church to remain open most weekdays.[10] The guides reported that visitors arrived from all over the country, drawn by a desire to see the elegant church architecture and to be in proximity to the Lee and Davis pews and windows. "Many Service men are eager," wrote guide chairwoman Nellie T. Harris in 1951, "to see the pew, and memorial window, of our matchless Chieftain, Robert E. Lee, and to pay reverent homage." She noted the following year that "one must feel that they are either seeking guidance or courage to meet some issue or make some momentous decision, as did General Lee in his 'upper room.'"[11] At St. Paul's, then, men in need of courage could pray for guidance from both God and General Lee.

Rituals sustained St. Paul's Confederate identity. Church members and Lee descendants in the Antrim family went as ambassadors to the State Capitol to lay wreaths at the Lee statue in the House of Delegates in 1950 and in 1960.[12] St. Paul's next rector Robert Brown helped dedicate a bust of Jefferson Davis at the statehouse in 1952.[13] Within the church, the Tucker Club, devoted to cultivating civic virtues of the young adults at St. Paul's, featured popular historian Clifford Dowdey's speech on "Lee's Character under the Strain at Gettysburg."[14] The church regularly served as the site for memorial services in conjunction with the United Daughters of the Confederacy (UDC) during their biennial national conventions and in annual citywide observances of Jefferson Davis's and Robert E. Lee's birthdays. The Lee birthday services usually featured Confederate flags flown from the portico and at the Lee pew in the sanctuary. In the Cold War era, the UDC marshaled history for contemporary lessons in the same way that their grandmothers had done. One speaker at the group's 1962 Veterans Day service at St. Paul's noted that "the Confederate soldier became the symbol of valor all over the world." Recalling the Cuban Missile Crisis just the previous month as a "crossroads of history," she suggested that modern America be inspired by Confederate military loss. "Americans need to practice the sacrifice of self for the love of principle and become indifferent to material things if we are to survive this crisis." As the essential character of Confederate soldiers proved meaningful for those reestablishing a racially conservative regime in the 1890s, so it was deployed as encouragement to Americans facing the threat of global communism in the Cold War.[15]

The Richmond Light Infantry Blues, as much a social club for elite Richmond men as it was a historic National Guard unit, regularly held anniversary services at its "official church," St. Paul's.[16] It was a perfect match: St. Paul's, the one-time religious home of Virginia's most famous military leader, and the Blues, a United States Army unit that marched in modern parades beneath a Confederate flag. The relationship reached its pinnacle in 1954 when the Blues celebrated its 165th anniversary at St. Paul's with President Dwight David Eisenhower as a guest.[17] Rector Robert Brown's invitation to the sitting US President included an exhortation to come and worship at the "Church of the Confederate President."[18]

Centennial observances of the American Civil War began in 1961. Despite rumbles from the unfolding Civil Rights Movement that threatened to intrude on the four-year long celebration, the Centennial marked the apogee of the reconciliationist narrative of the Civil War. That narrative viewed the war as an unfortunate struggle between honorable brothers, leaving ample room to accommodate southern honor and pride and, at the same time, to celebrate national reunion and modern American strength. It offered no space whatsoever to consider slavery, race, or the tragedy of failed Reconstruction for Black Americans.[19] St. Paul's rector Joseph Heistand participated at the groundbreaking for the Commonwealth's Civil War Centennial Visitor Center in 1961,[20] and the church opened its doors as part of a March 1962 walking tour of Richmond's Civil War sites.[21] Through the ongoing emphasis of St. Paul's as a historic Confederate site, the stories of the worshipful Lee and Davis, the wartime marriage and funeral of John Pegram, and the notification of Davis about the fall of Petersburg were once again firmly planted in the public mind as indelible markers of St. Paul's public identity.

St. Paul's marked the Centennial for itself with a bronze tablet. The vestry naturally found it "fitting that the Church of the Confederacy should at some appropriate time during the Centennial of the Civil War dedicate a tablet in honor of all members of St. Paul's who gave their lives in the service of the Confederate States." The battle flag-embellished tablet, "to the glory of God and in everlasting memory of those members of this congregation who served loyally the Confederate States of America," was unveiled in October 1961. (Interestingly, the church had wanted to install a plaque with the names of St. Paul's Confederate dead in 1909 and revisited the possibility several more times in subsequent decades, but the move faltered when a complete list of names could not be recovered. The vestry revisited the issue again in 1916, 1918, 1939, and 1956 before settling on a general memorial without names.)[22] In 1967, St. Paul's accepted the gift of a coat of arms designed by Harry Temple, a retired officer and expert in military heraldry.[23] Thereafter, the heraldic shield, which incorporated the Confederate battle flag, adorned two altar kneelers in the sanctuary and bookplates in the library.

The early twentieth-century events of reunions and funerals ended when the Confederate generation finally passed. Now, history at St. Paul's had become routinized in brochures, postcards, and guided tours. Advertised as a stop for automobile tourists on America's new interstate highway system, Richmond civic boosters and tourism managers promoted the church as a must-see destination for out-of-towners. The Lee and Davis pews continued to be the main attraction. In 1951 the guides reported on the high number of servicemen visiting the Lee pew. "One outstanding soldier," Nellie Harris wrote, "when invited to sit in General Lee's pew, stepped forward and said, 'I would think it an honor to *kneel* where General Lee stood,—and he did kneel in the pew while his comrades stood silently."[24]

At midcentury, the vestry, at least once, became troubled by the shrine-like quality of the church and the complacency toward present-day societal needs that accompanied it. In a 1950 discussion of "Evangelical Work," the agenda included a consideration of the "function and mission of St. Paul's as a militant church—not as a shrine or museum to be protected and preserved."[25] The outcome of that discussion was not recorded.

For St. Paul's young people, however, new relationships to the Confederate identity yielded new meanings. Dr. Hunter "Mac" McGuire, a St. Paul's member and grandson of the famed Confederate surgeon and St. Paul's vestryman Hunter Holmes McGuire, developed a rueful alienation from Confederate memory because he had spent his childhood being schooled by Confederate veterans about his famous ancestry.[26]

Another young member, Anne Hobson [later Freeman], also developed a critical detachment from St. Paul's story of the Civil War. On a Saturday night in May 1948, a drunk, off-duty sailor broke into St. Paul's and punched his fist through several stained-glass windows. The Sunday morning service commenced before the sanctuary could be entirely cleaned. Young Miss Hobson, who had been conditioned to see Robert E. Lee "as bloodless and symbolic as the statues that we saw all over town," entered to find a scene of bloody smears on the pews, prayer books, and glass shards from the broken windows. She immediately recalled newsreels of bombed out cathedrals from the war in Europe as she glanced at a man opening a blood-soaked hymnal. "As I stood there, horrified, staring at the hymnbook, I was struck with an almost unbearable knowledge—the knowledge that war—any war—means not just statues and hero-saints, or even broken glass. It means, mainly, bloodshed. Dark, red, *human* blood." She continued, "From that day on, I began to notice something I had missed before in General Lee's ubiquitous postwar photographs and portraits, and even in the statues. An air of almost indefinable sorrow.... As I grew on through World War II and then Korea, then Vietnam, as an adult, I came to see Lee more and more not as a god or saint, but simply as a man, who would bleed if he were shot or cut or weep if he were hurt. A world-weary, prematurely *old* man at that."[27]

Confederate memory proved useful in twentieth-century white supremacist action. Early in the century that memory had been used to justify the imposition of a Jim Crow regime. In the late 1940s, conservative southern Democrats began again to adopt Confederate symbols to signal opposition to President Harry Truman's nascent integration agenda.[28] St. Paul's never harnessed its Confederate identity for overtly political ends, even if its parishioners personally supported a conservative approach to race. The church's Confederate identity in the 1940s and 1950s instead signaled consensus, comfort, and complacency. It explored no new theology or challenging social issue, and in that way, it stagnated while this larger context once again shifted around it.

World War II fundamentally altered the political rhetoric of American democracy, and with it, that of religion as well. Facing race-based totalitarians in Nazi Germany forced the United States to emphasize the value of a pluralistic democracy and condemn discrimination against religious and racial minorities. Influential Episcopal Bishop Henry Hobson wrote in 1942 that "nothing is more important than an educational program which will emphasize the relationship between various religious groups, and between members of the different races." Certainly, segregationist white southerners idealized harmonious and organic relationships between races, but the underlying expectation of the dynamics of power between them was remarkably different in the new postwar world. Segregation in America outlasted Nazi Germany, but the war critically set American national ideals against it.[29]

So, too, did the Cold War between western democracies and communist nations. The Soviet Union and its allies readily drew attention to America's racial inequalities in the 1950s, and the United States government responded by beginning to advocate, through the Department of Justice, the end of Jim Crow laws.[30] The American narrative about itself could no longer abide legal and cultural discrimination, even if many Americans could.

The postwar pluralistic ethos of American democracy blended with popular Protestant thought. Theologians at work in early and mid-twentieth century, including Dietrich Bonhoeffer, Paul Tillich, Rudolph Bultmann, and Reinhold Niebuhr, all contributed to the growing consensus among mainline Protestants that Christians should engage in secular and social affairs by improving the Kingdom of God in this world.[31] These impulses were firmly settled in mainstream thinking in 1955 when the Episcopal Church's Department of Christian Education published a series, *The Church's Teachings*, which declared that "[s]ince all worldly power is derived ultimately from God, Christians have a religious duty to engage in political activities in order to ensure that society conforms to God's purposes."[32] And God's discernible purposes had shifted yet again. The series culminated in 1963. At the National Conference on Religion and Race, scheduled to coincide with the centennial of the Emancipation Proclamation (not marked in Virginia's official centennial celebrations), Protestant, Catholic, and Jewish clergy and laypeople affirmed positive denominational stances toward the American Civil Rights Movement and "acknowledged the collective guilt of racial bodies" in perpetuating segregation. Not only did the Conference advocate integration, but keynote speaker Martin Luther King Jr. declared that "racial discrimination and segregation are an insult to God."[33] Exactly one hundred years had passed since Confederate clergy convened in Richmond to affirm that slavery had been God's plan.

However, not everyone agreed that segregation was an insult to God. Increasingly, denominations and their clergy became far more committed to progressive racial outlooks than did the great majority of their congregants. This was true in Episcopal parishes. Complacency, not resistance, remained the strongest countervailing force against the Civil Rights Movement. One Episcopal critic in the 1950s condemned the "suburban captivity of the churches," meaning a focus on parish, family, and social life that detached middle-class and elite white churches from the social struggles of the day.[34]

Complacency also extended to theology, where racialist thinking showed surprising resilience among laypeople. It did so at St. Paul's. In 1956, when rector Joseph Heistand asked the congregation to pray on the issue of a constitutional convention that would empower Virginia's Massive Resistance effort after the *Brown v. Board of Education* decision, vestryman Turner Arrington took exception. Arrington wrote to Bishop of Virginia Frederick Deane Goodwin to complain. Whimsically adopting the voice of God as revealed in a dream, Arrington explained His—and his own—approach to race: "After 1950 years or even 80 years I am not changing my mind and deciding that segregation is contrary to the teachings of my Son. Your Heavenly Father is not that kind of person. My past teachings have set down a definite line and I have not changed because nine politicians in Washington take a different line."³⁵ Of course, Jesus had not taught American racial segregation in his own lifetime, so Arrington instead referenced a proslavery theology articulated by Episcopal clergy in the nineteenth century.

Arrington cited G. Maclaren Brydon in his letter. A fixture in the Diocese of Virginia, Brydon, as a young priest, had served as the diocesan Archdeacon for Colored Work in the 1910s and 1920s, and as the executive secretary of the Diocesan Missionary Society, the treasurer, and register of the diocese. He later served as a rector in Ashland and then as the diocesan Historiographer. In this latter position he could indulge his interest in Virginia's Episcopal history.³⁶ Brydon held tight to his segregationist convictions. He expressed his "firm and unalterable conviction based upon 43 years of experience in the ministry of my church to the Negro race . . . that integrated public schools would be an utmost calamity and tragedy to the children of both races." In the late 1950s, Brydon sincerely wished that Black youth could aspire to and achieve their full potential. He always had. However, he was also "strongly convinced that Almighty God created differing races of men with different abilities and powers of mind."³⁷ Therefore, he vehemently insisted that Black students could only achieve their potential by maintaining segregation. "[F]or the average rank and file their own institutions will do more to make them leaders among their own people than the institutions primarily for the white students can ever do." This was an argument common to earlier architects of Jim Crow—that Black people would flounder in white institutions but succeed in their own. He protested that "I am as deeply interested in the welfare of the children of the white race as I am of the children of the Negro race." However, "they are two separate races, each with its own innate character and past history, and each with the God-given right to have the opportunity to develop according to the genius of its own race." Bishop Randolph from 1882 would have heartily agreed with the Reverend Brydon of 1957. Brydon squared his professed interest in Black people with his insistence on segregation by rejecting the assertion that the Apostle Paul had used the phrase "one blood" in his original letters. "My Negro brother," Brydon wrote, "can agree with me that we are of one Spirit, and of one fellowship, and that is a stronger bond than any idea of 'one blood' can be."³⁸

Such racialist theology had lain somewhat dormant in the 1920s during the era of the Social Gospel. Yet it remained sustainable and acceptable because the Social Gospel had never challenged segregation in the South. Therefore, in the 1950s, racialist theology arose surprisingly alive and completely at odds with the prevailing direction of mainline theology and action. These influential men—Arrington and Brydon—knew they harbored old-fashioned ideas. Bishop Goodwin told Arrington as much in his letter of response. Playing along with Arrington's conceit of having channeled the word of God— the bishop flatly—if cheekily—told him that "the very nature of what you received as official from above contains certain earthly errors which would throw some doubt on the authenticity of the material."[39]

St. Paul's people, at the dawn of the Civil Rights decades, likely harbored complicated mixtures of theologies and of historical imaginations that increasingly leaned conservative as they continued to go out into the world and, through personal effort and public policy, to shape the racial landscape of Richmond.

Segregation compounded hardship upon hardship in the lives of African Americans, especially in the South. Lingering stories about benevolent masters and happy slaves reinforced an expectation that Black men and women would fill menial labor and low paying jobs and accept inadequate housing, health care, and education. Their political disfranchisement meant that city government—including that of Richmond—did not have to respond to the municipal needs of Black families. Race-based housing ordinances confined Black people to crowded and dilapidated neighborhoods with minimal city services. In this marginalized environment, African Americans found it nearly impossible to accumulate the generational wealth to which white families had access. St. Paul's people played policy roles in perpetuating this cycle of oppression.

Black Richmonders and white progressives had worked together in the 1910s and 1920s to marginally increase city services for Black neighborhoods, but without questioning the fundamental inequities of segregation. The long festering state of housing continued to plague Richmond in the 1940s. With a city government patently unmotivated to serve the disfranchised African American community, the problems persisted. Well into the 1950s, decades long after Monument Avenue and the streets in the West End received paving and lighting, Black neighborhoods in Church Hill still lacked modern sewer services and, in many places, paved streets.

In Harland Bartholomew's 1946 Master Plan for the City of Richmond, the author noted that "the improvement of conditions for Negro housing is the most serious problem facing this community since the base majority of slum and badly blighted areas in Richmond are occupied either entirely by Negroes or by mixed population." Based on census data from 1940, the plan laid out by the nationally acclaimed urban developer noted that African Americans were concentrated in neighborhoods where up to 50 percent of houses lacked "private flush toilets" and where between 25 and 50 percent of dwellings needed "major repairs."[40]

While Richmond's policymakers in the 1930s did not invest in poor neighborhoods, they did favor another way of tackling the problem of dilapidated housing—tearing it all down and building modern houses and apartments. Planners called the strategy "slum clearance" and "urban renewal." St. Paul's vestryman E. Randolph Williams participated on Mayor Fulmer Bright's committees that, beginning in the 1930s, formulated urban renewal plans for Richmond. But since the governing regime consistently chose low taxes over spending on Black neighborhoods, it enacted no plans.

The opportunity to use federal money available through New Deal spending broke the impasse—but not without opposition. St. Paul's vestryman Thomas C. Boushall, founder of the Bank of Virginia and advisor to Richmond city government, favored slum clearance in the 1930s but opposed the use of federal funds in the endeavor. The very suggestion, he said, was "anti-American and fundamentally against democracy."[41] Richmond, therefore, declined New Deal funds. Instead, during World War II, it used federal money intended for wartime housing for workers in industry to begin building public housing in what became Gilpin Court. St. Paul's member H. Laurie Smith's Lawyers Title Insurance Corporation worked with the newly chartered Richmond Redevelopment and Housing Authority (RRHA) to examine the titles for the units that began opening in 1943.[42]

Boushall was a civic-minded banker who served on various city advisory commissions, as president of the Chamber of Commerce, and on the Richmond School Board. He was a lifelong conservative who adhered to increasingly obsolete language of white supremacy. In 1946, as part of an education conference, he touted the advantages of funding education in the South—or at least for its White population—when he claimed that "the South has a very potent Anglo-Saxon citizenry, quite susceptible to high economic and cultural development."[43]

In 1943 Boushall voiced his opposition to subsidized housing, declaring "[m]ore slums can be cleared by honest enforcement of existing ordinance than by the erection of all the slum-clearing housing that the government could ever afford to amortize through public taxation."[44] Yet he was flexible in his ideology. Bartholomew's Master Plan, with its businesslike approach to addressing Richmond's urban blight, seems to have played an important role in convincing Boushall to change his mind and support federally subsidized public housing. When the Federal Housing Act of 1949 released even more money for urban renewal projects, Boushall—then president of the Richmond Chamber of Commerce—chaired a citizens' advisory committee that worked with the City Council, the City Planning Commission, and the RRHA to study the potential use of that money. It also established guidelines for the 1,800 new low-rent housing units that such funding enabled. Creighton Court and Hillside Court were the result. Boushall, while supporting the use of federal money, also produced a "sanitary" housing code that would "give the city power to enforce certain minimum standards of health and sanitation on owners and occupants of substandard housing that would become an irredeemable slum if allowed to deteriorate unchecked."[45]

Changes in the racial landscape of Richmond that began with the movement of Black residents from neighborhoods long neglected by the city into high-density public housing during the 1940s only accelerated with the construction of interstate highways in the 1950s. Again, St. Paul's members provided guidance in the project.

The same 1946 Master Plan that directed slum clearance and urban renewal also recommended the building of an "interregional highway" through Richmond. Voters, alongside a fiscally reluctant City Council and Planning Commission, defeated initial concepts for a Richmond-Petersburg Turnpike route through the city (including a proposed stretch down Broad Street) in 1947.[46] Political opinion began to turn after 1950. Thomas P. Bryan Jr., a young lawyer and St. Paul's vestryman, proved a key figure in maneuvering the Turnpike through political and planning approval processes. Newly elected to the City Council in 1952, Bryan chaired a Council subcommittee that negotiated with the City Planning Commission and the Commonwealth Turnpike Corporation (represented by another vestryman, H. Merrill Pasco) to develop a new proposal for a highway, its route, and its funding.[47] These civic bodies, led by Bryan, recommended the creation of a toll road authority that could determine a route and secure financing without submitting plans to voters. It passed in 1954.[48]

Thomas Bryan subsequently became Mayor of Richmond while the toll road authority began the demolition of nearly 400 homes and the displacement of around 1,000 families, mostly African American, from the Navy Hill and Jackson Ward neighborhoods. Bryan worked with Thomas Boushall on the relocation of Black Richmonders. In addition to those displaced by the toll road (later Interstate 95) Bryan oversaw the use of federal funds from the Housing Act of 1954 in the bulldozing of dilapidated Black neighborhoods near Lombardy Street—because no amount of city investment could bring them into compliance with the new sanitary housing codes that Boushall had developed. The displaced people from Lombardy moved into newly opened Fairfield and Whitcomb Courts.[49]

One of the few laments from St. Paul's over the swath of destruction caused by the massive development campaign came from historic preservationist Mary Wingfield Scott, who wrote that "in the destruction of old buildings, this plan will have a more far-reaching effect than any event in the history of Richmond except the Evacuation Fire." Unfortunately, Miss Scott's prominent advocacy focused more on the historic buildings than on their displaced residents, whose homes she described as "a curious cottage . . . like a giant pigeon-house, the pigeons tumbling out of every opening being innumerable Negro children."[50]

In public campaigns for racial equality, Black men and women, freed from the obligation to be subservient to white people, began to challenge the legal doctrine of "separate but equal" that had been established by the *Plessy* v. *Ferguson* case in 1896. Led by the National Association for the Advancement of Colored People (NAACP) and its Legal Defense Fund, Black lawyers like Oliver Hill Sr. and local activists Jesse Tinsley and Antoinette Bowler set to work in the 1940s filing lawsuits against segregation in public schools. St. Paul's members participated in and shaped Virginia's policy response to NAACP challenges and, at the very beginning of the modern Civil Rights Movement, embraced conservative moderation.[51]

Dabney Lancaster, a St. Paul's vestryman, directed Virginia's initial response to the NAACP lawsuits in his position as the Virginia Superintendent of Instruction (1942–1946) by attempting to "equalize" resources for Black schools. In 1942 he issued a response to a lawsuit filed seeking Black student bus transportation equal to that furnished to white students. "I feel," Lancaster wrote, "that transportation should be provided for Negro populations just as rapidly as arrangements can be made."[52] When the NAACP filed lawsuits demanding equal pay for Black teachers, Lancaster reported that "a recent survey showed 26 of [Virginia's] 100 counties have equalized salaries or will have done so by 1943–1944, and plans for equalization have been adopted in 19 other counties."[53] The effort to make resources equitable as an attempt to forestall more serious challenges to segregation did not work. The United

States Supreme Court issued its *Brown v. Board of Education* decision in 1954, and, in strong response, Virginia's government embarked on its most notorious series of pro-segregationist strategies.

Another vestryman, Archibald G. Robertson, a Richmond lawyer, assisted the Virginia Attorney General in representing Prince Edward County in its defense against school integration in *Davis v. County School Board of Prince Edward County,* one of five lawsuits ultimately bundled into *Brown v. Board of Education*.[54] A year following the *Brown* decision, the Supreme Court ordered states to integrate their schools with "all deliberate speed" but left the details up to localities with no imposed timelines. Governor Thomas B. Stanley and the State Board of Education, which included Thomas Boushall, announced that Virginia's public schools would remain segregated for the next school year as it developed a strategy for implementing the Court's decision.[55]

In November 1955, a committee appointed by Governor Stanley issued its report. The Gray Plan, named for the committee chairman, Virginia Senator Garland Gray, allowed integration decisions to be made by local school districts, permitting compliance with the *Brown* decision in jurisdictions that desired it. It also authorized state tuition grants for parents who opposed integration to send their children to private schools. The moderate path—not demanding integration, avoiding overt resistance, and facilitating a way around it—received the support of Dabney Lancaster, Thomas Boushall, and Buford Scott,[56] who all signed public resolutions supporting the Gray Plan. Lancaster expressed his desire to keep Virginia's public schools open while stating, "I am opposed to integration and have said I believe it will set education back 50 years in the state. I still feel that way." The majority of Virginia's voters agreed with Lancaster, approving constitutional changes to allow for private school tuition grants.[57]

Virginia's powerful Democratic political machine headed by Senator Harry F. Byrd, however, eschewed moderation. It did not implement the Gray Plan and called a special session of the General Assembly in August 1956 to enact what it called "Massive Resistance"—empowering state control (as opposed to local control) of pupil placement schemes and ordering the closure of any public school and cutting of state funds to any public school forced (or choosing to) integrate.[58]

Boushall and Scott supported segregation but opposed Massive Resistance, noting that they "firmly believe segregated schools should be continued in the best interest of white and Negro races, and Virginia should fight to preserve segregation 'to the greatest possible extent by all lawful means.'"

Yet they also "urged continuation of public schools" and sanctioned again the local option.[59] Boushall's moderation cost him his position on the State Board of Education. Pro-segregationist leaders from Southside Virginia, who led his ouster, viewed Boushall as "'too moderate' and not wholly dedicated to the state's official policy of cutting off state funds and closing schools, if necessary, to prevent integration."[60] The moderates at St. Paul's nurtured their grievances in private. Anne Hobson Freeman recalls condemnation by various church members of the incendiary commentary of James J. Kilpatrick, the *Richmond News-Leader* editor and chief public advocate of Massive Resistance.[61]

Massive Resistance ultimately succumbed to legal challenges, and Virginia policymakers returned to a modified version of the Gray Plan with local option and tuition grants. Moderates supported it. Dabney Lancaster spoke to segregated meetings of teachers in Charlottesville and claimed that "[w]e need both public and private schools" and that education could be delivered "in fairness to every human being."[62] This "freedom of choice" plan permitted a gradual integration of public schools in Virginia, but at the same time it facilitated the massive migration of white students into private schools.

The cautious moderation bordering on conservatism that characterized St. Paul's at the beginning of the Civil Rights Movement continued to mark its approach as white religious people in Virginia and in Richmond began to tenuously stand up for the destruction of Jim Crow. The Virginia Commission on Interracial Cooperation limped into the 1940s. Its ties to St. Paul's weakened following the 1938 departure of rector Beverley Tucker. In 1943, the group met at the church for a symposium on race relations entitled "Present Situation and Paramount Needs," but the *Times-Dispatch* coverage did not—as it had when Tucker presided—mention participation by the rector, Vincent Franks, or anyone else associated with St. Paul's. White participation, instead, was led by Baptist ministers.[63] Losing momentum, the CIC merged with the newly formed Virginia Council of Churches and became its Department of Interracial Cooperation in 1944.[64]

In the 1920s and 1930s, the vestry had readily approved biracial services at St. Paul's on a couple of occasions (Robert Damell's funeral and the Race Relations Sunday featuring Dr. Robert R. Moton speaking on the inequities of "separate but equal" accommodations) as long as Black and white people sat in separate areas of the sanctuary. Mixed race services drew more controversy, however, in the 1940s and 1950s. In 1949, shortly after Virginia gubernatorial candidate Frances Pickens Miller addressed an integrated audience at St. Paul's for a world fellowship service sponsored by the Richmond YMCA, parishioner W. G. Taylor wrote a letter to the vestry "protesting mixed gatherings of white and colored people in the Church."[65] The following year, the Southern Association of Church Related Colleges requested to hold a service at St. Paul's in conjunction with its annual meeting. The rector reported that the service would be attended by college presidents, "about twelve of whom are negroes." The vestry approved, but with conditions: "It was the sense of the meeting that permission should be granted [for a biracial gathering] if the service would be for worship and not for discussion of political or racial issues of the day."[66]

In the 1940s, as the dynamics of racial change fundamentally shifted, St. Paul's members in positions of public influence continued to act as benevolent paternalists. In 1942, Odell Waller, a Black sharecropper, faced the death penalty in a case that reached the United States Supreme Court. Vestry members E. Randolph Williams and Thomas Boushall signed a petition to the governor asking for clemency.[67] In 1946, another vestryman, Judge John L. Ingram, oversaw the trial and conviction of two white police officers for raping a Black woman.[68] These meager gestures had limits. When former councilman and civil rights lawyer Oliver Hill asked the Richmond City Council in 1954 to petition the General Assembly to repeal segregation laws related to common carriers and public places, Thomas P. Bryan Jr., responded that it was a matter of state law and there "wasn't much the City of Richmond can do about that."[69]

Such efforts, the bare minimum required of a paternalistic elite, were reflected in the employment of sextons at St. Paul's. Men like John Lightener, Major Lewis, James Coleman, Harry Thompson, and Dones Anderson performed maintenance and steward duties in the church and Parish House for pay ranging between $60 to $75 per month. An economic safety net beyond the capricious benevolence from women's auxiliary groups or the vestry did not exist. In 1948, the Social Service Committee agreed to pay $107.72 in hospital bills for Dones Anderson.[70] In 1945, the vestry bestowed a modest pension for one year on John Lightener when he developed a terminal illness and was given two years to live.[71] Eight years later, the vestry also proposed a pension for Anderson in honor of his decades' of service but suspended it when Anderson squabbled with fellow sexton Harry Thompson. The vestry released him on the eve of his retirement.[72]

The complacency toward social needs troubled rector Robert Brown. In 1951 he confessed that "it is a matter of real concern to me that practically everything we have done thus far as a congregation—we have done for ourselves!" Contributions to the Diocesan Missionary Society aside, "we have been working to guarantee our own future, we have, in a word, failed to accomplish as much for others as we have for ourselves." He envisioned more active outreach and charity across Richmond, though he might have considered the security of St. Paul's sextons. Brown recognized that the church possessed great "power to provide," yet it had failed to do so. "We must not, we dare not, lose our Christian vision by continuing to look down our noses at ourselves."[73]

This creeping inertia increasingly placed St. Paul's in opposition to ecumenical advocacy of civil rights. In place of the Commission on Interracial Cooperation, several associations of white and Black ministers challenged local segregation laws in the 1940s and 1950s. Those organizations (the Protestant Ministers' Association, the Richmond Ministers' Union, and the Interdenominational Ministerial Alliance) merged to form the biracial Richmond Ministers' Association (RMA) in 1953. The RMA, noted one supporter, was "an expression of the Christian doctrine of the brotherhood of man and it will make possible a greater effectiveness in working for the Kingdom of God in Richmond."[74]

Even before the 1954 *Brown* decision, the RMA pushed for the dismantling of Jim Crow laws. A year earlier, it petitioned the General Assembly to repeal segregation laws in public transportation.[75] In 1957, the organization adopted its "Statement of Conviction on Race," criticizing Governor Stanley and the General Assembly for "their exceedingly inept handling of the current racial situation," referring to Massive Resistance. The statement, reported the *Times-Dispatch,* was "designed as a credo about which Virginians who oppose the Stanley non-integration plan and anti-NAACP bills can rally."[76] Despite the policy moderation of Thomas Boushall and the private odium of parishioners like Anne Freeman and her friends, the St. Paul's vestry condemned the RMA's resolution by expressing "its pleasure, its commendation, and its thanks to [St. Paul's] Clergy for their refusal to be drawn into public controversy on the Richmond Ministers Association resolution."[77] Although he was privately involved with certain RMA causes, including efforts to desegregate public facilities, rector Joseph Heistand dutifully had responded "no comment" when the *Times-Dispatch* surveyed Richmond clergy regarding the RMA resolution.[78]

Few, if any, sermons or events like Tucker's earlier condemnation of the Klan or support of a Race Relations Sunday remain in the historic record for the years after World War II. In fact, Vincent Franks, serving as rector from 1940 to 1946, never spoke directly about race until after he had moved on to a church in Jackson, Mississippi. Six years later, he returned to preach for the Lenten Lunch series and told his listeners that "we Christian white folks have a direct responsibility to the Negro, and we are not meeting it."[79] His time in volatile Mississippi and distance from St. Paul's seems to have loosened his tongue.

The position of St. Paul's toward race relations in the 1940s and 1950s might be summed up by resolutions adopted in 1949. In that year the Virginia Council of Churches opposed an amendment to the state constitution to repeal the poll tax and replace it with another disfranchisement measure—a literacy test—as too vague and broad. The vestry at St. Paul's, a member of the Council, did not like the attempt to stymie an initiative intended to maintain Black political disfranchisement. "It was resolved," vestry minutes state, that "this church does hereby regret and protest any such action of the said Council on purely political questions and its undertaking without due authority to express the views of member churches or individual parishes. The said Council is also requested and admonished not to attempt matters of this kind for or on behalf of or as representative of this parish."[80] The declaration suggests that members of St. Paul's vestry implicitly approved of efforts to strengthen segregation.

At the same meeting, the vestry passed another resolution, condemning the actions of the Federated Council of Churches, which had filed an amicus brief to the Supreme Court in the *Sweatt* v. *Painter* case regarding admission of a Black man to the University of Texas Law School. This time, the vestry noted "[t]he effort by a church agency to enforce by law the admission of a student to a State educational institution is hardly consistent with the claims for separation of church and state."[81] Frustrated with the liberal advocacy of the Virginia Council of Churches, the vestry voted in 1951 to withhold St. Paul's contributions.[82]

In the same church where the biracial CIC had once discussed ways to address racial issues of their day a generation before, the vestry now declared such discourse off-limits. Racial discussions were now viewed as political, not religious. Advocacy for racially liberal politics was permitted in the 1920s, but not in the 1950s. What had changed? In the 1920s, the church's most prominent members did not challenge fundamental assumptions about theology, about the paternalistic role of white people, or about the bedrock of segregation. Advocacy within those limits could be deemed a faithful enactment of religious belief, even a progressive one. But the advocacy in the 1950s challenged the role of white people and particularly the assumptions of Jim Crow. Therefore, advocacy, at least at St. Paul's, was deemed beyond the bounds of comfortable consensus on issues of theology, race, and politics, and therefore not rooted in proper religious purview. When religion and politics agreed, activism and action were acceptable; when they differed, they were condemned. Still, the Diocese, alongside other white Protestants in Richmond and beyond, continued to push the boundaries of theological and political consensus.

St. Paul's public face countenanced the survival of segregation long after the Diocese of Virginia began to chip away at its ecclesial underpinnings. In 1949 the diocese did away with all mentions of race in its canons and dissolved the Colored Convocation in which Black clergy and parishes were long consigned.[83] Five years after the *Brown* decision, the Council of the Diocese of Virginia adopted a resolution calling upon its members to provide leadership in implementing desegregation and resolved that "the problems created by such a decision presents to it an opportunity for intelligent, deliberate, Christian leadership." Yet the final form of the resolutions saw the diocese hedge on any comprehensive condemnation of segregation. Stricken from the initial draft was a reaffirmation of "our belief that discrimination between persons solely because of race or color is contrary to the spirit of Christianity." A frustrated Black clergyman, Charles W. Fox of Charlottesville, vented, "if Council doesn't take a stand under God, there's no need for the Negro clergymen to teach children they are under this church."[84] A subsequent resolution the following year asked for the removal of "all barriers preventing free fellowship in the church's life of people of different races."[85]

In the St. Paul's archives is a draft resolution from 1956 likely composed by vestryman McDonald "Mac" Wellford, based on one that had been introduced to the Diocesan Council of South Carolina, that expresses the conservative approach to what he called "the integration problem caused by the Supreme Court decision of 1954." Wellford, following the South Carolina resolution, framed the solution to the problem as a matter of personal conscience. Instead of legislating integration, he preferred that "greater emphasis needs to be placed on those things which are basic and Christian attitudes those daily contacts with people of other races where courtesies, consideration and love should be shown everyone, regardless of color. If in certain areas this should involve membership in the same church as a natural procedure, then the Christian thing is to welcome one of another race into the fellowship of that particular congregation. However, it seems unnatural and unwise to insist on bringing those of another race into a specific congregation just because they are of a different race."[86]

The diocese began integrating its youth camps at Roslyn and Shrine Mont in 1956. When some parishes objected, Bishop Frederick Goodwin declared that "the big job of the church today was reconciliation, not prophecy" and proposed a Racial Study Commission to be composed of "laymen and clergy of both sexes and of both races."[87] Two St. Paul's members served on the 1959 commission: Eppa Hunton IV and Mary Tyler Cheek (later McClenahan). Cheek, the daughter of newsman and Lee biographer Douglas Southall Freeman, urged respectful dialogue between races. In a prepared statement about the *Brown* decision delivered to fellow committee members, she wrote, "Social change is as inevitable as it is slow. Growth is painful, but it cannot be stopped because it is the essence of life."[88]

Hunton, a principal lawyer for the Richmond firm that represented Prince Edward County in upholding school segregation, also prepared a long memorandum outlining his opinions. He cited two documents that he regarded as establishing diocesan policy on race relations. Remarkably, the first was the 1860 "Report of the Committee on the Religious Instruction of the Colored People." Hunton's core lesson from that "able committee" was the advisability of creating separate and distinct congregations for people of color. The second document Hunton cited was the 1955 resolutions from the Diocesan Department of Christian Social Relations that recommended joint meetings "between representatives of the white and Negro races," interracial choir exchanges, interracial "vacation study groups" for children, the exchange of clergy, and that offered the opinion that "each member should do everything possible to see children in the churches and the church school grow up free from prejudice and ill-will toward members of other races."

Hunton approved of those recommendations. He did not, however, mention the 1949 resolutions that scrubbed racial descriptors from diocesan canon. In the absence of any remaining statutory barriers, he questioned whether "segregation in fact exist[s] today in this Diocese." He concluded, "I am not at all sure that it does." He further noted that "I do not believe there are any such [barriers] despite the call of the Council for their removal."

But Hunton—without apparent self-awareness—described situations in which social and cultural mores would continue to work toward enforcing *de facto* segregation. He lamented that because of the present "deterioration in the relations between the two races that has occurred since the school decisions," he could not host a fundraiser for a Black Episcopal school in the whites-only Westmoreland Club, "the walls of which were almost obscured by the portraits of Confederate officers in uniform," as he had done in the 1930s.

He also fretted that "colored clergy" would be left without jobs if churches integrated. In his imagination, no predominantly white church would hire a Black clergyman. As for laymen, "if they [Black Episcopalians] become members of a church in which white members are overwhelming in numbers, it will be almost unheard of for any colored man to be elected to the Vestry, or any colored person to occupy one of the top positions in the parish organizations." Hunton recalled a conversation with former rector Robert Brown regarding the hypothetical application of a Black man for membership at all-white St. Paul's. Hunton remembered Brown saying that, "he would point out to such a man the lack of community interest which he would have with the other members of the congregation, the unlikelihood that he would be welcome, and the almost certainty that he would never occupy a position of prominence or influence in the congregation, and the desirability that he should attend a colored church where he could be more fully accepted and make his influence more effective." Like his idols in 1860, Hunton had concluded that, even though the church allowed interracial worship, social reality—the inability of white people to imagine they could mingle with Black people as equals—demanded a continued separation in the house of the Lord.[89]

Many of the St. Paul's vestry rallied around Turner Arrington, Mac Wellford, and Hunton to express their guarded opposition. In a November 1958 letter to the Bishop, Arrington cautioned that his missive was not an official vestry action, but that eleven of twelve vestrymen (out of sixteen) consulted agreed. They regarded the bishop's leadership as "non-divisive," but they took exception to statements by "non-parochial clergy" that "we believe show a lack of understanding of the beliefs and wishes of the overwhelming majority of the laity." They "deplore[d]" a statement from the national church that condemned a tendency to "lock ourselves up behind the walls of our fears," and "the race mixing position of the Department of Christian Social Relations, both National and diocesan." In Virginia they "deplore[d]" the "sponsoring of mixed racial groups of young children and teen-agers by the Diocesan Department of Christian Education." They went on to "deplore" the nascent integration efforts at Rosyln and Shrine Mont, and the employment of a faculty member at the Virginia Theological Seminary "who heads a pro-integration organization" (though they hastened to add that they would similarly object to a "pro-segregation organization").

With Wellford's earlier appeal to individual conscience as the solution to "the integration problem" and this group's charges against church policy changes, a basis for a subtle opposition to integration (that would elide a politically unpalatable segregationist stance) emerged. To these men, the language of policy changes that identified racial barriers as a moral problem and a sin offended their self-defined sense of their racial benevolence—perhaps the most outrageous thing one could do to a paternalistic Virginian—that therefore should be avoided. Throwing the solution onto an appeal to individual conscience in a way that avoided addressing the ongoing systemic inequalities, then, gave tacit approval for segregation at the local level to continue. Hunton had already admitted this with his example of a Black man seeking membership that his individual conscience—and the realities of racial etiquette he maintained—would not allow it.

The extent to which most members of St. Paul's harbored this group's opinions is not known, but it is likely that most agreed. Perhaps others did not. Hunton reported in his memo that a bishop friend of his had chastised him for his "old-fashioned" views that only a few other "old-fogies" would share. Certainly, Mary Tyler Cheek disagreed. The Commission on which they sat ultimately concluded that white ministers should serve white churches and Black ministers Black churches. It also affirmed the move to desegregate youth camps but made provisions to continue segregated camps for those who desired them. The Commission couldn't hide the differences that led to its modest conclusions. "In our deliberations," they wrote, "there have been honest disagreements upon particular issues, and we individually do not necessarily endorse each proposal this report contains. If we as members of a Commission which has met monthly for a year cannot agree completely, we cannot expect complete agreement among other Christians of the Diocese." The diocesan council met the report with similar ambivalence, accepting it without comment.[90]

Integration of diocesan schools proceeded slowly. In 1963 Richmond's Episcopal school for girls, St. Catherine's, voted to accept a limited number of applications from Black students. In that year they placed one Black girl on a waiting list. St. Paul's vestryman Robert Gordon, chairman of the St. Catherine's board that made the decision, received letters of support as well as condemnation. One Richmond Episcopalian no doubt represented hundreds of others when he told Gordon that St. Catherine's was not ready for such a "revolutionary move." Mary Tyler Cheek, however, praised the decision in a letter to Bishop Robert F. Gibson as a "courageous and just action." She declared, "To say to a human being, 'You are welcome to join our church but you may not cross the threshold of our church school because your skin is brown,' seems a contradiction on the deepest level of Christian relationship."

The first accepted applicant chose to go elsewhere; St. Catherine's admitted its first Black student in 1968, the year all nine of the diocesan schools had integrated.[91]

As the Diocese debated integration, others deployed a story from St. Paul's to advocate for Southern acceptance of the *Brown* decision. The old tale of Robert E. Lee kneeling beside a Black man in 1865—once a tribute to the maintenance of white supremacy but reinterpreted by Black intellectuals as a potential symbol of interracial cooperation in the 1930s—reappeared once again. Interestingly, several Richmond historians discounted it out of hand. Lee biographer Douglas Southall Freeman declared that it had "absolutely no foundation in fact." Virginius Dabney, who in 1966 termed it a "Lee-gend" that drew its "only nourishment from the breath of rumor."[92]

Despite their skepticism, the story thrived during the integration crisis. white liberal journalists mimicked the interpretation of Benjamin Brawley and Carter Woodson, and projected Lee as a Confederate hero who defied societal norms to extend the hand of welcome and equality to Black people. Of course, this was the complete opposite of the intended message of Broun's original narrative. In the immediate wake of the 1954 *Brown v. Board of Education* decision, *Washington Post* columnist Benjamin Muse used it to advocate for white churches to accept Black worshippers in 1954. I.F. Stone published the story in *I. F. Stone's Weekly* in 1956 to condemn Alabama students who lacked the "moral courage" to sit beside a lone Black student integrating a public university. Perhaps the story gained its most widespread exposure from evangelist Billy Graham, who twice used it to call for racial tolerance in the growing turbulence of the Civil Rights Movement. First, in *Life* magazine in 1956, Graham called the moment when the Lee knelt "beside his colored brother," a "simple, eloquent example," of magnanimity. Graham deployed the story yet again in 1960 in the pages of *Reader's Digest*, amid a Student Nonviolent Coordinating Committee campaign of "kneel-ins," designed to call attention to the intransigence of white churches. In the early 1960s, white advocates, including Ralph McGill, liberal editor of the Atlanta *Constitution*, continued to use the story to shame segregationists. Despite the skepticism of historians and the lack of contemporary evidence to prove the story, the notion of a kindly Lee extending Christian brotherhood to a Black man proved too tempting for most commentators.[93]

Certainly, Lee's Christian character had been a staple of Lost Cause history, but through this tale, integrationists could utterly appropriate it (while misunderstanding it) in support of Black equality. In their rebuke of vicious segregationists, they had given moderate white people cover by mobilizing Confederate history in a liberal cause. Yet, while versions of the story flourished and transformed elsewhere, it still made little impact at a St. Paul's, which remained stagnant in the face of the Civil Rights challenge.

The caution toward the rapidly unfolding Civil Rights Movement exhibited by the Diocese of Virginia and St. Paul's had become relative intransigence in its passive resignation. In the same year that the diocesan Racial Study Commission released its moderate conclusions, impatient liberals in the Episcopal Church began to stake out more progressive aspirations. In 1958, northern and southern clergy and lay people (including Charlottesville Episcopalian Sarah Patton Boyle) met in New Hampshire to develop strategies for opposing the massive resistance now engulfing all southern states. When the national church balked at endorsing that meeting's resolutions, the group formed the independent Episcopal Society for Cultural and Racial Unity (ESCRU) to actively overturn segregation.[94]

Changes in Richmond also accelerated the progress of civil rights. During Virginia's Massive Resistance strategy in the late 1950s, the General Assembly passed laws intended to hobble NAACP activism. In response, Black men and women in 1956 created the Crusade for Voters, a highly effective voter education and mobilization organization. Among its chief tasks was to raise money with which Black voters could pay the poll tax that remained a hurdle to voting. By the early 1960s, the Crusade regularly endorsed bipartisan and biracial slates of progressive candidates for City Council and, in 1964, helped elect B.A. "Sonny" Cephas to become the city's second Black councilman since 1902, following Oliver Hill's notable 1949 turn. On top of the Crusade's successes, the passage of the Civil Rights Act the same year and the US Voting Rights Act in 1965 served to dismantle the bulwark of Jim Crow. In 1966, the elimination of the poll tax through the *Harper v. Virginia Board of Elections* (in which St. Paul's vestryman George D. Gibson represented the Board of Elections) proved a watershed in Black participation and power in Richmond's politics.[95]

A 1961 attempt to consolidate the City of Richmond with Henrico County failed, partly because of Crusade opposition.[96] Frustrated that Richmond had mismanaged the opportunity, a group of white business professionals formed a non-partisan lobbying group called Richmond Forward in 1963 in order to support effective candidates for City Council. Thomas Boushall served as its first president. The organization also included St. Paul's members S. Buford Scott and William V. Daniel.[97]

Richmond Forward played savvy racial politics. Acknowledging the growing electoral power of Black Richmond, it endorsed African American physician and Crusade co-founder, W. Ferguson Reid, for the Democratic nomination for the General Assembly in 1965.[98] Some St. Paul's members sponsored a fundraising cocktail party for Dr. Reid at their home—an event that many believed to be the first instance of hosting a Black candidate in a white residence in Richmond.[99] Reid's campaign was successful, making him the first Black Virginia delegate elected since Reconstruction. Yet Richmond Forward, despite its regular endorsement of Black candidates for office, remained firmly rooted in the white business establishment. Eventually it became a fierce competitor with the Crusade over the course of the 1960s.

The specter of a majority-Black Richmond haunted many white Richmonders, and they moved to annex parts of Chesterfield County to restore a favorable white monopoly to dominate city politics in the late 1960s. Representatives of Richmond Forward led the effort, particularly Councilman James Wheat Jr. who accused anti-annexation council members of a desire to "see the city converted into a Black ghetto for their own purely political interests."[100] Following a protracted legal struggle in the court system, Richmond Forward and other advocates prevailed and twenty-three square miles of Chesterfield County—with its predominantly white residents—became part of the city. A three-judge panel of the Virginia Supreme Court, including vestry member Thomas C. Gordon Jr., turned back an attempt by anti-annexation opponents to reverse the decision.[101] The effort to preserve white dominance of Richmond politics, however, had limited reach. As the civil rights lawsuit over the annexation made its way to the US Supreme Court, the Justice Department ordered Richmond to suspend all City Council elections. The high court's ruling in 1975 held that the city could keep the annexed land but had to change its form of government to a racially balanced nine-ward system. As a result, Richmond elected its first Black majority City Council in 1977, which in turn elected Richmond's first Black mayor, Henry L. Marsh III.[102]

During the 1960s, conservative and moderate white people across the South recoiled at the increasingly radical stances taken across the activist spectrum, and particularly by militant African Americans who took to the streets mid-decade. Even before the devastating assassination of Martin Luther King Jr. in April 1968 and the widespread protests that followed, over two dozen riots laid waste to urban centers across the country between 1964 and 1967. Scrambling to respond to unfolding events, racial activists clamored within the US Episcopal Church. At the 1967 General Convention, Presiding Bishop John Hines established the General Convention Special Program (GCSP), a $9 million fund designed to be disbursed as block grants to Black community and economic empowerment organizations in urban areas. The controversial GCSP immediately galvanized Episcopalians into factions. Moderate white churchmen condemned the lack of oversight of grants, some of which went to groups they considered to be violent separatists. Administration of the GCSP also bypassed and therefore alienated Black Episcopal clergy and congregations. The program attracted the attention of an ecumenical coalition of Black clergy who had formulated the *Black Manifesto* in 1969, with which they approached the Episcopal Church and demanded millions in reparation payments.[103] At a Special General Convention held in South Bend, Indiana that year, representatives of the Union of Black Clergy and Laymen took over the podium, civil rights and anti-war activists disrupted the meeting, and protestors variously accused the Episcopal Church of racism, paternalism, and failing to trust the leadership of its Black clergy and laypeople as leaders in the denomination. The convention assented to the many demands and committed yet more money from the church's coffers.[104] White southern Episcopalians, conservative and moderate, viewed the religious, social, and political tumult in 1969 with a great deal of trepidation. They fearfully perceived a complete loss of control of the management of racial politics and huddled in fear. A few, like Mary Tyler Cheek, stepped forward.

In 1950, former St. Paul's rector Russell Bowie retired from a professorship at Union Theological Seminary in New York and returned to Virginia. He settled at the Virginia Theological Seminary in Alexandria but made frequent trips back to Richmond. His time away from Virginia had permitted him the space in which to cultivate his Social Gospel practice and to critically reexamine his own understanding of race and segregation, an evolution that he described in his autobiography *Learning to Live* (1969). Recalling his childhood nostalgia for "mammies" and his later efforts to relieve Jackson Ward of poverty, he felt a tinge of guilt. He had been among the foremost of Richmond's white racial liberals in the 1910s but now he saw his limitations. "Where there needed to be a sensitive social conscience," he lamented, "there was often a blind spot. It was hard for the privileged, even the most kindly ones, to conceive that the Negro might have aspirations equal to their own." In his long years, he had matched Anne Hobson Freeman's critical detachment from the Lost Cause that he himself had preached as a young man. "One looks back in personal recollection and can see how fixed the old ideas were—and how intertwined with sentiment which made the old seem to have a halo around it." His personal reexamination of his own beliefs fitted him with a new perspective on more recent events in the 1950s and 1960s.[105]

Virginia's massive resistance to the *Brown* decision dumbfounded Bowie. In 1957, he penned an angry letter to the editor of the *Times-Dispatch,* accusing the paper of using language designed to provoke violence against civil rights leaders. "You and your columnist have the advantage of entrenched white supremacy. Have you then no noblesse oblige? As in Montgomery, Alabama, under the leadership of their minister [Martin Luther King Jr.], so in many of our states Negroes have shown an integrity of conviction and a patient nonviolence which deserves the respect of just and thoughtful men—and may we not say are worthy of the approval of God?" Bowie counseled the embrace of leaders like King and Fred Shuttlesworth and their aspirations while his peers in the elite Episcopal world of Virginia became ever more resistant.[106]

Bowie noted in his memoirs, completed in the wake of King's assassination, that he had "looked with sadness upon what was happening in public affairs. The balances which might have risen toward creative change sank instead toward a darker consequence." Religious and secular leadership had failed to rise to the occasion, but instead had cultivated "hostility to school desegregation and to anything else that might seem to threaten white privilege and white superiority found its elegant embodiment in Senator Harry Flood Byrd of Virginia, with his slogan of 'massive resistance...'" Perhaps most painful to the old rector was that "even the people of my beloved St. Paul's, who in the earlier years had become the standard-bearers for liberal thought and positive purpose, for the most part dropped back into reaction."[107]

5 | Effective Witness

RACIAL RADICALISM WASHED onto the portico of St. Paul's in late May 1969. Three weeks earlier, Black activist James Forman created a national stir by interrupting services at Riverside Church in New York City to demand $500 million in reparations from wealthy white churches. In Richmond, two Black clergymen did the same on the steps of Second Presbyterian and of St. Paul's. Howard C. Moore and Linwood Corbett demanded that white Richmond churches dedicate $1.5 million toward alleviating causes of racial disparities. The reaction from St. Paul's—then under the interim rectorship of the Reverend Uly Gooch—is not known, but the Richmond Area Clergy Association (RACA) considered the demands. At their summer meetings, RACA passed "a mild resolution" to acknowledge Moore and Corbett's claims and to study the problems and recommend courses of action. A committee blandly affirmed that Richmond churches should, indeed, become "more involved in alleviation of Negro problems."[1] The threat of radicalism had pushed Richmond's moderate mainline Protestants to act, even if in a deliberate way.

Critics called Forman, Moore, and Corbett's demands for reparations extortion and bribery, and they condemned the implied threat of violence. Yet the uncompromising and urgent demands had the effect of driving frightened white centrists into accepting mainstream liberal action. Either embrace the vision of Martin Luther King Jr., Russell Bowie had warned, or suffer at the hands of radicals like Stokely Carmichael.[2] The rector of St. John's Church in Lynchburg, Virginia, John Shelby Spong, agreed that reparations demands were an outrage. "To the Forman manifesto," he wrote, "I think it is quite clear that, corporately and individually, we must say a polite but quite firm NO!"[3]

However, Spong, like most mainline white Protestants, sympathized with the continuing social and economic plight of African Americans even after the political successes of the Civil Rights Movement. Many white southerners realized that the Civil Rights Movement had been a revolution that had overturned the fictions of their worldviews and challenged the rootedness of racial thinking in the everyday assumptions about their society, culture, and faith. While some retreated into bitter racial revanchism as the 1970s dawned, others more pragmatically embraced new realities.[4] Spong, then, readily acknowledged the complicity of white people in the historical oppression of Black people. "We make no effort to justify our failure to right the wrongs," of the past, he told his Lynchburg flock. "We are painfully aware today that we are, in fact, paying the price of the slavery of our great grandparents, the segregation and second-class citizenship of our parents and of ourselves, and our failure to provide equal opportunity for all citizens until we were forced to do so by the power of the Federal Government and by the threat of violence. Our history is not clean and we know this." Spong firmly rejected the call for his contemporaries to pay for the sins of their fathers through reparations, "but let us never forget that we are responsible, quite responsible, for what we do about what we have inherited." Spong finished his message to St. John's: "We are held accountable for making our world today a fair and just world, for removing every symbol that downgrades or insults a fellow human being," and he ended with a rigorous endorsement of the nascent and controversial General Convention Special Program.[5]

When St. Paul's called Jack Spong as its rector in 1969, he made good on his commitment to remove insulting symbols. St. Paul's had regularly flown a Confederate flag from its portico to mark Robert E. Lee's birthday and other significant Confederate anniversaries. "To me," he later wrote, "that flag was nothing but a symbol of slavery and segregation." Spong demanded that the flag not be flown, or else he would vacate the pulpit on those occasions. "My passion surprised the vestry, who had never thought much about this issue," Spong recalled. Indeed, St. Paul's people may have associated the flag with genteel ceremony, but Jack Spong had been the target of the flag-brandishing Edgecombe County Ku Klux Klan in Tarboro, North Carolina, because of his support for integration. At St. Paul's, vestrymen Catesby B. Jones and James Rawles vehemently objected to the proposal for removal, but their cohorts agreed to a compromise: stop flying the flag outdoors and only display it on appropriate occasions in the sanctuary. "[A]fter one or two years," Spong recalled, "the altar guild simply forgot to put the large and cumbersome flag out and so the custom died."[6]

Perhaps even more shocking, Spong rallied St. Paul's to make a public support of the national church's General Convention Special Program. Speaking to the Men's Association of St. Paul's, the new rector tackled the Special Program resolutions line-by-line. He assured his listeners that the initiative did not arise as a response to the reparations demands of the Black Manifesto, but from the concerns of Black Episcopal clergy, and that the conditions of financial disbursement of funds depended on the meeting of strict criteria by receiving organizations. In short, Spong assured his cautious audience that the GCSP did not intend to disburse funds to revolutionaries. He candidly admitted that the Special Program was a risk, but one worthy of consideration. Success would mean "a tremendous contribution our church has made to the problems of our times." Members of the gathering were so inspired that they published Spong's address as a full-page paid advertisement titled "An Address to ALL Episcopalians." St. Paul's members Nora Lee Antrim, Walter W. Craigie, Sr., William H. Mann, Hunter "Mac" McGuire, H. Merrill Pasco, S. Buford Scott, and H. St. George Tucker Jr., all signed their names to it alongside a handful of members from other Episcopal congregations.[7] Where churches in the Diocese of Virginia had spent a generation languishing in cultural complacency, moderate and progressive Episcopalians in Virginia found in Spong and St. Paul's an unexpected example of courageous leadership in the church.

Jack Spong's rectorship at St. Paul's marked a turning point in the church's history just as significant as the tenures of Minnigerode and Bowie. In his years, St. Paul's identity underwent a transformation. Many customs—like the raising of Confederate flags—died unnoticed. In their place, St. Paul's people built new traditions for a post–Civil Rights Movement world.

Jean LeRoy, a St. Paul's staff member and key aide to Spong insightfully assessed the church in 1969. Post–World War II suburban expansion and white flight had long before drained the old Franklin and Grace Street corridors of the middle- and upper-class residents who made up the historic core of St. Paul's membership. "We have a loyal congregation of people drawn from the suburbs," LeRoy noted, "who come to church downtown because it offers them something special." She noted that congregants might be attracted to St. Paul's social prominence, its superior music performed by a professional organist and choir, or the consistency of high-quality liturgy and sermons. Interestingly, she did not mention the pull of St. Paul's historical identity, though families with deep genealogical connections no doubt cherished that aspect of their St. Paul's experience. LeRoy last observed that the civic-minded businesspeople that frequented St. Paul's on Sundays felt affinity for a church "perceived to be a place where issues of the whole city are addressed, or in which various outreach programs are sponsored."[8] The prevailing perception was that Richmond's well-connected downtown businesspeople played at the Country Club of Virginia and they worshipped at St. Paul's. The church was a social marker just as much as it was a historical one.

Indeed, in the late 1960s, businessmen among the congregation could attend forum series discussions sponsored by St. Paul's on essential issues facing Metropolitan Richmond. As part of the Downtown Cooperative Ministry (DCM)—which also included St. Peter's Roman Catholic, Centenary Methodist, and Second Presbyterian—the church scheduled talks and debates on such topics as "liquor by the drink," "public welfare," "the limits of protest," "bridges across the generation gap," and "the church's role in the racial crisis."[9] At such forums regarding public issues, St. Paul's offered ways for its congregants to network informally and accumulate social clout among influential people of the city and state.

St. Paul's did have an active outreach program under the umbrella of the Christian Social Relations Committee chaired by Evans Brasfield and its efforts served traditional objects of church charity—the poor. In response to feedback by public health nurses, the church opened a food and clothing pantry for needy families.[10] St. Paul's operated a Benevolent Fund, and in 1970, its Episcopal Church Women chapter opened and began fundraising for further outreach causes selected annually by its members.[11] The church also sponsored the St. Paul's Church Home Fund, a restricted charitable endowment formed from monies remaining after the closing of its orphanage in the late 1920s. Set up in 1959 as an independent non-profit corporation with a separate board, the fund's ongoing mission was to give charitable grants to nurture and educate children and to aid destitute sick people regardless of age.[12] In 1966 and 1967, two additional endeavors brought focus to special-needs groups on weekdays. The Adult Development Center operated out of the undercroft and provided physical and occupational therapy for people with serious disabilities.[13] The Oral School, housed in Sunday School classrooms, provided training and activities for up to fifty pre-school deaf children. At some point after opening, the Oral School began accepting Black children with no documented objection from parishioners.[14]

St. Paul's approached racial matters differently now than in earlier generations. In the 1920s, Richmond's Black and white city leaders gathered at St. Paul's to discuss white people's obligations to Black people and to promote Black uplift. By the late 1960s, however, the Civil Rights Movement had changed the dynamics of Black-white relationships in public. White municipal leaders grudgingly accepted and worked with Black leaders, often on the latter's terms. Conscientious, church outreach initiatives began to intentionally approach recipients of money as partners in charitable decision-making and not just as the objects of benevolence.

Certainly, white leaders and church members began to gain their footing in the novel environment of Black autonomy in the late 1960s. For the rising young clergy, contemporary theological innovations undermined any sense that segregation could be benevolent and instead insisted that it represented the sin of prejudice and nothing more. Spong arrived at St. Paul's—the church of Eppa Hunton IV and Thomas Boushall—as a committed anti-segregationist and elaborated his theological view of diverse humanity in a 1972 address. Regarding Jesus's post-Crucifixion admonition that "ye shall also be my witness in Samaria," Spong insisted that "if the Gospel is proclaimed, it must invade and witness in the areas of our prejudice." Whereas in earlier generations Hunton and Mary-Cooke Munford had considered segregation compatible with Gospel fulfillment, Spong officially declared that the problem within segregation was not the shortcomings of the Black race, but rather, the sinful tendencies of white segregationists. "A segregated, exclusive church," he preached, "has never heard the Christian Lord;" and he dared St. Paul's to "raise the issues of race, housing, schools, jobs, war, and let the

FIGURE 8. Rev. John Shelby Spong and parishioners in the St. Paul's library, ca. 1974. (*Richmond Times-Dispatch* Collection, The Valentine)

Gospel shed its uncomfortable light upon them."[15] Subsequent engagement by St. Paul's in the secular world would never be the same.

Outreach became the chief means of engagement with race. Spong tasked Evans Brasfield of the Christian Social Relations Committee to evaluate an initiative of the Richmond Area Clergy Association to raise $310,000 to "help Richmond black poor" that had been demanded by Howard Moore and Linwood Corbett. Spong and Brasfield recommended to the vestry that St. Paul's contribution should be $7,500 and dispatched a special fundraising letter to members.[16] The vestry also authorized the Benevolence Fund to donate money to the Bainbridge Richmond Community Action Program Center (RCAP). When Mary-Cooke Munford, Richard Carrington, and St. Paul's acted in the 1920s, they had lent their social and political influence toward urgent advocacy of public policy regarding Black Richmonders. The programs of the late 1960s instead utilized St. Paul's growing physical plant and leveraged its considerable wealth to directly aid people in poverty, particularly in African American neighborhoods.

The new rector, however, did not want his "years to be spent in simply continuing or even expanding things previously done." Spong lamented that St. Paul's lacked "focused outreach in the poor and Black communities of Richmond." Inspired by the General Convention Special Program, he proposed a major new outreach initiative. The "Isaiah 58:12 Program" would, in partnership with proposed communities and with other funding institutions, make significant block grants to create "real and long-term differences." He desired that it involve the congregation in hands-on work, and specifically, "serve to repair the breach between races and economic groups in this city." He proposed to fund it using revenue from the church parking garage that was constructed in 1961 and for which the debt would be retired in 1971. Spong met some resistance from the vestry but overcame his chief obstacle, Eppa Hunton IV, by appealing to the latter's "noblesse oblige" and also his "ultraconservative" opinion about the futility of public welfare programs.[17] In his formal presentation to the vestry in December of 1970, Spong noted the long-term decline in outreach spending from St. Paul's, from 60 percent of church income in Russell Bowie's time to 30 percent in his own. Over a handful of objections the vestry approved the allocation of $100,000 from parking garage income to be disbursed in $25,000 grants over the next four years. The grant, administered by each community endeavor and not the church, was intended to be seed money to attract additional sustaining funds. Conscientiously stepping away from past outreach approaches while mollifying conservative concerns, Spong hoped that "this committee would administer this fund in such a way as to avoid the pitfalls of paternalism on one side, and irresponsibility on the other."[18] Associate rector Walton Pettit, who had been tasked with Isaiah's logistic operations, reported that the congregation had met the initiative with "wonderful acceptance."[19]

The Isaiah 58:12 Program, chaired by Thomas Boushall, made its first grant toward establishing a medical clinic in Fulton. This historically Black neighborhood in Richmond's East End lacked any medical services, and the committee was drawn particularly to the opportunity for parishioners to volunteer in the clinic, to serve on the board alongside community members, and to significantly impact a struggling neighborhood. St. Paul's committed $22,000 to the clinic, an amount increased by $4,000 from the General Convention Special Program and $7,000 from other local funders. The clinic opened on November 5, 1972. Among the visitors on opening day was Governor Linwood Holton.[20]

While St. Paul's people helped get the Fulton Medical Clinic underway, the Isaiah committee—now chaired by Eugene Sikorosky—moved forward with its next grant opportunity. In February 1973, the vestry, at the Isaiah committee's recommendation, approved the expenditure of two years' worth of program funds ($50,000) to support a private alternative high school on Grace Street for high school dropouts still seeking an education.[21] The Street Academy opened in April 1974 and served as a pilot project in the city. Isaiah and Street Academy planners intended for Richmond Public Schools ultimately to assume administration and funding of the project.

The vestry, in 1974, voted to extend the Isaiah project for two additional years.[22] In 1976, the Isaiah committee recommended supporting a Family Crisis Shelter on Grove Avenue, which would provide refuge for family members suffering violence or neglect at the hands of relatives.[23] However a downturn in annual giving and membership at St. Paul's in the late 1970s prompted the Isaiah Project to pause for a period of evaluation and planning.[24] Its last recorded round of grants included $2,000 for the Church Hill Area Revitalization Team, $1,000 for the Center on Aging of the Presbyterian School of Christian Education, and $500 for the Family Crisis Center.[25]

Evans Brasfield and the Christian Social Relations Committee (CSR) had not been idle during years that the Isaiah Project got underway. The CSR began a multifaceted relationship with St. Peter's Episcopal Mission, a biracial congregation in the East End's historically Black Fairmont neighborhood.[26] St. Paul's partnered with St. Peter's to create a legal aid program that grew to a long-term involvement of St. Paul's people in Richmond's Offender Aid and Restoration (OAR) program.[27] Further, St. Paul's made multiple grants to a supplementary education program sponsored by St. Peter's. One grant, in 1971, called Black Education Teams, "undertook to give specialized training to disadvantaged Black children in the vicinity of St. Peter's." This project eventually grew into the Peter Paul Development Center.[28] In 1972 Walton Pettit reported on a "Black-White dialogue group composed of members from St. Paul's and Second Baptist Church on Randolph and Idlewood Avenue," but he did not record its agenda.[29]

Members of the Christian Social Relations Committee took a particular interest in the problem of housing in Richmond, including discrimination that violated the Federal Housing Act of 1968 and an increasing scarcity of affordable housing. In 1972, it began studying ways that St. Paul's might help "alleviate the shortage of low- and moderate-income housing in Richmond."[30] The CSR's interest began with the arrival of Jim Hecht to Richmond. Hecht, a scientist at DuPont, had come from Buffalo, New York, where he had been active in open-housing advocacy. At Jack Spong's urging, he and his wife, Amy, became communicants at St. Paul's and took an active interest in its outreach efforts. In the fall of 1971, Hecht helped organize the non-profit Housing Opportunities Made Equal (HOME) to educate and pressure local real estate firms to offer equitable housing. Moreover, it worked alongside the US Justice Department to investigate and bring suit against violations of racial steering, redlining, and blockbusting. The group's efforts had the endorsement of Governor Holton, who sponsored Virginia's fair housing legislations.[31]

Jack Spong intended to make HOME the Isaiah project for 1973. The Isaiah committee agreed, but the effort floundered when the vestry took up the question. In his later autobiography, Spong recalled that group's conservatives claimed that HOME had more of a political and economic bent than a religious one, and that it would divide the church. They successfully rallied a veto of the project—over the yes votes of H. St. George Tucker and S. Buford Scott—in what Spong called "my greatest failure in Richmond." Hecht, on the other hand, recalled that the St. Paul's rejection turned out to be a crucial turning point. "Quite simply," he said, "if it had not happened, HOME would not have become what it did." Despite the defeat, the organization built on the rigor of the Isaiah vetting process and, with the key assistance of S. Buford Scott, and John and Virginia Ritchie, found crucial backers and outside funding to initiate and sustain operations.[32]

St. Paul's dramatic burst of outreach in the early 1970s earned the praise of Bishop Robert Hall of the Diocese of Virginia. "Indeed," he wrote, "there are few churches in the United States . . . that have as powerful and as effective a witness to the heart of the Gospel of Jesus Christ as St. Paul's. You and your people are really awe-inspiring to behold as you wrestle with theological and social programs that could tear apart many churches."[33] The church's approach to outreach withdrew from the paternalism of earlier generations, but it still relied on St. Paul's wealth and enormous influence. Doing so, certainly, they risked continuing patterns of paternalism or maintaining a narrative of racial difference that—while in the context of acknowledging the sinfulness of racism—continued to link Blackness with poverty.

Jack Spong's larger ministry profoundly reshaped St. Paul's identity. To begin with, he reframed the church's history. In his address on the church's 125th anniversary, Spong referred to "the War Between the States" with a few sentences of pabulum but then unleashed a torrent of praise for Russell Bowie's civic activism and anti-fundamentalist stances. He directly connected Bowie's integrity to "the heroic leadership that emanated from this church during the recent controversy engendered by the South Bend Convention" (meaning the General Convention Special Project). Pointedly, in his anniversary address, Spong made no reference at all to the Confederacy, Robert E. Lee, or Jefferson Davis. He did, however, mention Charles Minnigerode's mission-planting efforts around Richmond and his embrace of Black members. (Spong missed the proslavery intentions of Minnigerode in sponsoring a Sunday Schools for Black people and attributed it to open-hearted liberality—and the fact that it ended after a single year.)[34] By the 1970s, members and clergy of St. Paul's had taken up the repurposed integrationist version of the Lee Communion story as a redemptive act of racial liberalism. S. Buford Scott recalled it as an inspirational anecdote to welcome potential Black members—as he did when he and Susie Scott recruited Ruby Grant Martin to the church in 1978.[35] The Reverend Rodney Rice, St. Paul's first Black clergyman from 1987 to 1989 used the story in a sermon to disarm visiting members of the United Daughters of the Confederacy who still held annual Lee Birthday services in the sanctuary.[36]

The narrative change about the church's identity, however, was secondary to the spiritual vitality Spong and his staff (including assistants Jean LeRoy and Lucy Negus) introduced to parish life. They reinvented and strengthened the Christian education and formation programs on Sunday. They transformed an existing sense of goodwill toward strangers and new members into an aggressive welcoming campaign. Spong's willingness to be a public figure in the political realm was matched only by his high-profile evangelism. He instituted a Sunday morning Bible class that featured open and critical engagement with the theological assumptions of the Christian faith. When the class regularly packed Scott Hall in the Parish House, the Union Presbyterian Seminary sponsored its broadcast over WRFK radio.[37] The Bible class's intellectual rigor and excitement about the activist outreach programs made St. Paul's a beacon for new, young, progressive-minded Richmonders.[38] Adrian Luxmoore, drawn by St. Paul's newfound energy in 1970, recalled a transition from "a church that was the home of the Old Virginian high society—First Families of Virginia—to a church that was much more of an activist, progressive, forward-looking" place.[39] Scott Sirles, who joined in 1972 recollected that prior to his time, "if you wanted to be a big shot lawyer, banker, what have you ... you'd have to go here or to First Baptist. And you probably had to belong to the Country Club.... Those days are long gone." Luxmoore added that "they went in the middle of the Seventies."[40] Mary Ann Ready, who joined with her family in 1978, remembered that "you didn't come to St. Paul's unless you planned to do some sort of urban ministry."[41] The total number of parishioners at St. Paul's eventually declined over the course of the 1970s, but the influx of new members who had come of age in admiration and support of the civil rights struggle—and had not been steeped in Lost Cause narratives of benevolent owners and loyal slaves—seized the social identity and public initiative at St. Paul's.[42] By decade's end, and for the first time since the antebellum era, St. Paul's congregation numbered African Americans among its official congregants.

In subsequent decades, St. Paul's would develop an even more intentional voice on race and interracial dialogue, but Spong's departure in 1976 left the church aware that it may have overextended itself. The Parish Profile prepared by the new rector search committee noted that "on occasions St. Paul's has publicly endorsed controversial policies for the good of the community but at its own risk."[43] Risk of financial liability and risk of dissent and division within the congregation existed. Yet the profile did not call for a retreat from that activity but boldly sought out a new rector who could successfully guide St. Paul's through ever more risk.

When the vestry called the Reverend Craig Biddle III to be St. Paul's thirteenth rector in April 1977, they recommitted the church to its focus on a race-conscious downtown ministry. A self-described "liberal orthodox" Episcopalian, Biddle arrived from Trinity on the Green Episcopal Church in New Haven, Connecticut. There, he had been a board member of the New Haven Downtown Cooperative Ministry, president of the national conference of Rectors of Urban Churches, and a staunch supporter of the ordination of women—a controversy then eclipsing the issue of race in the Episcopal Church.[44] Before his arrival, Biddle told the *Richmond Times-Dispatch* that "affluent white downtown churches, like St. Paul's, have a great deal of responsibility for social action." The young rector, whose large family included an adopted "Black-Vietnamese" child, gained attention in Richmond by refusing the customary step of joining the still-segregated Country Club of Virginia and by enrolling his children in the city's public school system.[45]

Biddle arrived in Richmond within a month of a historic transformation in the racial power dynamic in the city—the special elections (after a seven-year court-ordered suspension) that ushered in the city's first Black majority council and mayor. The election results appeared to be the culmination of Black political empowerment and the capstone of the Civil Rights Movement in this storied southern city. Instead, it revealed the comprehensive inequities in the distribution of formal and informal influence in Richmond's corridors of power. Struggles a year into the new regime demonstrated that much of Richmond's economic and cultural power still resided in traditionally white—and exclusive—spaces like the private clubs, boardrooms, and business associations to which, on the eve of the 1980s, Black people still had no access. Mayor Henry Marsh noted, "I am not privy to many of the situations where leaders of the white community meet.... A lot of this is done in socializing and a lot of the socializing is done where Blacks are not present." These enclaves of power proved reluctant to entrust Richmond's Black leadership with a share of its influence. By 1980, racial acrimony between white and Black council members dominated Richmond's government and public life.[46] Biddle oversaw the continuation of former outreach efforts, but he also guided a turn toward addressing the racial imbalance in Richmond's power structures that the Black majority council had revealed.

Biddle immediately joined the year-old Downtown Cooperative Ministry, now a group of five churches, including Third Street AME Bethel, dedicated to addressing the unique problems faced by Richmond's urban churches—homelessness and poverty. The DCM had already initiated a prison visitation program that sponsored weekend shuttle service to Powhatan Correctional Center, to which St. Paul's began contributing time and volunteers. Biddle saw the opportunity to "help the poor and voiceless" in the city and helped establish a "walk-in" ministry for homeless people that not only provided food on a rotating basis between churches, but also counseling services, referrals, and emergency lodging aid.[47] Assistant rector Jeffrey Fishwick administered

St. Paul's participation in the walk-in ministry, and later the church hired John Coleman—the influential African American activist who helped found the Peter Paul Center—as its urban missioner.

The DCM partnership also birthed the Richmond Urban Institute. With the guidance of the Reverend Benjamin P. Campbell, who had been editor of the *Virginia Churchman*, DCM partners proposed an ecumenical non-profit organization designed to be an advocate "for the poor and voiceless, and mediators in an effort to break down class and racial barriers." St. Paul's, in January 1979 provided $45,000 of the $65,000 seed money, office space, and half the steering committee, including chair Don Switz, to help launch the Institute's first year.[48] At a September 1979 retreat, a biracial steering committee created operating principles. The group decided that the Urban Institute would "develop methods for identifying, studying, evaluating, and publicizing issues [that] need to be brought to the attention of the greater community."[49] The membership of its council would deliberately be half-Black and half-white. It would be, in effect, an informal, biracial think tank that otherwise did not exist in Richmond.

The new organization was led by Campbell and his associate Edythe Rogers, an African American woman, each of whom bore the title of Urban Missioner. The Urban Institute council sought to undertake projects devoted to overcoming racial polarization, encouraging "Black capitalism," strengthening police-community relations, prompting a reinvestment in housing, and cultivating youth employment.[50] The twenty-member steering committee, again split equally between the races, determined to spend their first year in operation studying racial polarization and reinvestment in housing.[51] Eventually, St. Paul's contributed seven members to the Institute's operating council.[52]

For most of the early 1980s, the Urban Institute conducted major research, administered ongoing programs, hosted symposia, and sponsored one-off projects. Its 1981 study, "Racial Tensions in Richmond," revealed areas in city governance and policy where support for racial cooperation and harmony would be effective. Responding to the study's findings, the Institute sponsored a number of programs dedicated to addressing the crisis of youth unemployment in the city. Wednesday's Child scheduled weekly summer bus trips to the beach for up to seventy young people in the early 1980s. It also created the Youth Employment Program that helped them find summer jobs. St. Paul's member Julia Seward served as administrator of the Urban Institute. Parishioner Carter McDowell took the lead, with Campbell and Seward, in researching and publishing a fully documented study on redlining by Richmond banks, supporting the work of Richmond United Neighborhoods (RUN), an ecumenical community organizing effort. The study enabled RUN to challenge a bank merger under the Federal Community Reinvestment Act. The organization also gained a regulatory order to cease the illegal cordoning off of majority-Black inner-city neighborhoods from loans and won a financial settlement that helped support a housing counseling operation for low-income persons.[53]

Other Urban Institute endeavors included a Grassroots Economic Development initiative that served as a neighborhood business incubator and a project to provide resources to the city for navigating federal budget cuts to public transportation. Working with Mary Tyler Cheek and others, the Urban Institute helped to develop the Richmond Renaissance downtown redevelopment project. It organized the Citizens Transportation Council, sponsored a Black-Jewish dialogue and an African Art & Cultural Collective at Highland Park Methodist Church, contributed to the East End Fuel Program, and participated in the Richmond Human Rights Commission's Martin Luther King Jr. Learning Week.[54] Where the early twentieth-century efforts of St. Paul's advocates at nudging Richmond's racial politics proved futile in the face of conservative resistance, the Richmond Urban Institute produced tangible successes in spotlighting and tackling some legacies of the Jim Crow structure.

Yet the Institute struggled to overcome deep-rooted cultural assumptions that hindered its effectiveness. An incoherent operating structure and activities directed by passionate members, rather than by well-understood procedures, in the Institute's first three years produced confusion just as often as tangible results. In this hopeful, but unhealthy, mix, the accumulated weight of generations of racial distrust emerged. Campbell and Rogers each brough different leadership styles and apparently clashed. Elsewhere, a feeling that St. Paul's held an outsized influence on the Institute contributed to a sense that the Institute consisted of white members accustomed to wielding power in a certain way that disregarded Black members who pursued public activism with fundamentally different methods, despite intentional efforts to train in consensus building techniques. This dynamic apparently discouraged Black members, and in 1982, the Institute noted an alarming decline in Black participation, prompting a restructuring of the organization and the resignation of Campbell and Rogers.[55]

The Urban Institute also spawned several other initiatives associated with St. Paul's people. Having resigned as the co-missioner for the Urban Institute but remaining associated with St. Paul's, Ben Campbell next headed up Home

Base, Inc., a non-profit dedicated to securing quality housing for low-income residents. The most prolific participant in the Urban Institute proved to be Mary Tyler Cheek. As an influential, monied Richmonder she had been an old-line racial liberal, as her support of the diocese's 1959 recommendations on integration suggests. But, as she later recalled, her participation in Richmond Urban Institute provided personal insights into shortcomings of her racial vision up to that point. Cheek told the *Times-Dispatch* that she "felt for the first time that I understood what was going on in the minds of Black people." An exercise that demonstrated to her the blatant discrimination Black people encountered when applying for loan applications deepened her understanding of the structural inequalities baked deep into economic and social systems.[56] "Once you see with a clearer perspective," she said, "it's ridiculous to move in a society that does not accept the obvious fact that we are all equal in the sight of God."[57] Like Mary-Cooke Munford, Mary Tyler Cheek could not sit still when confronted with social problems.

Cheek founded, as an adjunct of the Urban Institute, the Richmond Urban Forum, a dinner and speaker series for "upper-echelon Blacks and whites of the area who meet periodically on a social level in order to overcome attitudes of racism." As such, the Richmond Urban Forum attempted to create venues and opportunities that overcame the racial exclusivity of traditional locations of clout. At one dinner, in 1983, participants listened to Black psychologist Dr. Kenneth B. Clark from New York University describe the roadblocks faced by the rising generation of Black professional managers. "Young Blacks" in business, Clark told his audience of businessmen, "had to prove their competence, while young whites brought in had to demonstrate incompetence."[58] The Urban Forum had an enthusiastic beginning, but after fifteen years, it ended when participation declined in the mid-1990s.[59]

Cheek's newfound interest in the economic affairs of Black Richmond led her to cofound with Carter McDowell the Richmond Better Housing Coalition (RBHC) in 1988. The RBHC devoted itself to advocating access to quality housing for underserved populations. A 1993 grant of $200,000 from St. Paul's vestry enabled the Better Housing Coalition to partner with the Local Initiatives Support Corporation to provide a revolving loan fund for residents in need of assistance.[60] A decade later the Better Housing Coalition had become the major non-profit producer of low-income housing in metropolitan Richmond.

During this time, St. Paul's Outreach Board supported a bewildering number of organizations that battled issues endemic to American urban life in the 1980s. Chief among them was homelessness. In addition to the ongoing walk-in ministry, St. Paul's contributed to the acquisition and administration of an emergency homeless shelter in 1984, supported a program to collect and distribute clothes and other necessities, and granted funds to *The Daily Planet*, a non-profit resource center that provided shelter, food, and medical care to the city's homeless population. In 1989, the Outreach Board reported that two-thirds of its grants had gone to address homelessness in Richmond.[61]

Concurrently, St. Paul's hosted many allied programs in the Parish House. The vestry resolved to dedicate 75 percent of its space to be in productive use 75 percent of the time. It housed offices, for instance, for Dignity/Integrity, a joint Catholic and Episcopalian ministry that advocated for gay and lesbian people for which Episcopal priest Edward "Pope" Gregory celebrated a weekly eucharist in the St. Paul's chapel. The scope of supported outreach projects kept expanding. In 1986, Outreach Board chair Jane Nelson reported that St. Paul's had issued $17,425 in grants to eighteen different charitable projects in just the first six months of 1986. Those included the Central Virginia Food Bank, Volunteer Emergency Foster Care, the Good News Jail Mission, Freedom House and Gateway House halfway houses, the Peter Paul Development Center, the Virginia Institute for Pastoral Care, the Richmond Aids Information Network, and the Virginia Interfaith Center for Public Policy. St. Paul's sponsored a refugee resettlement project that assisted the transition of immigrants from Vietnam into American life. In the 1980s as well, the church began to develop the Prison Visitation Project, an initiative that provided shuttle services to family members visiting the incarcerated in central Virginia prisons. It would grow to become one of St. Paul's premier ministries in the 1990s.[62]

The suite of outreach initiatives benefited from the partnership approach, as did St. Paul's congregants, who sat with homeless people at lunch, met the requests of the formerly incarcerated, and answered to community education leaders. Charitable causes in general exposed rank and file church members to a greater spectrum of Black Richmond's working class and the hardships of poverty and discrimination. Through forums like the Richmond Urban Institute and the various programs it inspired, St. Paul's people also forged enduring relationships with middle- and upper-class African Americans, opening myriad professional, social, and spiritual connections.[63]

Nevertheless, the feverish pace of St. Paul's outreach initiatives exhausted the church. Congregants had always been cautious—whether the cause had been race-based or not—about supporting projects that might have crossed the always-subjective line between religious and political action. Through the 1970s and 1980s occasional grumbles arose regarding the large number of recipients of the church's largesse. And, in fact, the church's almost fifteen-year, intense engagement with contemporary issues had, by 1983, placed financial strain on a slowly dwindling congregation and tested its interior sense of community. Upon the resignation of Craig Biddle, a special vestry meeting in July 1983 reviewed St. Paul's circumstances. Interim rector Hunsdon Cary noted that "giving is not keeping pace with inflation." Not only was the church $52,000 in debt, but its annual stewardship pledge campaign had significantly fallen short of expectation. Further, donors consisted of a small group of families with elderly members, portending further financial distress. "Programming is 'starved' from too little funds," Cary said, "and garage income once earmarked for outreach is now spent on the church."[64]

The call for a new rector signaled a significant change in tone. The Parish Profile stated flatly: "Many parishioners were attracted to St. Paul's by a desire

FIGURE 9. An AIDS vigil passes before St. Paul's, ca. 1987. (*Richmond Times-Dispatch* Collection, The Valentine)

to be a part of a congregation that 'does things,' 'is committed,' and 'is involved.' On the other hand, some expressed concern about the appropriateness of the Church being the focus of social and political action. The Church needs to wrestle with this issue and the theology of community involvement." Further, despite St. Paul's reputation for wealth, "those intimately involved with the financial aspects of the parish know, however, that the Church struggles to make ends meet." The search committee sought a rector who could cultivate "a new sense of community among its members ... an effective pastoral counselor," whose primary concern should be "the spiritual health of the parish."[65] The next rector, the Reverend Canon Robert Hetherington, did not back away from St. Paul's extensive outreach commitments and proved an active but subtle player in Richmond's justice causes. But he also responded to St. Paul's need for inner work.

The tone and direction of conversations about race and racism within the larger Episcopal Church underwent its own transformation in the mid-1980s. The Civil Rights Movement in the nation, and within the church, had focused on breaking legal barriers to full Black inclusion in American (and church) political life. It worked, and while the transition to Black political power—as Richmond's experience had indicated—had been contentious, the fierce urgency of the movement faded in apparent success and other cultural battles rose to prominence in the 1980s.

Yet Episcopalians looked at their church in this decade and still saw— accurately—an overwhelmingly white institution with sparsely integrated congregations alongside a small number of traditionally Black parishes such as Richmond's St. Philip's. This observation bothered some white members and perturbed the few Black members. The national church, in declaring its support of national affirmative action policies in 1982 noted the continued existence of racism. The House of Bishops charged each diocese with the formation of a Committee on Racism and the performance of a racial audit. The Diocese of Virginia's Committee on Race convened in 1983 to "study, identify, and confront the root causes of racism in all people, systems and institutions," and to create educational programs supporting ecclesial and public policies that would "lend support for truly desegregated communities, schools, and house[s] of worship."[66]

After performing their audit, the Virginia diocesan committee homed in on the problem of representation in both the clergy and lay ranks of the church. They made twelve recommendations to reform clergy and staff hiring practices, recruit Black and Hispanic students to grade schools and seminaries, promote Black history and Black theology in church publications, invest in Black owned banks, and provide scholarships to Black youth for church camps.[67] Despite the strong start and endorsement of the diocese's executive council, the Committee on Race had no real authority or budget to compel the implementation of its recommendations. The 1986 report to the diocese claimed some success in promoting greater Black participation on diocesan committees but lamented that all they could do was "prod, push and cajole" those in authority. Altogether, they sighed, "no positive changes have taken place" in overcoming racial imbalances on church and school staffs. The stymied Committee asked, "Is it the highest possible office or is it just that of janitor or a sexton," that Black people might fill?[68]

The Committee's continued frustration emerged in its 1988 report where it noted, "sadly . . . there are some areas in which little progress has been made." They called for "new goals" and "new blood" for the committee, particularly "more majority (white) representation within its structure." They flatly stated that "the problems and issues that the Commission [sic] is attempting to address should not be the concern of only the minority faction within the Diocese of Virginia."[69] While well-meaning, white support of integration had not translated into demonstrable action and results.

At the national level, a flurry of activity seized the Episcopal Church. In 1991, the General Convention passed eight resolutions, calling the church to require interracial representation on interim bodies, to examine the effects of racism, to reduce discrimination in clergy hiring, to commit to further racial audits, and to commit to ending racism in "the life of the nation."[70] The House of Bishops' pastoral letter on the sin of racism gave new vocabularies to the issue in the 1990s. The end of the bi-polar orientation of the Cold War (to white Americans, at least) with the fall of the Soviet Union had revealed a world wracked with interethnic conflict. The bishops looked to apartheid in South Africa, ethnic cleansing in central Europe, and religious tensions in South Asia. They also looked at home to changing national demographics. They noted that globalism, pluralism, and multi-culturalism defined the future, and they stated that the "challenge of people with differing backgrounds having to live together has never been greater." Maintaining mono-cultural enclaves in secular neighborhoods and in church communities would not only be untenable, but the expectation of assimilation was itself a problem.

> Various resolutions in the past have proposed ways for victims of discrimination to participate in the prevailing system. Many have chal-

lenged the system itself to become more inclusive. The unspoken assumption of these resolutions is that victims will adapt and assimilate into the existing system. Their message, in essence, has been: "You are welcome to become like us."

Such efforts may have represented progress in their time, but they are seen by many today as the product of a dominant racial attitude, which is at the heart of institutional racism.

The bishops wondered, "Can the old melting pot image of assimilation be replaced by a better metaphor that reflects the value of difference?" African Americans had entered political life through voting rights legislation. But political equality had revealed deeper societal intolerances—if not in individuals, in systems and assumptions—that caused harm by not accounting for historical, cultural, and economic differences. The bishops asked, "How can the inherited privilege and unearned advantage of some people be used to bring about the reconciliation of all?" Implicit in the question was the death of the noblesse oblige that had sustained St. Paul's occasionally liberal outlook in former generations, and the insistence that reconciliation required the dismantling of "inherited privilege" and "unearned advantage." In 1994, the bishops covenanted themselves and their Dioceses to a slew of reflections and actions in their efforts to "commit ourselves afresh to combat racism in church and society."[71]

Clergy and laity at St. Paul's felt their way into these new expectations of race and reconciliation in the late 1980s and 1990s with variable success. Rector Robert Hetherington, as a young seminarian, had been convicted by theologian Harvey Cox's call for church activism in secular settings, by his acquaintance with classmate and civil rights martyr Jonathan Daniels, and as a witness to Martin Luther King Jr.'s preaching.[72] He maintained St. Paul's active outreach programs and, while he hesitated to follow the diocesan call to withdraw memberships in racially exclusive clubs, he stepped into positions of vulnerability in Richmond's social causes.[73] In 1991 Hetherington attended an organizational meeting of an anti-crime and anti-drug crusade convened by a coalition of Black Baptist preachers. He inadvertently tweaked lingering resentment by remarking that some Black ministers in attendance were "strangers." One pastor responded that "the only time we come together is when y'all (white clerics) start something and we're around in." A second pastor noted the relative absence of White clergy and remarked that this "is rather symbolic of what happens in Black-White relations . . . there is a resistance, as a fact of life, for white folk to follow the leadership of Black folk." Hetherington, despite the chastening remarks, continued to support the crusade, serving on its fundraising committee. However, the second pastor's prediction had proved out—white clergy had largely failed to show up to the crusade's opening event. Hetherington did and prayed, "give us the power to persevere to make the city of Richmond like the City of God."[74]

Perhaps in response to the Diocese's call to explore Black theology, Hetherington proposed an "African Method of Bible Study" as part of a catechumenal process "whereby a diverse group of people within the church move toward a more mature commitment as Christians."[75] He later took a sabbatical in South Africa, and St. Paul's hosted a visit by a Black South African priest in return.[76] It was during Hetherington's tenure that St. Paul's welcomed its first Black clergyman, the Reverend Rodney Rice, who was ordained to the priesthood during his two-year deaconate. In the same year, 1987, the church elected its first African American vestry member, Ruby Grant Martin. A former staff attorney with the US Commission on Civil Rights, Martin had served as the founding director of the civil rights office in the Department of Health, Education and Welfare in the Johnson administration. She relocated to Richmond with her family in 1978. Her husband, Dr. Henry S. Martin Jr., had a remarkable tie to St. Paul's: he was the grandson of the church's former sexton, Robert Damell, whose funeral made front-page news in 1925. Ruby Martin's expertise and vision helped shape state policies when she served as Virginia's secretary of administration under L. Douglas Wilder, the nation's first elected African American governor. She would also prove an influential leader in guiding St. Paul's outreach programming in a new, innovative, direction.[77]

St. Paul's reputation for social activism had drawn the attention of Rob and Susan Corcoran, British-born veterans of the international movement known as Moral Re-Armament (since renamed Initiatives of Change).[78] When the Corcorans arrived in Richmond in 1980 following intense peace work in South Africa, they discovered a nascent biracial network of individuals— some old Richmonders and some newcomers—devoted to bridging racial divides through the development of trustworthy personal relationships. The network, which included influential St. Paul's members like Frank Mountcastle and Don Cowles, ultimately emerged as Hope in the Cities, a group devoted to fostering honest conversations about race, reconciliation, and responsibility. Hope in the Cities' first major program, "Healing in the Heart of America" in 1993, consisted of a four-day conference that focused on finding common truths in shared histories and developing ways to use them in racial healing and trust building. The conference culminated in a "Unity Walk" that saw hundreds of people follow a pathway from Church Hill and Confederate monuments, through the Shockoe Bottom slave trading district, to the state capitol in a ritual embrace of a more inclusive Richmond history.[79] The city eventually continued the efforts with the establishment of the Slave Trail Commission, the "discovery" of Richmond's central role in America's domestic slave trade, and the excavation of Lumpkin's Slave Jail. St. Paul's parishioner and Virginia Commonwealth University history professor, Philip J. Schwarz, served as the endeavor's primary researcher and historical consultant.

Similar conferences and dialogue series helped St. Paul's people realize the depth of systemic racism. One, a "Role Reversal in Race Relations," particularly affected Lee Switz. Then chair of the Richmond Urban Forum, Switz had been a civil rights activist in her youth; but, as she later recalled, it was through this 1994 program that she came to realize the shocking degree of entrenched racial assumptions faced by professional Black women.[80] That year, S. Buford Scott, perhaps keeping in mind the Diocese's Committee on Race's admonition on the racial makeup of administrative boards, resigned his position on the University of Virginia's Board of Visitors to make way for a Black candidate.[81] Rob Corcoran similarly stepped aside from an "Eyes on Richmond" panel on Richmond's history in 1997 because of its lack of nonwhite participants.[82]

In 1995, parishioner Alton Ayer spearheaded a Racial Reconciliation Task Force at St. Paul's. Convinced that "when two people of different races can get to know one another, racism declines," Ayer proposed inviting Black congregants from St. Peter's Episcopal Church to St. Paul's regular foyer dinners and other efforts at relationship building with Black congregations around Richmond.[83] Ayer's proposal dovetailed with a Long-Range Planning initiative that the vestry had undertaken. It included among its seven goals that St. Paul's "become a recognized leader in racial reconciliation, shifting from a role of moral support to proactive leaders, possibly in partnership with an African American congregation."[84] The Task Force spent the next couple of years attempting to initiate relationships with other churches. It conducted several meetings with St. Philip's Episcopal Church, which eventually withdrew when it undertook a new rector search.[85] They also nurtured a budding relationship with members of 31st Street Baptist Church.[86] The Task Force promoted participation in Hope in the Cities' "A Call to Community" programs and the diocese's Region IX workshop titled "Racism, It's Everybody's Problem."[87] The Task Force sputtered to a close in 1997, with Ayer reporting on "the great deal of energy required to maintain interaction."[88]

A case study on St. Paul's that parishioner Don Cowles presented to the 1999 meeting of the Consortium of Endowed Episcopal Parishes adequately defined the church's evolving identity at the turn of the twenty-first century. "The congregation is predominantly white," the report noted, "with a small but active number of Black members." Despite this, "the congregation is far from a homogeneous group, with members covering the entire economic, political and social spectrum." St. Paul's "powerful outreach," added Rev. Hetherington, "attracts and retains most of St. Paul's parishioners. The entire parish has a passion for social justice." The report continued that "race relations in the City has been a major issue for years. Historically, the conservatives among the leaders of both races have contributed to a rather peaceful co-existence, with the races generally maintaining their distance." The highly acrimonious days of the late 1970s and early 1980s had seemed to wane. Organizations like the Richmond Urban Institute and the Richmond Urban Forum had certainly helped. In more recent years, the case study noted, "racial reconciliation has progressed as Hope in the Cities and Richmond Hill Retreat Center, each founded by St. Paul's parishioners, has provided needed leadership and dialogue on the painful issues of the past." Within the church, however, aspirations to biracial relationships had not met expectations. "Several parishioners are actively involved in racial reconciliation initiatives," the report stated, "however, attempts to partner with an African American congregation have not borne fruit."[89]

The 1999 church profile—like Jack Spong's 125th anniversary address— did not mention Confederates. True, the ongoing church tours drew attention to the Lee and Davis pews and related well-known stories; and the United Daughters of the Confederacy still held annual services in the sanctuary. But as the congregation continued to comprise non-native Richmonders who embraced St. Paul's social ministry, its Confederate and Lost Cause past did not stand as the church's chief calling card to the world. Where St. Paul's had previously advertised itself as the "Shrine of the South" and "The Church where Lee and Davis Worshipped," it now conscientiously positioned itself first (in 1978) as "An Urban Church for ALL People," and later (1996) as a church "Proclaiming Christ in the Heart of the City."[90]

In a 1986 *Times-Dispatch* article that described the draw of various Richmond churches, the author noted that church attraction could be anything from convenient parking to "Bible teaching." Reverend Robert Hetherington, quoted in the article, noted that St. Paul's "draws a wide variety of people because of its historic background, its location, and its involvement in urban ministries." He added that "because St. Paul's social ministry may be considered by some as a little more controversial than the ministries of suburban churches, it will attract some while turning others away."[91] By the turn of the twenty-first century, St. Paul's had continued to maintain a vigorous outreach program that both connected parishioners to the social problems of urban America and pulled them further from their church's historical grounding. New initiatives—the Prison Ministry and the Micah Initiative—exemplified these efforts.

St. Paul's had been engaged in a cooperative prison visitation program in which the church donated money and volunteers to a shuttle service for family members visiting kin in prison. In 1995, however, the supervisor of the walk-in ministry, Mary Atterholt, piloted a program in the church that provided counseling and transition services to five women recently released from prison.[92] Within three years, the Prison Ministry served four counseling groups from two different prisons and engaged up to 275 volunteers from within and without the church.[93] It provided pre-release planning, therapy, and counseling to 130 women in 1998. Two years later, the Prison Ministry established the Spring Hill House, a transition residence for post-release women.[94] Atterholt used her experience to train volunteers from other Episcopal churches and to create training materials for the Diocese of Virginia.[95]

In the late 1990s St. Paul's outreach programming took a dramatic turn. At the time, the prosperous national economy in the late 1990s proved a boon to St. Paul's stock portfolio. Increasing revenue encouraged the Outreach Board to establish a "vision task force" to "determine how, instead of spending the money available from St. Paul's among ten or fifteen different organizations . . . to find one organization to make a difference." Encouraged by rector Hetherington, the church leadership established the "Outreach Dream" task force to discern a new direction. Chaired by Ruby Martin, the Outreach Dream committee guided the church through a year-long process where it explored ideas and heard proposals for potential programs to fund. The group determined that the selected project would be child-focused, have a transformative effect on parishioners, and in the words of S. Buford Scott, could "change the world."[96]

In 1998 St. Paul's launched the Micah Initiative in the predominantly Black Woodville School in Richmond's East End. Micah was intended to be a different kind of outreach—not a grant program or other initiative intended to leverage St. Paul's wealth, but rather one that responded to stated needs of program recipients. "The very first thing that was done," recalled Lee Switz, "people went over [to Woodville], and they listened. They didn't go over there and say, 'we're going to do this.' But instead, 'what do you need?'" Key to its formation was discussion with the school's principal, Alberta Person, the faculty, and PTA leaders. The primary St. Paul's liaison was Betsy Carr, who would later be hired by the church as Micah coordinator and outreach director. It was a multilayered program; St. Paul's parishioners served at-risk students in the underfunded East End elementary school as tutors, mentors, volunteers, and advocates. In time, the program added a summer camp component directed by parishioner Page Luxmoore. In the early 2000s, St. Paul's had up to seventy volunteers in Woodville, and the school measured a significant increase in end-of-grade Standards of Learning scores over those years. Through the facilitation of Reverend Ben Campbell, then the pastoral director at Richmond Hill and St. Paul's priest-in-residence, the Micah Ministry grew far beyond the church. By 2009, it encompassed 1,300 volunteers from 105 faith communities to serve 24 Richmond elementary schools.[97]

The financial good fortune that floated new outreach efforts in the late 1990s failed in the 2002 recession. St. Paul's budgeted $475,000 to five different outreach programs in 2003. Budget gaps began to appear in 2003 when the church reduced its donation to the diocese, and late that year, the vestry projected a $38,000 shortfall.[98] In the budget pinch, the vestry decided that the Prison Ministry and Spring Hill House would have to be spun off. However, failure to find an outside funder resulted in the shuttering of the programs.[99] Acrimony over the discontinuing of the prison ministry riled the congregation, compelling the vestry to hire an outside consultant.[100]

At the same time, in 2002, the vestry oversaw a new strategic plan that committed the church to—among other things—"reaffirming our identity as a downtown church 'proclaiming Christ in the heart of the city.'" The plan noted that "people come to St. Paul's for all kinds of reasons and from all kinds of backgrounds.... Given this disparate membership [it] is difficult to create a sense of focus and identity." Nevertheless, the vestry determined that St. Paul's should play a role in the revitalization of downtown Richmond and "to appreciate in our parish the diversity of the body of Christ and the presence of God in all people." They intended the latter aim to be pursued through mindful and intentional approaches to diverse spiritual practices, interfaith dialogue, inclusive hiring practices, and critical thinking about what welcoming means in a diverse society.[101]

Under rectors Hetherington and his successor Wallace Adams-Riley, St. Paul's contributed volunteers and money to a variety of initiatives. It continued to participate in and give to the walk-in ministry and other DCM projects. The Thursday food program for the poor and homeless took on a new name and concept: Emmaus, which conveyed the Biblical approach of "welcoming the stranger." Guests would receive lunch, yes, but St. Paul's members would engage them in active listening and conversation. St. Paul's also established itself as a townhall for dialogue, launching "Eyes on Richmond" in 1996. This weekly forum, held each fall, brought speakers from business, civic, government, and cultural leadership. Frequent themes address issues of racial justice and equality. St. Paul's participated in a policy advocacy consortium that supported the work of the Virginia Interfaith Center for Public Policy. Members called the group the "Friends of Fletcher," after the Interfaith Center's director, the Reverend Canon Fletcher Lowe—and later changed its name to AMOS.[102] Under that umbrella, St. Paul's people committed again to Richmonders Involved to Strengthen our Communities (RISC), an intentionally biracial faith community organization devoted to exploring and advocating for policy issues in the city's public education, health, transportation, employment, and affordable housing in Richmond.[103] In 2008 St. Paul's received a $10,000 grant from the diocese to support a relief organization, the Carpenter's Kids, in Mwitikira, a rural town in central Tanzania. This grant began a long-term relationship between St. Paul's members and people in Mwitikira, guided by liaison C. Roger Whitfield. The ongoing, expanded program included a $20,000 fundraising drive by the St. Paul's youth to provide famine relief in 2009. In an innovative cross-venture, the St. Paul's Faith-in-Action Committee (the new name of the Outreach Board) enlisted the aid of the Micah Initiative's students in Woodville in the fundraising efforts.[104]

In 2012 the vestry again committed St. Paul's to a ministry focused on downtown Richmond when it hired the Reverend Melanie Mullen in a revived position of Downtown Missioner. Mullen, St. Paul's second Black clergyperson, engaged the church in a greater range of activism beyond service to the homeless population. She continued and developed an Ashes-to-Go program on Ash Wednesday and a Grace Street block party to attract young professionals. Mullen participated in a conversation on race that resulted in an "Absalom Jones Service," spoke at citywide interfaith gatherings, began the

Laundry Love campaign, and partnered with St. Philip's Church on a joint viewing of the 2015 film *Selma*.[105]

The conceptions of race, racism, and racial relationships had undergone a transformation at St. Paul's since 1969. The remarkable catalog of outreach that answered the long-held call to render charitable mission work—historically rooted in the paternalism of the slave regime, imperatives of the Social Gospel, or the urgency of easing urban unrest in the volatile Civil Rights era—now evolved alongside an understanding that acts of benevolence could go only so far without equitable relationships. A new consciousness and desire for meaningful engagement between St. Paul's predominantly white congregation and Black Richmonders ultimately went beyond outreach-as-racial engagement and included deeply personal and social relationships, and a congregation that included a fair (but not large) number of Black members. This post-1969 generation at St. Paul's entered into challenging dialogues and tested the financial and spiritual capacity of the church, and the tension within that journey served as the basis of a new identity. St. Paul's had become a faith community that understood itself as living into decidedly liberal theological and social realities.

Reviewing St. Paul's remarkable run since 1969 is not simply a prideful record of accomplishments, a suggestion that the church had atoned for its history or had necessarily approached racial matters in the best possible ways. What is important is that through the work, and the people the work attracted, St. Paul's built a post-Confederate identity that served to give deep meaning to members' church life, their sense of themselves as political entities in a multiracial world, and an entirely new reputation for the church in downtown Richmond. Certainly, tourists still came to see Lee and Davis's pews, but parishioners came to do interracial work, as they understood it, in the city. That, more than the memorial windows, is what mattered.

At the same time, St. Paul's receded from its former heights of prominence and influence—if not wealth and upper-middle-class status of its members. This decline was not unique to St. Paul's, but a result of long-term trends sometimes called "Mainline Decline." The Civil Rights Movement and the Vietnam War had certainly stressed the Episcopal Church, but later disputes fractured it. Debates over ordination of women and afterward of gay people, and a reform of the prayer book, caused some parishes to break off from diocese and countless disgruntled members to simply walk away. An even deeper cultural shift shaped late twentieth century church life as well: the post-1960s secularization of society had caught mainline churches off guard and incapable of offering a competing social meaning to congregants. In their place, the theologically conservative evangelical churches of the Moral Majority and the larger religious Right movement stepped in. Americans simply stopped joining the Episcopal Church and memberships atrophied. In 1970, St. Paul's boasted 1,443 members. In 2006, 759 remained on the rolls.[106]

As had become routine by the beginning of the twenty-first century, parishioners took little to no notice of St. Paul's Confederate past and identity. At the same time, the clergy and staff continued to distance the church intentionally and unintentionally from expressions of Confederate nostalgia and move toward an embrace of a more comprehensive history. The annual service held by the United Daughters of the Confederacy had become so invisible in parish life that when their sibling organization, the Sons of Confederate Veterans requested space at the church as part of a "National Heritage Rally" in 2012, Adams-Riley reported that the staff had scheduled it with a "shrug & carry on attitude." When media coverage revealed the event would be something more than just a memorial service, St. Paul's canceled the booking and returned the SCV's deposit. When Reverend Melanie Mullen had her installation service, the congregation fell to sheepish embarrassment when they realized that a UDC memorial service had been scheduled to follow as hoop-skirted ladies awaited their turn in the sanctuary.[107] In 2014, the vestry, in response to a letter of concern about the ongoing relationship with the UDC, implemented a policy requiring Confederate heritage groups to "disclose their views" and be advised that their mission and presence would be measured against St. Paul's understanding of the Baptismal Covenant of "upholding the dignity of every human being." Requests from the UDC and SCV ceased thereafter.[108] While St. Paul's pushed away old-fashioned notions of Confederate celebration, it embraced a more expansive view of Civil War history. During the 150th anniversary observances of the Civil War in Richmond, St. Paul's participated in events with "The Future of Richmond's Past," a consortium of museums and community organizations devoted to telling an inclusive story that celebrated emancipation as the key legacy of the failed Confederate experience.[109] The stories St. Paul's told itself had changed completely, and as former stories faded, that changed St. Paul's historical imagination and its identity.

The Charleston murders that caused Reverend Wallace Adams-Riley to challenge St. Paul's, and the national conversation about the place of Confederate iconography in American public life, happened at the intersection of several long-term historical trends. For one, academic historians had long since debunked the notion that the slaveholding states had seceded for any reason other than the protection and perpetuation of slavery and the society that slavery undergirded. No credible scholar could maintain that the defeated Confederates had been righteous and innocent victims in Reconstruction and that Confederate leaders had been saintly figures. They were just men, and flawed men in light of contemporary views of race relations. Also, in the post-Civil Rights era—particularly in the 1970s and 1980s after the development of Black political power in regional politics—any public expression of uncomplicated Confederate nostalgia met opposition.[110] In truth, an unconscious reckoning with St. Paul's Lost Cause identity had commenced—if obliquely and semi-intentionally—in 1969 when Jack Spong and the vestry resolved to never again fly the battle flag from the portico. By the 2010s, a new St. Paul's recoiled from its former connections when reminded of them, and sought ways to understand this history.

The early twenty-first century saw another revolution in the vocabulary of historical understanding about race that St. Paul's increasingly drew on. The US Episcopal Church, for example, continued to affirm anti-racism initiatives within the denomination. In 2006, however, voices within the national Church began to call for reparations for slavery and for congregations to pursue restorative justice and Truth and Reconciliation-style methods in anti-racism work.[111] Both required searching and self-critical historical inquiry, based on the presumption that deep and structural racism cannot be eliminated unless its historical foundations are understood and its perpetuators take part in the process. The urgency of understanding the historical roots of oppression only accelerated after the fatal 2014 shooting of an unarmed Black man by Ferguson, Missouri, police prompted national protests. The subsequent emergence of the Black Lives Matter movement focused widespread national attention on chronic inequities that had remained despite the apparent successes of the Civil Rights Movement. Historian Nathan Connolly contextualized that moment, stating: "the politics of diversity and inclusion have not kept there from being massive numbers of people killed by law enforcement officers; they have not dealt with the wealth gap; they have not dealt with the public housing, or the public health crises in so many parts of the country." No longer would ostensibly color-blind policies and an optimism over inevitable racial progress be used to paper over very real racial inequities that still plague America. Acknowledgment of the past and a recognition that the historical landscape has a tangible impact on race relations has become an essential tool and a front in the ongoing struggle.[112]

To some this moment of realization was not a revelation. Black Christian commentator Jemar Tisby pointedly asked, "Why did it take the murder of nine Black people in a Bible study for some people to finally reject the racism associated with the Confederate emblem? Why do people have to literally be killed before we confront racial prejudice?"[113] A fair question. Yet most St. Paul's parishioners in 2015 honestly did not know the extent of their church's long-embraced connection to the Confederacy and had never really noticed that four of the many stained-glass windows were memorials to its most prominent leaders Lee and Davis. (Indeed, a longtime member sheepishly approached this author in early 2019 to ask just which windows we were suddenly so interested in.) When one St. Paul's member commented, "who we are now and what we are about now is what's important," he no doubt thought of the contemporary identity of St. Paul's as a socially liberal place. Contemporary imagination had failed to recognize the artifacts of racism, yet when shaken by the crisis of the Charleston murders, congregants saw them anew and felt the newfound weight of St. Paul's submerged historical identity. The church's decision to remove battle-flag motifs from the sanctuary in November 2015 brought a significant inflection point in its 170-year history. A *Times-Dispatch* editorial entitled "St. Paul's lives up to its namesake" marveled that, after deep prayer and painful conversation, the congregation "decided to liberate itself" of Confederate symbols that "do not belong in a church for all people" and "insult the memories of those held in bondage."[114]

Adams-Riley hoped that St. Paul's, in subsequent prayerful conversations, might endure the test of painful self-examination. "Where these conversations will go, we don't yet know. What we will decide to do, is not clear yet. Does sorting that out feel daunting to you?" he asked his congregation. "Impractical? Impossible, maybe?"

Charting a new future without the old historical imagination would seem daunting, indeed.

Epilogue

THE VESTRY AFFIRMED the Reverend Wallace Adams-Riley's call for a racial self-study in November 2015. "Given that the mission of the church is to restore all people to unity with God and each other in Christ," they resolved that St. Paul's would "embark on a new journey of racial reconciliation."[1] The vestry immediately removed all of the Confederate flag motifs from the sanctuary and vestibule, including memorial tablets to Robert E. Lee, Jefferson Davis, a plaque to St. Paul's Confederate veterans in the foyer, and embroidered kneelers with the St. Paul's coat of arms.

In the months leading to the resolution, the congregation undertook a series of "Prayerful Conversations" facilitated by Don Edwards from Washington, DC's Justice and Sustainability Associates. A consensus emerged from those discussions that "[t]here was a call to understand St. Paul's past role in slavery and racial segregation as well as the legacies of ongoing discrimination and racial inequities—all necessary for the church to more fully address Richmond's present and future needs."[2] To undertake that work and to plan for continuing prayerful conversations, the vestry created the ad hoc History and Reconciliation Initiative (HRI) with a four-year agenda of study, programs, memorialization, and reflection intended to culminate as the church observed its 175th Anniversary year beginning in November 2020. These four years have witnessed a group of well-meaning congregants—white and Black—come together to grapple with a hard history. It has been revelatory, painful, imperfect, and at times raucously joyous. It hasn't always been easy.

The historical research that produced this work has not been the entirety of the HRI endeavor. While Elizabeth O'Leary, Anne S. Hayes, and I, along with half a dozen other volunteers, waded through the manuscript sources that produced this work,[3] the HRI Memorials and Liturgy subcommittee, helmed sequentially by the Reverend Melanie Mullen, Lee Switz, and then Michelle Walker, hosted often searching and painful conversations about what St. Paul's means when it says it is a welcoming church—and whether our sanctuary really proclaims those values to which we aspire.[4] The memorials committee—consisting of some of the church's oldest and some of its newest members—ultimately decided that it did not. Remove *all* the memorial tablets, it proposed, and rededicate the windows honoring Lee and Davis.[5]

In the meantime the HRI Steering Committee hosted a variety of discussions and activities for all interested parishioners. We presented periodic updates on our historical research. We invited Katrina Browne for a viewing of her documentary *Traces of the Trade*.[6] We visited other historical locations grappling with the legacy of slavery and racism in American history, including the groundbreaking exhibition *The Mere Distinction of Colour* at James Madison's Montpelier, and the Equal Justice Initiative's National Memorial for Peace and Justice in Montgomery, Alabama. We invited Black and white churches in Richmond to join us in prayer and conversation. A significant moment occurred with the March 2018 visit of the Episcopal Church's Presiding Bishop Michael B. Curry. Following a public seminar in which a summary of our recently excavated history was discussed by local historians, ministers, and social rights activists, Bishop Curry blessed us. And he encouraged us by saying, "What you are doing is so important, not only for Richmond, but for our country, and indeed, for our whole world, for our common humanity. The truth of the matter is that we cannot continue as we have been going. We cannot continue, and we must find a better way, and you are modeling how we can find that better way."[7]

The process, and our modeling of such an endeavor, has not been without challenges, but not how an outside observer might expect.

As would be anticipated, a handful of congregants early on rejected any examination of Confederate connections—not to mention removal of its emblems within the church. Accusations of "erasing" history echoed similar charges arising in discourse around the possibility of removing the Confederate monuments that had occupied the city's public space and imagination for an equal amount of time. But few, if any, appeared to have objected to HRI because of any reflexive love for the Lost Cause. After all, as chapter 5 reveals, St. Paul's is not that church anymore, and hasn't been for some time. Early on (but not so much recently), I noticed the expression of a deflective discourse that I see in many public conversations about history: *We can't do anything about it, so why bother dwelling on it? You can't change history.* True, we can't change history. But we aimed to prove that it is worth dwelling on. We aimed to prove that seeing it differently is a fruitful endeavor.

The chief objection that we heard from both parishioners and members of the public regarded the pace of our work. The gist of that has been expressed as, *we know that slavery and racism were bad; we know that St. Paul's participated; we don't need to waste time studying the details but instead we should get out and do something about it.* This is, after all, a congregation that has been impatient about *doing something* and historically been able to effectively act on those impulses. The urgency also reflected the internal understanding of St. Paul's contemporary identity: liberal on racial matters and wanting to do *more*.

Similar criticism about our pace has come from non-parishioners but rooted in a different view of who St. Paul's currently is. Why didn't we immediately strip out the memorial plaques and the windows and denounce racism? The implication is that we hesitate because of some affection for the civil religion of the Lost Cause and all of the racial implications therein. The assumption sometimes strays into an odd perception that nothing we do has mattered, or will matter, unless we physically remove "the windows."

That may be, and perhaps it represents my own blind spots that I don't regard such dramatic gestures as substantive when they are not authentically rooted in our experience and contexts. Instead, I've seen benefits to a slow and deliberate pace.

Taking time in these matters—despite the risk of public criticism—has value. As a Christian body, we are, of course, determined to avoid alienation of our immediate family (even if that result may be inevitable or necessary). The longer-term impact is that initially skeptical members of our congregation have had ample chance to express reservations and also to learn that these sorts of endeavors can be accomplished with grace and love. (A common concern has been that this work might be prosecutorial, or that it is a pathetic exercise in self-flagellation. I pray that we have proven otherwise.) While HRI has been underway, we have witnessed at least two other Episcopal congregations sustain damaging schism by sudden efforts to confront their racial history through the removal of plaques and the changing of names. One spun apart after its move to renounce its history. Taking time for trust building yields rewards.

Determining to take a studious and prayerful pace has also helped us avoid the temptation of making a dramatic but shallow display of "performative allyship" that, once completed, would allow us some emotional satisfaction that risks slipping into smug complacency upon its accomplishment. It has left St. Paul's with a nascent desire to make lasting change in the way it approaches the world. That discernment is only now beginning and will take an equally long time, and the challenge of resisting that smug complacency of having begun this work will always be with us.

A slow process, too, has allowed for exploration of the deep structural working of racism in America in the past and today, and to see St. Paul's place in it. We are able to identify more than just a generic complicity in slavery and segregation and express more than just outrage about the veneration of Jefferson Davis. We can see specifically how slavery and segregation worked for the people of St. Paul's and how they in turn shaped the racial landscapes around them and harmed the dignity and bodies of Black people in the process, such as through the social practices in church that led to separate Black congregations and the historical imagination that confined Black people to low-wage jobs and redlined residences. These came into our view simultaneous to the movement by Black Lives Matter to make these historical oppressions visible to all America.

In peering into the complexities of how racism worked in certain times and places, we see that it is more than an essentialism called "white supremacy" at play, easily brushed aside with a change of heart or a "reconciliation" with Black people. The narrative of racial difference and the white supremacy that it supported did (and does) not exist as a subject in and of itself. Instead, it is composed of a wildly diverse and ever evolving series of facts and beliefs in science, literature, history, social organization, gender revolutions, theology, and political theory that just as often had nothing to do with race, as they did. The complex worldviews demanded, justified, and accepted white supremacy, but did so along the tendrils of those other contexts, so that history, theology, and science did not initially appear to be about white supremacy. A theory about germs may be about science and a theory about the evolution of democracy in English-descended societies may have been about history but combined in the American South in the Gilded Age, we get Bishop Alfred Randolph's conviction that Black people could not participate equally in American democracy, and John Kerr Branch's belief that Black people passed along diseases to white people. The eugenicist Racial Integrity Act directly resulted. The pieces and parts of that worldview changed over time, and white supremacy has adapted to new circumstances such as the end of slavery, the rise of science, or the democratization of civil rights. By the late twentieth century circumstances aligned to destroy the Jim Crow state, if not white supremacy. So, saying that we are against "racism" is a hollow claim unless we are willing to critique the various elements of our worldview that don't initially appear to be directly about race relations. Almost any long-lived white church in the United States can admit to these general trends and these general sins, and undertake the inquiries demanded of us, but these are historical complexities that few white Americans have grappled with in the sustained way until our present moment. It is daunting and humbling, indeed, to even imagine the work ahead that will be required to interrogate our own myriad galaxies of values, beliefs, and assumptions in order to expose the blind spots that we undoubtedly possess.

A slow and deliberate process also allows us time to discern St. Paul's unique contribution to this cluster of beliefs that pervaded white southern Christianity for long after the Civil War.

What is unique about St. Paul's experience?

St. Paul's is a storytelling church. More than most southern white churches, it has made a significant contribution to the history, literature, and public conversations about white supremacist beliefs through the stories it has told about itself and about race in the former Confederacy. Of all the things to which St. Paul's has an obligation to is history, perhaps none is more unique and authentic than to re-deploy the power of its historical imagination.

By that I mean a framework for moral rectitude and possibility in the present day that is derived from the boundaries established by historical example. The presence of Lee and Davis at regular worship at St. Paul's affirmed for its members their sense of self-importance in their own time and enabled them to sit comfortably in the halls of political and economic power while elevating those two figures to quasi-divine status alongside Jesus, the Prophets, and the Apostles. The historical fact of Davis receiving the fateful message from Lee while sitting in a St. Paul's pew gave its members a claim to the central national drama of American history well into the twentieth century. It also enabled them to advance their profile in the prestigious memorial landscape of Civil War tourism alongside Monument Avenue and Richmond's battlefields. In looking to Lee kneeling next to a Black man, they learned to approach challenges to white supremacy with restraint and "character" instead of with violence and hateful rhetoric. The story about Robert Damell's funeral, dripping with language drawn from the justification for slavery, affirmed for them the righteousness of paternalistic white oversight of a permanent Black underclass and their advocacy for more segregation laws. And the later reimagined Lee Communion story offered them by proxy that, from that same communion rail they, too, were going forward to fulfill a new sacred obligation to be welcoming to Black people.[8]

That dangerous historical imagination is alive today in America. While few people seriously think of slavery as a positive good, an alarming number offer comments on the internet, in public forums, and in print media that fundamentally misconstrue proslavery Christianity and the self-styled benevolence of white people before and after emancipation. The Sunday school taught to Black people by Thomas Jonathan "Stonewall" Jackson in Lexington, Virginia before the Civil War, for instance, is frequently held up as a subversive pseudo-abolitionist venture. Robert E. Lee's overly parsed declaration that "in this enlightened age, there are few, I believe, but that will acknowledge, that slavery as an institution, is a moral & political evil in any country" is another. Both assertions, unmoored from context, promote terrible historical misunderstanding of people who accepted slavery as God's design and strove to make slavery work in what they regarded as a more humane fashion, not end it. The misunderstanding serves to distance the Confederate cause from slavery.[9] Yet it is about more than the reputation of the Confederate States.

This faulty historical imagination at work in these assertions serves a slightly different purpose today. Adherents to these beliefs firmly maintain that race relationships in the past were harmonious and, therefore, that charges of systematic inequality rooted in the legacy of slavery and segregation must be intentionally bogus. Such arguments often conclude with the specious assertion that attempts to address racism are really attempts to sow racial division that had otherwise never existed. It remains a remarkably resilient and potent idea.

Twice during the Black Lives Matter uprising of the early summer in 2020, letters to the *Richmond Times-Dispatch* attempted to defend the Robert E. Lee Memorial on Monument Avenue by citing the Lee Communion story. In one letter, Mr. T. Scott Fields of Haymarket, Virginia recalled the story and noted that "only Lee could have set this example that we should all try to follow today." Therefore, he concluded, "the Lee monument should be replaced with a monument of Lee kneeling beside a former slave." A full-page paid advertisement from an anonymous group calling themselves the "Friends of Lee Statue" argued a whole raft of inaccurate and misleading assertions about Lee, including the claim that "He knelt to take communion with a Black man when no one else would."[10]

It should be the obligation of St. Paul's to actively work against these narratives that, defying reason, continue to have power today.

St. Paul's spent the summer of 2020 humbly thinking about its historical and contemporary blind spots and wrestling with how difficult—even with this history at hand—it is to discern them.

Why is it difficult when they seem so clear?

In a series of discussions about the report that is the basis of this book in October 2020, a number of St. Paul's parishioners expressed surprise that their history has been laid bare for the first time. Histories that they had never known or had never learned about the church in particular and about race in American history in general. The realization became personal. *Why*, a few reflectively asked, *didn't I act then as I know how to act now?* Or, *Why didn't I see things as clearly then as I do now?* Another lamented that someone she had known and loved—widely regarded as a generous and toweringly gregarious personality at St. Paul's—had been revealed to have resisted integration, and she didn't know how to feel about him anymore. *How could any of this have happened?* History had blindsided them.

I believe these self-reflections can be explained by the opacity created by the complexity of the past. People and institutions are so much more complex than we give them credit for, but that complexity—of interests, discomforts, actions, contexts, family, faith, politics, health, economics, and race—mix together in such a way as to make the things we are interested in knowing about initially obscure. That obscurity makes it difficult to see people as we seek to understand them both then, and now. No one (or, rather, no white people) understood the deeply poisonous meaning behind the happy façade of Robert Damell's funeral until we asked how the ceremony fit into what we know about race relations of the 1920s. The same works today. No one, for instance, can really know how I feel about, say, the National Football League, if all you know about me is what you have read here, unless you ask me a very specific and perhaps awkward question that will force you to peel away so many other (possibly) agreeable things about me and doing contextual research on the 1980s NFC East to get a clear answer. You might say, I knew Chris, but I didn't *know* Chris, before reconsidering me in a new light. In fact, I haven't thought about that subject too deeply myself, but answering pointed questions might reveal something about myself that even I might not like. I might be blindsided myself.

And that journey is what this inquiry has been. It is not intended to be a comprehensive history of St. Paul's or of the lives of its members, or a retelling of familiar old tales. It asks very specific questions: *How did the people of St. Paul's understand race in a religious context? How did they act on those beliefs in their own lives?* And it attempts to give a very specific answer, one that appears suddenly new and troublingly obvious because it had not been asked before. In fact, several parishioners expressed surprise when discovering that St. Paul's people actually enslaved Black people, so innocent of history had they been. They're not alone: many Americans are ignorant about slavery.[11]

St. Paul's people had never thought about it because historical thinking, as history educator Sam Wineburg says, is an "unnatural act."[12] Understandably, few people interrogate their own past with the same specificity and with the same cognitive moves with which academic historians approach a topic.[13] Nevertheless, in the October 2020 discussions, some participants did perform spectacular historical thinking by leaning into the *foreignness* of the past to distance us from it, and perhaps from any obligation to it.

But the past—at least in this case—may not be so foreign as we hope.

If St. Paul's has transformed in the last few generations, why should it be troubled about its history now? Why should it do anything about it? Many participants picked up on a central theme of the report and drew out great meaning about change over time. Yes, St. Paul's has evolved. It is absolutely not the same as it was in 1850, 1898, 1954, and even in 2000. The theological paradigms of proslavery Christianity, the Social Gospel, the liberal universalism of the Cold War, for instance, no longer shape our parish life. Instead, a progressive liturgy, an embrace of an inclusive Gospel, and a generational commitment to racially conscious outreach that has characterized St. Paul's since 1969, do. But one thing that remains consistent through all eras is that every generation *believed* that they acted on their best and most liberal impulses, and out of love, when it came to matters of race. This may have been the most difficult concept for many parishioners to grasp; that our historical subjects did not operate from a place of hypocrisy, conniving evil, or willful self-deception, but that they framed their actions on race in what they considered to be moral virtue, kindness, and decency.[14]

Do we not think the same thing about ourselves today? This is the most challenging question not just for St. Paul's, but for all well-meaning white people.

We are different, but have we changed that much that we avoid forming blind spots about the harms caused by our own good intentions? One participant in the discussions pointedly asked, "what are the slave markets that we are walking by today?" Are they underperforming and underfunded schools, poverty, and housing? Yes, and St. Paul's has been admirably working on those, and more, for a generation now in partial recognition that its spiritual ancestors created these problems.

But question's point is to direct us to what we *don't* see or, more importantly, to get us to explore our assumptions about what we regard as good actions in the way that we wish Russell Bowie, Mary-Cooke Munford, Richard Carrington, and others could have examined their own embrace of white racial paternalism and belief in segregation. In that remarkable Social Gospel era in St. Paul's history, they possessed many of the qualities to which parishioners today aspire to: They were generous. They were out front. They were leaders. And they risked many things for their beliefs.

They also did damage because they were so blinded by their own historical imagination that they couldn't see the harm they did—the harm that was before their very eyes.

What are ours? We have them. Perhaps mine lies in my assurance that a measured pace for self-study is more important than an urgent need for dramatic action. Who is being harmed because I am searching historical records when I could be supporting the efforts of affordable housing activists to badger local politicians to alleviate the impact of gentrification? How do we cut through the complexity of the present to see them in the same way that we have unnaturally and uncomfortably cut through the complexity of the past to see them? We still possess that impulse to lead a charge; to attack race-based poverty with charity—even if the charity is relational and recipient-directed. Perhaps we need to question our contexts. Perhaps we need to think of this work not as reconciliation, but as justice. Jennifer Harvey, for instance, notes that reconciliation is an outmoded model that prioritizes togetherness while at the same time it papers over causes of alienation while threatening the integrity of Black churches. Reparations, on the other hand, forces attention to causes of alienation, and their remedies. Similarly, Jemar Tisby and Austin Channing Brown have said that reconciliation and a sense of togetherness is a fundamentally flawed course unless justice is first approached.[15] As a "confession," as the subtitle to this book hints, this work is not the end, but the beginning of that process of justice.

Congregational review of this report had initially been planned for the Spring of 2020. We had scheduled discussions among parishioners to digest and discern an appropriate and authentic course of action, including acknowledgment of the church's past, a liturgy of repentance, a confession of sins, and an exploration of ways that the performance of reconciliation, reparations, and justice can be incorporated more firmly into the parish life of this church. Just as we were about to get the discussions underway in March, the COVID-19 pandemic shut down everything.

Two months later, Minneapolis Police murdered George Floyd, and the Black Lives Matter uprising gripped the nation—including Richmond. Throughout June and July, daily and nightly protest marches coursed up and down Grace Street, Broad Street, and Monument Avenue. One of the largest

FIGURE 10. The names of Black men and women killed by police on the St. Paul's portico, 2020. (Elizabeth L. O'Leary)

marches, on June 2, began between St. Paul's and the State Capitol at the intersection of Grace and Ninth Street. St. Paul's clergy, staff, and parishioners did not just stand on the portico watching; they marched along. On different occasions, Richmond police met demonstrators with teargas, and protestors left a wordy trail of spray-paint graffiti in their wake. In a likely indiscriminate move, someone tagged "BLM" on one of the columns on the portico, and others marked the steps with the names of victims of police brutality, including Floyd, Trayvon Martin, and Breonna Taylor.

The Reverend Dr. Charles Dupree, recently installed as St. Paul's sixteenth rector, and the vestry decided to leave the marks of protest, in humble solidarity with the BLM cause, noting that "we can't sweep it under the rug."[16]

Over the summer, protestors converged at the Confederate statues on Monument Avenue and thoroughly transformed them with art, vibrant music, peaceful gatherings, and a sense of community relief and joy at having claimed space in a historically exclusionary landscape. Protestors recast Lee Circle as Marcus-David Peters Circle to honor a 2017 victim of police violence in Richmond. In earlier years, a small but growing movement calling for the removal of Confederate statues struggled against the intransigence of city and state bureaucracy. Now, it flourished and forced its way into widespread public attention and acceptance. The Mayor of Richmond, the City Council, and the Governor of Virginia (enabled by a recent reversal of state laws enacted by a newly elected Democratic General Assembly) quickly caught up to public sentiment and initiated the process to remove the Confederate monuments. Five of the major statues came down that July.

St. Paul's acted at the same time. In preempting a move that would likely have taken place at the November 2020 anniversary celebration, the vestry, with no fanfare, removed the remaining tablets dedicated to Lee, various members of the Jefferson Davis family, a plaque dedicated to the Macgill family, and the pew plaques marking the spots where Lee and Davis worshipped.

Moreover, at a service dedicated to reconciliation on September 27, where the Reverend Melanie Mullen spoke about the freedom found in telling a truthful history and the capacity to continue to see good news in the windows' *religious* messages (not historical), the clergy ritually retracted the dedications to Lee and Davis of the stained-glass windows. We now call them, simply, the Moses and Paul windows, when we refer to them at all.

After altering what had been, St. Paul's offered new commemorations based on new stories. On All Saints' Day in November 2020, clergy dedicated three commissioned needlepoint kneelers honoring Nancy Scott, Margaret Tyler, John Hilton, and Walker Wilson (Black members—enslaved and free—in the antebellum years), Robert Darnell, and Ruby Grant Martin.

In 2022, the church installed fourteen papercut art pieces created by artist Janelle Washington in the sanctuary. Called "The Stations of St. Paul's," they replicate the "Stations of the Cross," but instead of Jesus's Passion, they recount stages of St. Paul's racial history. Parishioners and visitors are encouraged to contemplate the historical stories portrayed and to offer prayers. In this church once known as a destination for those wishing to bask in the reflected glory of Confederate saints, it is our hope that the Stations become a more compelling draw.[17]

Memorials emanate power through the tangible effect of the stories they tell. These kneelers and the Stations are small gestures toward turning around a narrative, but they cannot be the last.

NOTES

Introduction

1. "In Mr. Davis's Honor," *Richmond Dispatch*, June 30, 1896, 23.
2. Ta-Nehisi Coates, "Why Do So Few Blacks Study the Civil War?" *The Atlantic*, special commemorative issue (February 2012).
3. The Episcopal Church, Acts of Convention, Resolution 2015-D044, The Archives of the Episcopal Church, https://episcopalarchives.org/cgi-bin/acts/acts_resolution-complete.pl?resolution=2015-D044, accessed June 24, 2019; Michael Gryborski, "Episcopal Church Calls for Removal of All Confederate Flags; Says It's a Symbol 'at Odds With the Love of Jesus Christ'," *Christian Post,* July 3, 2015.
4. Michelle Alexander, *The New Jim Crow: Mass Incarceration in the Age of Colorblindness* (New York: New Press, 2010).
5. *Becoming Beloved Community,* https://episcopalchurch.org/beloved-community/.
6. Robert Orsi, "Everyday Miracles: The Study of Lived Religion," in *Lived Religion in America: Toward a History of Practice,* ed. David D. Hall (Princeton, NJ: Princeton University Press, 1997), 11.
7. Walter Russell Bowie, *Learning to Live: An Autobiography* (New York: Abingdon, 1969), 254.

1. The Sacred Obligation of Slavery at St. Paul's

1. "Unlawful Assembly," *Richmond Dispatch*, August 22, 1854, 2.
2. Benjamin Campbell, *Richmond's Unhealed History* (Richmond, VA: Brandylane, 2012), 90–91.
3. Matthew Karp, *This Vast Southern Empire: Slaveholders at the Helm of American Foreign Policy* (Cambridge, MA: Harvard University Press, 2018); Walter Johnson, *River of Dark Dreams: Slavery and Empire in the Cotton Kingdom* (Cambridge, MA: Belknap, 2017); Eugene D. Genovese, *Roll, Jordan, Roll: The World the Slaves Made* (New York: Vintage, 1976).
4. City of Richmond, Virginia, 1850 United States Census, Slave Schedule, 6.
5. Henry Brown, *Narrative of the Life of Henry Box Brown, Written by Himself* (Manchester: Lee and Glynn, 1851), 16–18, 25–26.
6. Midori Takagi, *"Rearing Wolves to Our Own Destruction": Slavery in Richmond, Virginia, 1782–1865* (Charlottesville: University Press of Virginia, 1999), 89; "Desperate Assault," *Richmond Dispatch,* January 18, 1855.
7. Barret appears on an 1845 list in Thomas Ellis's Record Book (1846–1870) in St. Paul's Church (Richmond, VA) Records, 1828–1963, Virginia Museum of History &

Culture, Richmond, VA; Brent Tarter, "William Barret," in John T. Kneebone, ed., *Dictionary of Virginia Biography* (Richmond: Library of Virginia, 1998), 1:353–54; *Daily State Journal*, March 24, 1874.

8. This term "narrative of racial difference" is inspired by Bryan Stevenson, who describes it as stories about White superiority and Black inferiority that undergirded and justified slavery, segregation, and mass incarceration. See for instance Corey G. Johnson, "Bryan Stevenson on Charleston and Our Real Problem with Race," *The Marshall Project*, June 24, 2015 (accessed November 3, 2020), https://www.themarshallproject.org/2015/06/24/bryan-stevenson-on-charleston-and-our-real-problem-with-race/.
9. Takagi, *"Rearing Wolves to Our Own Destruction,"* 37–70.
10. Richmond Ward 3, Henrico, Virginia, 1840 United States Federal Census, 63.
11. Diane Barnes's study of artisans in Petersburg suggests that skilled workers tended to be a mix of Whites and free blacks, who worked alongside enslaved Black laborers. Diane Barnes, *Artisan Workers in the Upper South: Petersburg, Virginia, 1820–1865* (Baton Rouge: Louisiana State University Press, 1996).
12. Campbell, *Richmond's Unhealed History*, 103; Charles F. Irons, "And All These Things Shall Be Added unto You: The First African Baptist Church, Richmond, 1841–1865," *Virginia Cavalcade* 47, no. 1 (Winter 1998): 26–35.
13. Meredith Henne Baker, *The Richmond Theater Fire: Early America's First Great Disaster* (Baton Rouge: Louisiana State University Press, 2012), 177–80.
14. Elizabeth Wright Weddell, *St. Paul's Church: Its Historic Years and Memorials* (Richmond, VA: William Byrd Press, 1931), 1:11–12.
15. Takagi, *"Rearing Wolves to Our Own Destruction,"* 17; Gregg D. Kimball, *American City, Southern Place: A Cultural History of Antebellum Richmond* (Athens: University of Georgia Press, 2000), 31.
16. "A Card," *Richmond Enquirer*, March 7, 1848, p. 3; Mary Wingfield Scott, *Houses of Old Richmond* (New York: Bonanza Books, 1941).
17. "New Grocery and Commission Store," *Richmond Enquirer*, March 21, 1845, p. 3.
18. "Auction Room," *Richmond Dispatch*, April 25, 1853, p. 2; "Davenport and Allen Auction Co.," *Style Weekly*, May 10, 2011, https://www.styleweekly.com/richmond/davenport-and-allen-auction-co/Content?oid=1477700/, accessed April 17, 2020.
19. "Auction Sales," *Richmond Enquirer*, February 26, 1845, p. 3.
20. "Local Matters," *Richmond Dispatch*, January 21, 1856, p. 1, "Limited Partnership," *Richmond Enquirer*, October 18, 1853, p. 3, "Wanted-Negroes," *Richmond Dispatch*, January 3, 1855, p. 3; "Coal Pit Hands Wanted," *Richmond Dispatch*, January 27, 1853.
21. "Death's Doings Yesterday," *Richmond Dispatch*, June 27, 1885, p. 1.
22. Virginius Dabney, *Richmond: The Story of a City*, rev. ed. (Charlottesville: University Press of Virginia, 1990), 62.
23. *Richmond Dispatch*, January 31, 1852, p. 2.
24. "William Marshall, Sr.," *Richmond Dispatch*, June 30, 1891, p. 3, Tucker 1850 Census. These are all derived from the 1849 parishioners list and the bondholders list.
25. *Richmond Dispatch*, December 17, 1854.
26. *Richmond Dispatch*, January 18, 1860.

27. *Richmond Dispatch,* March 15, 1855.
28. *Richmond Dispatch,* March 8, 1859; William Still, *The Underground Rail Road* (Philadelphia: Porter & Coates, 1872), 497–98.
29. Takagi, *"Rearing Wolves to Our Own Destruction,"* 71–95.
30. Takagi, *"Rearing Wolves to Our Own Destruction,"* 83–84. See also Charles B. Dew, *Ironmaker to the Confederacy: Joseph R. Anderson and the Tredegar Iron Works* (Richmond: Virginia State Library, 1999).
31. Biographical information on the Bolling family is found in Bolling Family File, St. Paul's Church; "Students of the University of Virginia," https://uvastudents .wordpress.com (accessed November 3, 2016).
32. Bolling Walker Haxall Account Book, 1851–1883, Virginia Museum of History & Culture, 24, 26.
33. *Richmond Dispatch,* December 10, 1858; January 21, 1856; January 3, 1855; January 13, 1855; October 7, 1854; January 7, 1853; January 1, 1853.
34. *Richmond Dispatch,* January 11, 1855, 2, *Richmond Enquirer,* January 3, 1860, 3.
35. *Richmond Dispatch,* October 7, 1864. Grandison probably ran the stand with Irving's tacit approval, but Irving agreed to shutter it when civil authorities arrested Grandison.
36. Joshua D. Rothman, *Notorious in the Neighborhood: Sex and Families Across the Color Line in Virginia, 1787–1861* (Chapel Hill: University of North Carolina Press, 2003), 92–129.
37. *Richmond Dispatch,* November 15, 1852, 2; November 11, 1852, 2; May 3, 1853, 2; *Richmond Enquirer,* July 19, 1853, 1. "Local Matters," *Richmond Dispatch,* April 11, 1860.
38. Marie Tyler-McGraw, *An African Republic: Black & White Virginians in the Making of Liberia* (Chapel Hill: University of North Carolina Press, 2007).
39. John C. Rutherfoord, *Speech of John C. Rutherfoord, of Goochland, in the House of Delegates of Virginia, on the removal from the commonwealth of the free colored population, delivered February 18, 1853* (Richmond, VA: Ritchies & Dunnavant, 1853); *Richmond Enquirer,* March 27, 1849, 3.
40. Kimball, *American City, Southern Place,* 119–20.
41. *Richmond Daily Dispatch,* February 2, 1865; February 15, 1865, 4; March 18, 1865, 4. See also Virginia Executive Papers, Letters Received, Library of Virginia, March 14, 1865.
42. Eugene D. Genovese, *A Consuming Fire: The Fall of the Confederacy and the Mind of the White Christian South* (Athens: University of Georgia Press, 1998), 3–33.
43. Campbell, *Richmond's Unhealed History,* 92–95. So, too, did Harriet Beecher Stowe take note of Meade's proslavery Christianity, quoting extensively from his writings and sermons in her work, *The Key to Uncle Tom's Cabin,* writing sarcastically that "Bishop Meade . . . thus expatiates to slaves on the advantages of their condition. One would really think, from reading this account, that everyone ought to make haste and get himself sold into slavery, as the nearest road to heaven." *The Key to Uncle Tom's Cabin; Presenting the Original Facts and Documents Upon Which the Story Is Founded . . .* (Boston: John P. Jewett, 1854), 488–89.
44. See *Journals of the Annual Convention of the Protestant Episcopal Church in Virginia*

for 1845 through 1860 and John Shelton Reed, *Glorious Battle: The Cultural Politics of Victorian Anglo-Catholicism* (Nashville: Vanderbilt University Press, 2000).
45. On proslavery Christianity, see John Patrick Daly, *When Slavery Was Called Freedom: Evangelicalism, Proslavery, and the Causes of the Civil War* (Lexington: University Press of Kentucky, 2004); Mitchell Snay, *Gospel of Disunion: Religion and Separatism in the Antebellum South* (Chapel Hill: University of North Carolina Press, 1997).
46. *Southern Churchman*, March 8, 1849.
47. Sarah Valentine to Edward V. Valentine, March 9, 1860, Valentine Family Papers, 1786–1920, The Valentine, Richmond, VA.
48. *Southern Churchman*, March 8, 1849. "Rules for the management of the negroes at Rock Castle," John C. Rutherfoord, Rutherfoord Family Papers, 1811–1946, Virginia Museum of History & Culture.
49. Susan Taylor Block, *Temple of Our Fathers: St. James Church, 1729–2004* (Wilmington, NC: Artspeaks, 2004), 56; T. Felder Dorn, *Challenges on the Emmaus Road: Episcopal Bishops Confront Slavery, Civil War, and Emancipation* (Columbia: University of South Carolina Press, 2013), 44–46.
50. *Southern Churchman*, March 8, 1849.
51. On the "mission to the slaves" initiated by Presbyterian Charles Colcock Jones, see Erskine Clark, *Wrestlin' Jacob: A Portrait of Religion in Antebellum Georgia and the Carolina Low Country* (Tuscaloosa: University of Alabama Press, 1999). On the mission as it developed in Virginia, see Charles F. Irons, *The Origins of Proslavery Christianity: White and Black Evangelicals in Colonial and Antebellum Virginia* (Chapel Hill: University of North Carolina Press, 2008). On the mission in the Carolina upcountry, see Christopher Alan Graham, "Faith and Family in the Antebellum Piedmont South" (PhD diss., University of North Carolina at Greensboro, 2013), 60–64.
52. See, for instance, *Journal of the Fifty-Seventh Annual Convention of the Protestant Episcopal Church in Virginia, 1852* (Washington, DC: Jno. T. Towers, 1852).
53. Anne Rose Page, *Sketches of Old Virginia Family Servants* (Philadelphia: Isaac Ashmead, 1847).
54. T. T. Castleman, ed., *Plain Sermons for Servants*, 2nd ed. (New York: Stanford & Delisser, 1858). Abolitionist Frederick Douglass excoriated this publication and its authors' pretenses to benevolence: "Why, Sir, the political parties in the United States that uphold the sin of slavery dwindle into insignificance, when compared with the power exercised by the church to uphold and sustain that system. It is from the pulpit that we have sermons on behalf of slavery; it is with reasonings such as you have heard from Bishop Meade . . . that the Abolitionists have to contend. What is worse, all the religious instruction given to slaves in the United States is mingled with just such sentiments as you have heard here. The slave-holders doom the slave to ignorance first, and then take advantage of his ignorance, and that highest element of the human character, the religious sentiment, to reduce him to slavery. . . . Only think of a religion under which the handcuffs, the fetters, the whip,

the gag, the thumbscrew, blood-hounds, cat-o-nine tails, branding-irons, all these implements can be undisturbed. Only think of a body of men thanking God every Sabbath-day that they live in a country where there is civil and religious freedom, when there are three millions of people herded together in a state of concubinage, denied the right to learn to read the name of the God that made them." Frederick Douglass, "Slavery in the Pulpit of the Evangelical Alliance: An Address Delivered in London, England, on September 14, 1846," *London Inquirer*, September 19, 1846; *London Patriot*, September 17, 1846, in John Blassingame et al., eds., *The Frederick Douglass Papers: Series One—Speeches, Debates, and Interviews* (New Haven: Yale University Press, 1979), 407. Henry Brown, who had been a member of First African Baptist and had witnessed first-hand the application of the "mission to the slaves" in Richmond, noted that "there actually does exist in that land where men, women, and children are bought and sold, calling itself the church of Christ; yes, my friends, it is true that the buyer and seller of the bodies and souls of his fellows; he who today can separate the husband from the wife, the parent from the child, or cut asunder the strongest ties of friendship, in order to gain a few dollars, to avert a trifling loss, or to please a whim of fancy, can ascend a pulpit to-morrow and preach, what he calls, the gospel of Christ! Yes, and in many cases, the house, which he calls the house of God, has been erected from the price of human beings; the very stones of which it is composed, have actually been dragged to their places by men with chains at their heels, and ropes around their neck!" Brown, *Narrative*, 63–64.
55. *Journal of the Sixty-Second Annual Convention of the Protestant Episcopal Church in Virginia, 1857* (Richmond, VA: Whig Book and Job Office, 1857), 112–13; Weddell, *St. Paul's Church*, 1:115–16.
56. *Journal of the Convention of the Protestant Episcopal Church in the Diocese of Virginia, 1847* (Lynchburg: The Virginian, 1847), 72.
57. *Journal of the Convention of the Protestant Episcopal Church in the Diocese of Virginia, 1847* (Lynchburg: The Virginian, 1847), 76.
58. See for instance *Journal of the Fifty-Seventh Annual Convention of the Protestant Episcopal Church in Virginia, 1852* (Washington, DC: Jno. T. Towers, 1852), 63.
59. Sarah Valentine to Edward V. Valentine, March 9, 1860, Valentine Family Papers, 1786–1920, The Valentine, Richmond, VA.
60. Blassingame et al., eds., *The Frederick Douglass Papers*, 407.
61. Charles F. Irons, "'And All These Things Shall Be Added Unto You: The First African Baptist Church, Richmond, 1841–1865," *Virginia Cavalcade* 47, no. 1 (Winter 1998): 26–35.
62. *Richmond Dispatch*, November 9, 1858.
63. First African Baptist Church, Richmond, Minute Book, 1841–1859, Library of Virginia, Archives Research Services, Richmond, VA.
64. Meeting minutes were recorded in St. Paul's Vestry Book, October 22, 1845, St. Paul's Church (Richmond, VA) Records, 1828–1963, Virginia Museum of History & Culture, Richmond, VA.

65. Irving ejected one free Black man named Green Smith for "behaving very badly in the galleries." Smith, or an associate, returned and threw a shoe through a window, "annoying the congregation." *Richmond Dispatch*, February 20, 1855.
66. *Journal of the Convention of the Protestant Episcopal Church, in the Diocese of Virginia, 1849* (Lynchburg: Blackford, Townley, 1849); *Journal of the Fifty-Seventh Annual Convention of the Protestant Episcopal Church in Virginia, 1852* (Washington, DC: Jno. T. Towers, 1862), 64; *Journal of the Fifty-Eighth Annual Convention of the Protestant Episcopal Church in Virginia, 1853* (Philadelphia: T. K. and P. G. Collins, Printers, 1853), 59; *Journal of the Fifty-Ninth Annual Convention of the Protestant Episcopal Church in Virginia, 1854* (Richmond, VA: C. H. Wynne, 1854), 83; *Journal of the Sixty-Second Annual Convention of the Protestant Episcopal Church in Virginia, 1857* (Richmond, VA: Whig Book and Job Office, 1857), 111–12; Weddell, *St. Paul's Church*, 1:66, 75, 77, 109, 131.
67. Nancy Scott Free Certificate, October 1, 1838, *Virginia Untold: The African American Narrative*, https://www.virginiamemory.com/collections/aan/, accessed February 12, 2019. *Richmond Dispatch*, February 11, 1857; February 18, 1860. The identity of Nancy Scott is not easy to discern. At least two free Black Nancy Scotts lived in Richmond in the 1850s and fleeting glimpses of others in central Virginia often appear. I am describing one of the free Nancy Scotts here because of the two, she best fits the profile of a single female member of St. Paul's.
68. Page, *Sketches of Old Virginia Family Servants*, 2.
69. This account is taken from "Appendix C: Report of the Committee on the Religious Instruction of the Colored Population," *Journal of the Sixty-Fifth Annual Convention of the Protestant Episcopal Church in Virginia, 1860* (Richmond, VA: Chas. H. Wynne, 1860).
70. On the growing tendency of southern religious people to emphasize religious practice in the home, see Christopher A. Graham, "Evangelicals and 'Domestic Felicity' in the Non-Elite South," *Journal of Southern Religion* 15 (2013): http://jsreligion.org/issues/vol15/graham.html.
71. St. Paul's Vestry Book, May 4, 1859, St. Paul's Church (Richmond, VA) Records, 1828–1963, Virginia Museum of History & Culture, Richmond, VA.
72. *Richmond Dispatch*, December 29, 1860, 1.
73. George H. Reese, ed., *Proceedings of the Virginia State Convention of 1861, February 13-May 1* (Richmond: Virginia State Library, 1965), 39.

2. St. Paul's in War and after Emancipation

1. "An Address to Christians throughout the World, by a Convention of Ministers, assembled at Richmond, Va., April, 1863," (Philadelphia: n.p., 1863). The Virginia Attorney General, John Randolph Tucker—a great uncle to future St. Paul's rector Rev. Beverley Tucker—delivered a remarkably similar speech two months later to the Richmond Young Men's Christian Association. See Hon. John Randolph Tucker, "The Southern Church Justified in its support of the South in the present War" (Richmond, VA: Wm. H. Clemmitt, 1863).

2. Rt. Rev. J. Johns, D.D., *A Memoir of the Life of the Rt. Rev. William Meade, D.D.* (Baltimore: Innes, 1867), 54.
3. *Journal of the Sixty-Eighth Annual Council of the Protestant Episcopal Church in Virginia* (Richmond, VA: Macfarlane & Fergusson, 1863), 38.
4. *Journal of the Sixty-Eighth Annual Council of the Protestant Episcopal Church in Virginia* (Richmond, VA: Macfarlane & Fergusson, 1863), 72; *Journal of the Sixty-Ninth Annual Council of the Protestant Episcopal Church in Virginia* (Richmond, VA: Macfarlane & Fergusson, 1864), 65.
5. St. Paul's Vestry Book (1855–1864), 508, in St. Paul's Church (Richmond, VA) Records, 1828–1963, Virginia Museum of History & Culture, Richmond, VA.
6. Thavolia Glymph, *Out of the House of Bondage: The Transformation of the Plantation Household* (New York: Cambridge University Press, 2008).
7. Judith McGuire, *Diary of A Southern Refugee During the War, by a Lady of Virginia* (New York: E. J. Hale, 1868), 108.
8. *Richmond Daily Dispatch*, April 27, 1861.
9. *Richmond Examiner*, May 26, 1862; *Richmond Dispatch*, May 29, 1862.
10. On Nancy Macfarland and the Soldiers' Aid Society of Virginia, see Caroline E. Janney, *Burying the Dead but Not the Past: Ladies' Memorial Associations & the Lost Cause* (Chapel Hill: University of North Carolina Press, 2008), 24–25.
11. "Richmond's Medical Miracle," *New York Times*, November 22, 2011.
12. Dave Ruth, "Chimborazo Hospital," *Encyclopedia Virginia*, Virginia Foundation for the Humanities, https:// https://encyclopediavirginia.org/entries/chimborazo-hospital/, accessed May 14, 2019.
13. *Journal of the Sixty-Eighth Annual Council of the Protestant Episcopal Church in Virginia* (Richmond, VA: Macfarlane & Fergusson, 1863), 31.
14. *Journal of the Sixty-Ninth Annual Council of the Protestant Episcopal Church in Virginia* (Richmond, VA: Macfarlane & Fergusson, 1864), 63; *Journal of the Sixty-Eighth Annual Council of the Protestant Episcopal Church in Virginia* (Richmond, VA: Macfarlane & Fergusson, 1863), 72.
15. Elizabeth Wright Weddell, *St. Paul's Church: Its Historic Years and Memorials* (Richmond, VA: William Byrd Press, 1931), 1:224–25.
16. McGuire, *Diary of a Southern Refugee*, 256.
17. *Diocese of Virginia. Sixty-Sixth Annual Convention, 1861* (Richmond, VA: Chas. Wynne, 1861); *Journal of the Sixty-Ninth Annual Council of the Protestant Episcopal Church in Virginia* (Richmond, VA: Macfarlane & Fergusson, 1864); Weddell, *St. Paul's Church*, 1:187–92.
18. *Parish Register*, Summer 1931, 2; Phillip J. Schwarz, *St. Paul's Episcopal Church: 150 Years, 1845–1995* (Richmond, VA: St. Paul's Episcopal Church, 1995), 13; *Report of the Sixteenth Annual Meeting of the Virginia State Bar Association, 1904* (Richmond, VA: Everett Waddey, 1904), 61–63.
19. Charles Minnigerode, *Power: A Sermon Preached at St. Paul's Church, Richmond* (Richmond, VA: W. H. Clemmitt, 1864).
20. *Richmond Dispatch*, March 3, 1863.

21. *Richmond Dispatch*, September 27, 1864.
22. *Richmond Daily Dispatch*, February 15, 1865, 4. *Richmond Daily Dispatch*, March 18, 1865, p. 4; "Record of trials of Oliver and George, February 14, 1865," Pardons, 1–4/65, Virginia Executive Papers, Letters Received, Library of Virginia.
23. *Richmond Dispatch*, July 24, 1861; May 2, 1862; May 13, 1862; September 2, 1862.
24. Bolling Walker Haxall, Account Book, 26, Virginia Museum of History & Culture, Richmond, VA.
25. Charles Minnigerode, *"He That Believeth Shall Not Make Haste": A Sermon Preached on the First of January, 1865, in St. Paul's Church, Richmond* (Richmond, VA: Chas. H. Wynne, 1865).
26. An account of the scene at St. Paul's on April 2 can be found in Nelson Lankford, *Richmond Burning: The Last Days of the Confederate Capital* (New York: Penguin Books, 2003), 60–69.
27. Michael B. Chesson, *Richmond After the War* (Richmond: Virginia State Library, 1981), 96–104; Charles F. Irons, "Urban Black Protestants and the Predicament of Emancipation," paper presented at Reconstruction and the Arc of Racial (In)Justice, Jepson School of Leadership, University of Richmond, September 16, 2016; Scott Britton Hansen, "Education for All: The Freedmen's Bureau Schools in Richmond and Petersburg, 1865–1870" (MA thesis, Virginia Commonwealth University, 2008).
28. *Journal of the Seventieth Annual Council of the Protestant Episcopal Church in Virginia* (Richmond, VA: Gary and Clemmitt, 1866), 22; Luke Harlow, "The Long Life of Proslavery Religion," in Gregory Downs and Kate Masur, *The World the Civil War Made* (Chapel Hill: University of North Carolina Press, 2015); Gardiner H. Shattuck, Jr., *Episcopalians & Race: Civil War to Civil Rights* (Lexington: University Press of Kentucky, 2000), 10–11. The Freedman's Commission likely funded St. Philip's for at least several years. St. Paul's Vestry Book, 250, St. Paul's Church (Richmond, VA) Records, 1828–1963, Virginia Museum of History & Culture, Richmond, VA.
29. *Journal of the Annual Council* (1866), 39–40.
30. *Journal of the Seventy-First Annual Council* (1866), 21–22, 40; *Journal of the Seventy-Third Annual Council of the Protestant Episcopal Church in Virginia* (Richmond, VA: n.p., 1868), 40–42; *Journal of the Seventy-Fourth Annual Council of the Protestant Episcopal Church in Virginia* (Richmond, VA: Gary, Clemmitt & Jones, 1869), 54, 56; *Southern Churchman*, "Church Intelligence. Virginia. 71st Annual Council," May 17, 1866.
31. Daniel W. Stowell, *Rebuilding Zion: The Religious Reconstruction of the South, 1863–1877* (New York: Oxford University Press, 1998), 65–79; Irons, "Urban Black Protestants." William Still, *Still's Underground Rail Road Records*, rev. ed. (Philadelphia: William Still, 1886), 545.
32. *Journal of the Annual Council* (1867), 57.
33. Edward L. Bond and Joan R. Gunderson, "The Episcopal Church in Virginia, 1607–2007," *Virginia Magazine of History and Biography* 115, no. 2, (2007): 284
34. *Journal of the Annual Council* (1875), 67.
35. Published in *Valley of the Shadow: Two Communities in the American Civil War*, Virginia Center for Digital History, University of Virginia Library.

36. William J. Cooper, *Jefferson Davis, American* (New York: Vintage, 2000), 590, 594.
37. *Richmond Dispatch*, May 28, 1893, 2; William Asbury Christian, *Richmond, Her Past and Present* (Richmond, VA: L. H. Jenkins, 1912), 288.
38. *Staunton Spectator*, September 5, 1865, 4; *Daily Progress*, September 15, 1865, 2.
39. *Richmond Dispatch*, April 16, 1867, 1.
40. *Harrisburg Telegraph*, April 20, 1867, 2.
41. *Richmond Dispatch*, March 16, 1868, 1.
42. *Richmond Dispatch*, December 20, 1867, 1. Monogenism had gained traction in educated circles in America in the antebellum period, and some White southern clergy insisted on it in arguments with polygenists. Eugene D. Genovese, *A Consuming Fire: The Fall of the Confederacy in the Mind of the White Christian South* (Athens: University of Georgia Press, 1998), 82–84.
43. Mary H. Mitchell, *Hollywood Cemetery: The History of a Southern Shrine* (Richmond: Virginia State Library, 1985), 64–65; Drew Gilpin Faust, *This Republic of Suffering: Death and the American Civil War* (New York: Vintage, 2009), 238–39.
44. "A Meeting of the Ladies of Richmond held at St. Paul's Church, May 3, 1866" in Hollywood Memorial Association Papers, Virginia Museum of History & Culture, Richmond, VA.
45. Mitchell, *Hollywood Cemetery*, 65–68; Caroline E. Janney, *Burying the Dead but Not the Past: Ladies' Memorial Associations and the Lost Cause* (Chapel Hill: University of North Carolina Press, 2012), 57; William Blair, *Cities of the Dead: Contesting the Memory of the Civil War in the South, 1865–1914* (Chapel Hill: University of North Carolina Press, 2004), 59; Faust, *This Republic of Suffering*, 238. Janney notes that most HMA leaders did not lose sons or immediate family members in the war.
46. Jane Dailey, *Before Jim Crow: The Politics of Race in Postemancipation Virginia* (Chapel Hill: University of North Carolina Press, 2000).
47. "Address of the Democratic State Committee to the People of Virginia," *Alexandria Gazette*, December 1, 1883. On the Danville riot, see Dailey, *Before Jim Crow*, 103–31.
48. *Journal of the Annual Council of the Protestant Episcopal Church in Virginia* (Richmond, VA: Wm. Ellis Jones, 1881), 74.
49. On the Zion Union Association, see Worth Earlwood Norman Jr., *James Solomon Russell: Former Slave, Pioneering Educator, and Episcopal Evangelist* (Jefferson, NC: Macfarland, 2012), 19.
50. *Journal of the Eighty-Fifth Annual Council of the Protestant Episcopal Church in Virginia* (Richmond, VA: Wm. Ellis Jones, 1880), 89.
51. Nicole Myers Turner, *Soul Liberty: The Evolution of Black Religious Politics in Postemancipation Virginia* (Chapel Hill: University of North Carolina Press, 2020), 81–83; Odell Greenleaf Harris, *Bishop Payne Divinity School, Petersburg, Virginia, 1878–1949* (Alexandria, VA: Protestant Episcopal Theological Seminary, 1980). The seminary took its name from the Rt. Rev. John Payne, a White Episcopal priest consecrated by William Meade as the First Missionary Bishop to Liberia.
52. *Journal of the Annual Council of the Protestant Episcopal Church in Virginia* (Richmond, VA: Wm. Ellis Jones, 1886), 32, 36. On William Norwood's enslavement of Caroline Bragg, see *Carolina Churchman* (August 1914), 14.

53. Lyon G. Tyler, ed., *Men of Mark in Virginia* (Washington, DC: Men of Mark, 1909), 5:361–62.
54. *Journal of the Ninetieth Annual Council of the Protestant Episcopal Church in Virginia* (Richmond, VA: Wm. Ellis Jones, 1884), 37.
55. *Journal of the Ninety-First Annual Council of the Protestant Episcopal Church in Virginia* (Wm. Ellis Jones, 1886), 46.
56. *Journal of the Ninety-First Annual Council of the Protestant Episcopal Church in Virginia* (Wm. Ellis Jones, 1886), 45–46.
57. *Journal of the Ninety-Fourth Annual Council of the Protestant Episcopal Church in Virginia* (Richmond, VA: Wm. Ellis Jones, 1889), 44–45.
58. Genovese, *A Consuming Fire*.
59. *Journal of the Ninety-Third Annual Council of the Protestant Episcopal Church in Virginia* (Richmond, VA: Wm. Ellis Jones, 1888), 42.
60. Lawrence L. Hartzell, "George F. Bragg (1863–1940)" in *Encyclopedia Virginia*. Virginia Foundation for the Humanities, https://encyclopediavirginia.org/entries/bragg-george-f-1863-1940/, accessed April 16, 2017.
61. *Afro-American Churchman*, January 15, 1887. See also in the same newspaper, February 19, 1887, and July 2, 1887.
62. *Afro-American Churchman*, February 5, 1887.
63. *Afro-American Churchman*, March 15, 1887.
64. Shattuck, *Episcopalians and Race*, 13–16; Bond and Gunderson, "The Episcopal Church in Virginia, 1607–2007," 287–288.
65. *Afro-American Churchman*, November 1, 1887.
66. Bond and Gunderson, "The Episcopal Church in Virginia, 1607–2007," 287–288.
67. St. Paul's Vestry Book, April 7, 1887, St. Paul's Church (Richmond, VA) Records, 1828–1963, Virginia Museum of History & Culture, Richmond, VA.
68. On the evolution of religious paternalism, see Elizabeth L. Jemison, *Christian Citizens: Reading the Bible in Black and White in the Postemancipation South* (Chapel Hill: University of North Carolina Press, 2020).
69. Carlton McCarthy, *Walks about Richmond: A story for boys, and a guide for persons visiting the city* ... (Richmond, VA: McCarthy & Ellyson, 1870), 115.
70. W. D. Chesterman, *The James River Tourist* (Richmond, VA: Dispatch Steam Print House, 1879), 7–8.
71. *Richmond Virginia, A Guide to and Description of its Principal Places* (Richmond, VA: J. W. Randolph & English, 1881), 21–22.
72. Gaines M. Foster, *Ghosts of the Confederacy: Defeat, the Lost Cause, and the Emergence of the New South, 1865–1913* (New York: Oxford University Press, 1987).
73. Caroline E. Janney, "The Lost Cause," in *Encyclopedia Virginia*. Virginia Foundation for the Humanities, https://encyclopediavirginia.org/entries/lost-cause-the/, accessed April 16, 2017; Christopher A. Graham, "The Lost Cause Myth," in *The Inclusive Historian's Handbook*, American Association for State and Local History and National Council for Public History, May 12, 2020, https://inclusivehistorian.com/lost-cause-myth/, accessed November 1, 2020.

74. James M. Lindgren, *Preserving the Old Dominion: Historic Preservation and Virginia Traditionalism* (Charlottesville: University of Virginia Press, 1993).
75. On the Lee Monument, see Kirk Savage, *Standing Soldiers, Kneeling Slaves: Race, War, and Monument in Nineteenth-Century America*, 2nd ed. (Princeton, NJ: Princeton University Press, 2018), 129–61. On the UDC, see Karen L. Cox, *Dixie's Daughters: The United Daughters of the Confederacy and the Preservation of Confederate Culture* (Tallahassee: University Press of Florida, 2003).
76. "Committee" to Powhatan Ellis, Esq., June 12, 1889, Powhatan Ellis Papers, 1856–1890, Virginia Museum of History & Culture, Richmond, VA.
77. St. Paul's Vestry Book, 1888–1898, p. 67, St. Paul's Church (Richmond, VA) Records, 1828–1963, Virginia Museum of History & Culture, Richmond, VA.
78. Mrs. Roger A. Pryor, et al., *Gen. Robert Edward Lee: Soldier, Citizen, and Christian Patriot* (Richmond, VA: Royal, 1897), 327, 337.
79. St. Paul's Vestry Book, December 30, 1889, Letter, December 12, 1889, St. Paul's Church (Richmond, VA) Records, 1828–1963, Virginia Museum of History & Culture, Richmond, VA.
80. St. Paul's Vestry Book, January 16, 1890; January 16, 1892; May 31, 1892, St. Paul's Church (Richmond, VA) Records, 1828–1963, Virginia Museum of History & Culture, Richmond, VA.
81. "The Windows Dedicated," *Times*, November 2, 1892, 5; R. E. Lee to Winfield Scott, April 20, 1861, Lee Family Digital Archives, https://leefamilyarchive.org/9-family-papers/708-robert-e-lee-to-winfield-scott-1861-april-20/, accessed May 2, 2019; Elizabeth L. O'Leary "'A Memorial to Those Who Made Her History': Material Acts of Remembrance at St. Paul's, 1845–2020," unpublished paper, 2020, St. Paul's archives.
82. Varina Howell Davis to Joseph Reid Anderson, March 19, 1890, St. Paul's Vestry Book, St. Paul's Church (Richmond, VA) Records, 1828–1963, Virginia Museum of History & Culture, Richmond, VA.
83. Undated flyer, and undated clipping "The Memorial to President Davis in St. Paul's Church: A History of the Movement," Jefferson Davis Memorial Window Committee Scrapbook, February 1900, St. Paul's Episcopal Church; O'Leary, "'A Memorial to Those Who Made Her History.'"
84. "Davis Window is Unveiled," *Richmond Dispatch*, April 19, 1898. On the hagiography of Davis, Lee, and Stonewall Jackson, see Christopher C. Moore, "Apostle of the Confederacy: J. William Jones and the Question of Ecumenism and Denominational Identity in the Development of Lost Cause Mythology" (PhD diss., Baylor University, 2016), 179–210.
85. Calder Loth, *Windows of Grace, A Tribute of Love: The Memorial Windows of St. Paul's Episcopal Church, Richmond, Virginia* (Richmond, VA: St. Paul's Episcopal Church, 2004), 16.
86. *Richmond Planet*, October 18, 1890, 1.
87. Loth, *Windows of Grace, A Tribute of Love*, 48–50.
88. On Winnie's life, see Heath Hardage Lee, *Winnie Davis: Daughter of the Lost Cause* (Lincoln, NE: Potomac Books, 2014).

89. "The late Dr. Macgill," *Richmond Dispatch,* May 6, 1881.
90. Elizabeth Hayes Turner, "Mollie Ragan Macgill Rosenberg," Texas State Historical Association, https://tshaonline.org/handbook/online/articles/froaw/, accessed May 18, 2019; St. Paul's Vestry Book, letter from Mollie Ragan Macgill Rosenberg, March 11, 1893; July 30, 1894; October 8, 1894; February 10, 1896, St. Paul's Church (Richmond, VA) Records, 1828–1963, Virginia Museum of History & Culture, Richmond, VA; *Richmond Times-Dispatch,* March 8, 1909, p. 7.
91. "Davis Window in St. Paul's," *Richmond Dispatch,* November 9, 1897.
92. "Dedication of the Davis Window," *Times,* April 17, 1898.
93. *Parish Register,* May 1909, 6–7.
94. *Richmond Dispatch,* April 5, 1896; *Parish Register,* April 1899, p. 5.
95. *Richmond Dispatch,* April 17, 1898.
96. "In Mr. Davis's Honor," *Richmond Dispatch,* June 30, 1896, 23.
97. Charles Reagan Wilson, *Baptized in Blood: The Religion of the Lost Cause, 1865–1920* (Athens: University of Georgia Press, 1980), 37–78.
98. John T. Kneebone, *Robert Stiles' Civil Wars,* unpublished manuscript; Robert Stiles, *Four Years Under Marse Robert* (New York: Neale, 1904).
99. See, for instance, Grace Elizabeth Hale, *Making Whiteness: The Culture of Segregation in the South, 1890–1940* (New York: Vintage, 1998), 98–104.
100. Elizabeth L. O'Leary, *From Morning to Night: Domestic Service in Maymont House and the Gilded Age South* (Charlottesville: University of Virginia Press, 2004), 54–56; Mrs. James H. Dooley, *Dem Good Ole Times* (New York: Doubleday, Page, 1906), 2, 5, 85.
101. Taylor Hagood, "Thomas Nelson Page," *Encyclopedia Virginia,* Virginia Foundation for the Humanities, https://encyclopediavirginia.org/entries/page-thomas-nelson-1853-1922/, accessed April 12, 2019; Thomas Nelson Page, "The Lynching of Negroes: Its Causes and Its Prevention," *North American Review* 173, no. 566 (January 1904): 33–48. In a response to Page's assertions, Black educator Mary Church Terrell also invoked history to explain lynching. "Lynching is the aftermath of slavery," she said. "The men who lynch negroes to-day are, as a rule, the children of women who sat by their firesides happy and proud in the possession and affection of their own children, while they looked with unpitying eye and adamantine heart upon the anguish of slave mothers whose children had been sold away, when not overtaken by a sadder fate." Mary Church Terrell, "Lynching from a Negro's Point of View," *North American Review* 178, no. 571 (June 1904): 853–68.
102. Beverley Bland Munford, *Virginia's Attitudes Toward Slavery and Secession* (New York: Longmans, Green, 1909); J. Douglas Smith, *Managing White Supremacy: Race, Politics, and Citizenship in Jim Crow Virginia* (Chapel Hill: University of North Carolina Press, 2002), 35–37; Cox, *Dixie's Daughters,* 96.
103. Reiko Hillyer, "Relics of Reconstruction: The Confederate Museum and Civil War Memory in the New South," *Public Historian* 33, no. 4 (November 2011): 50–52.
104. "Negro Communed at St. Paul's Church," *Richmond Times-Dispatch,* April 16, 1905, 5. The article was subsequently published under Broun's name and with some minor alterations in *Confederate Veteran* 8, no. 8 (August 1905): 360.

105. Myrta Lockett Avary, *Dixie after the War* (New York: Doubleday, Page, 1906), 136. This interpretation owes much to Philip J. Schwarz, "General Lee and Visibility," paper delivered to the Stratford Hall Plantation Seminar on Slavery, August 4, 2000. Schwarz, a member of St. Paul's and professor of history at Virginia Commonwealth University, was one of the leaders in the public discovery of the downriver slave trade and the excavation of the Richmond slave market in the first two decades of the twenty-first century.
106. Archer Anderson, "Robert Edward Lee. An address delivered at the Dedication of the Monument to Robert Edward Lee at Richmond, Va., May 19, 1890," (Richmond, VA: Lee Monument Association, 1890). Charles Minnigerode, at the time St. Paul's rector emeritus, gave the invocation at the Lee monument unveiling.
107. Susan Breitzer, "Constitutional Convention, Virginia (1901–1902)" *Encyclopedia Virginia*, Virginia Foundation for the Humanities, https://encyclopediavirginia.org/entries/constitutional-convention-virginia-1901-1902/, accessed April 13, 2017. "The Validity of the Constitution Tested," *Lexington Gazette*, December 3, 1902; "'Not an Ebony Belle'," *Richmond Dispatch*, December 18, 1902; "Mr. Wise's Effort," *Richmond Planet*, December 6, 1902.
108. "Episcopal Bishops," *Richmond Times-Dispatch*, October 25, 1903, 19.
109. Shattuck, *Episcopalians and Race*, 21–25, *Richmond Times-Dispatch*, October 2, 1907, quoted in Weddell, *St. Paul's Church*, 2:297.
110. Weddell, *St. Paul's Church: Its Historic Years and Memorials*, 2 vols.

3. The Social Gospel in a Lost Cause Church

1. "Fund of $100,000 Starts Campaign," *Richmond Times-Dispatch*, June 14, 1916, 12.
2. Marvin Chiles, "Down Where the South Begins: Black Richmond Activism Before the Modern Civil Rights Movement, 1899–1930," *Journal of African American History* 105 (2020): 56–82; John Egerton, *Speak Now Against the Day: The Generation Before the Civil Rights Movement in the South* (Chapel Hill: University of North Carolina Press, 1994); Glenda Elizabeth Gilmore, *Defying Dixie: The Radical Roots of Civil Rights, 1919–1950* (New York: W. W. Norton, 2009); Blair L. M. Kelley, *Right to Ride: Streetcar Boycotts and African American Citizenship in the Era of Plessy v. Ferguson* (Chapel Hill: University of North Carolina Press, 2010).
3. On Mary-Cooke Munford and White Virginians' racial paternalism, see Clayton McClure Brooks, *The Uplift Generation: Cooperation Across the Color Line in Early Twentieth-Century Virginia* (Charlottesville: University of Virginia Press, 2017), 11–33. Clayton McClure Brooks, "Mary-Cooke Branch Munford," *Encyclopedia Virginia*, Virginia Foundation for the Humanities, https://encyclopediavirginia.org/955hpr-fc763194ee39edc/, accessed September 12, 2018. Quote in J. Douglas Smith, *Managing White Supremacy: Race, Politics, and Citizenship in Jim Crow Virginia* (Chapel Hill: University of North Carolina Press, 2002), 241.
4. Walter Russell Bowie, *Sunrise in the South: The Life of Mary-Cooke Branch Munford* (Richmond, VA: William Byrd Press, 1942), 178.
5. "Dr. Bowie Speaks to Business College Students," *Richmond Times-Dispatch*, January 20, 1915. See also *Parish Register*, June 1915.

6. Samuel C. Shepherd Jr, "South and North: The Exceptional Seminary Education of Walter Russell Bowie," *Anglican and Episcopal History* 87, no. 1 (March 2018): 1–33.
7. Martin E. Marty, *Righteous Empire: The Protestant Experience in America* (New York: Harper & Row, 1977); Ronald C. White Jr., *Liberty and Justice for All: Racial Reform and the Social Gospel, 1877–1925* (New York: Harper & Row, 1990); Ralph E. Luker, *The Social Gospel in Black and White: American Racial Reform, 1885–1912*, 2nd ed. (Chapel Hill: University of North Carolina Press, 2000); George M. Frederickson, *The Black Image in the White Mind: The Debate on Afro-American Character and Destiny, 1817–1914* (Middletown, CT: Wesleyan University Press, 1971).
8. In the antebellum years, Christians warned against wealth because it tempted the wealthy away from faith. Here, Bowie critiqued wealth because the pursuit of it produced social inequality and "human pain" for the poor.
9. Walter Russell Bowie, *Learning to Live: An Autobiography* (New York: Abingdon, 1969), 83–84.
10. John M. Coski, *The Confederate Battle Flag: America's Most Embattled Emblem* (Cambridge, MA: Harvard University Press, 2009), 45–96. See also Gaines M. Foster, "Today's Battle Over the Confederate Flag Has Nothing to Do with the Civil War," *Zocalo Public Square* (October 23, 2018).
11. *Parish Register*, June 1907.
12. Elizabeth Wright Weddell, *St. Paul's Church, Richmond, Virginia: It's Historic Years and Memorials* (Richmond, VA: William Byrd Press, 1931), 2:367–71.
13. On Mrs. W. H. F. Lee, see "Funeral today at 4 at St. Paul's," *Richmond News-Leader*, March 7, 1924. On Fitzhugh Lee, see "Nation Weeps at the Grave of Fitzhugh Lee," *Richmond Times-Dispatch*, May 4, 1905, 1. On Anderson, the *Richmond Planet* continued, "When great pressure was brought to bear for the purpose of dismissing the coloured men in his mills, his reply was, 'Some of these men have been with me ever since I entered business and I shall never turn my back on them.' His reply was the key to his whole character. He was too great to know any prejudice, either on account of race or colour. The lowliest workman in his mills had the same access to him which the wealthiest merchant was accorded." Kathleen Bruce, *Virginia Iron Manufacture in the Slave Era* (New York: Century, 1931), 258. "End of a Noble Life," *Richmond Times-Dispatch*, September 10, 1892.
14. *Parish Register*, Thanksgiving, 1926.
15. *Parish Register*, June 1915; *Richmond Times-Dispatch*, June 1, 1915.
16. *Parish Register*, May 1909.
17. James M. Lindgren, *Preserving the Old Dominion: Historic Preservation and Virginia Traditionalism* (Charlottesville: University of Virginia Press, 1993).
18. J. Douglas Smith, *Managing White Supremacy: Race, Politics, and Citizenship in Jim Crow Virginia* (Chapel Hill: University of North Carolina Press, 2002), 235.
19. *Parish Register*, June 1915. For a more insidious articulation of the Lost Cause as not lost, see Bradley T. Johnson's keynote speech at the dedication of the Confederate Museum in 1896, in Confederate Memorial Literary Society, *In Memoriam Sempiternam* (Richmond, VA: Confederate Museum, 1896).
20. *Winkie: Mary Wingfield Scott* (n.p., ca. 2011), 36–38; Bowie, *Learning to Live*, 18–19;

Ellen Anderson Gholson Glasgow, *The Woman Within: An Autobiography* (New York: Harcourt Brace, 1954), 9–31; O'Leary, *From Morning to Night*, 53–54. See also Micki McElya, *Clinging to Mammy: The Faithful Slave in Twentieth-Century America* (Cambridge, MA: Harvard University Press, 2007). For an in-depth exploration of race relations and the complexities of employer-employee relationships during this period, see Elizabeth O'Leary, *From Morning to Night: Domestic Service in Maymont House and the Gilded Age South* (Charlottesville: University of Virginia Press, 2004).

21. "Housewives' League Seeks Servant Problem Solution," *Richmond Times-Dispatch*, March 22, 1922, p. 1; O'Leary, *From Morning to Night*, 42, 45, 83–84. "Servant Shortage Shows Lack of Good Training," *Richmond Times-Dispatch*, May 7, 1942.
22. "E. Mulford Crutchfield Shot Dead on Porch of His Home Here," *Richmond Times-Dispatch*, July 4, 1937; "Police Fusillade Kills Negro Sought in Death of E.M. Crutchfield," July 5, 1937, pp. 1, 3.
23. "White Friends Pay Tribute to St. Paul's Colored Sexton," *Richmond Times-Dispatch*, April 7, 1925; "Unique Tribute to St. Paul's Sexton," *Richmond News-Leader*, April 9, 1925.
24. "A Negro Man Was Buried," *Richmond Times Dispatch*, April 9, 1925. St. Paul's republished this editorial in the October 1925 *Parish Register*.
25. McElya, *Clinging to Mammy*, 116–59.
26. "House that Jack Built," *Richmond Times-Dispatch*, November 10, 1912; "House that Jack Built," *Richmond Times-Dispatch*, November 23, 1912.
27. Annie C. Moore, "Saint Mary's Memorial Church: In Memory of the Beloved Colored 'Mammies' of the South," *The Spirit of Missions* 82 (1917): 261–62. See also "Colored Memorial Church Consecrated," in *Churchman*, October 14, 1916, 513.
28. Richard B. Sherman, "The 'Teachings at Hampton Institute': Social Equality, Racial Integrity, and the Virginia Public Assemblages Act of 1926," *Virginia Magazine of History and Biography* 95, no. 3 (July 1987): 275–300; "Negro buried from a White Church," *Daily Press*, April 10, 1925, p. 4.
29. In 1930, All Saints Episcopal Church on River Road conducted a similar funeral for Junius Smith, their sexton of 27 years, including the vestry acting as pall bearers and a section of the church reserved for White people. "Sexton of All Saints to Be Buried Today," *Richmond Times-Dispatch*, December 3, 1930.
30. *Army Register of Enlistments*, 321; City of Richmond, Virginia 1900 United States Census, Population Schedule; *Parish Register, 1916*; *Parish Register, 1919*.
31. Lucy T. Taylor, Find a Grave, https://www.findagrave.com/memorial/5106487/lucy-t_-taylor/, accessed June 3, 2019.
32. "Fund of $100,000 Starts Campaign," *Richmond Times-Dispatch*, June 14, 1916.
33. "Woman's Suffrage Certain to Come," *Richmond Times-Dispatch*, December 29, 1913, 10; M. M. A. Williams, "Open Letter Against Equal Suffrage Given Legislators," *Richmond Times-Dispatch*, September 2, 1913, 3; Brent Tarter et al., *The Campaign for Woman Suffrage in Virginia* (Charleston, SC: History Press, 2020), 121, 133.
34. "The Rev. Dr. Russell Bowie and the Famous Choir of St. Paul's Episcopal Church at Fifth St. M.E. Church," *Richmond Times-Dispatch*, May 26, 1921.

35. See Mark Ellis, *Race Harmony and Black Progress: Jack Woofter and the Interracial Cooperation Movement* (Bloomington: Indiana University Press, 2013).
36. Samuel C. Shepherd Jr., *Avenues of Faith: Shaping the Urban Religious Culture of Richmond, Virginia, 1900–1929* (Tuscaloosa: University of Alabama Press, 2001), 13–14.
37. Gustavus A. Weber, comp., *Report on Housing and Living Conditions in the Neglected Sections of Richmond, Virginia* (Richmond, VA: Whittet & Shepperson, 1913).
38. "Church and Saloon are Antagonistic," *Richmond Times-Dispatch*, July 6, 1914.
39. "Campaign for Hospital Indorsed by Merchants," *Richmond Times-Dispatch*, June 13, 1916; "Local Manufacturers Asked to Raise $50,000," *Richmond Times-Dispatch*, June 23, 1916; "Plans Are Approved for the Colored Hospital," *Richmond Planet*, October 7, 1916.
40. *Southern Churchman*, February 2, 1929.
41. *Journal of the 117th Annual Council of the Protestant Episcopal Church in the Diocese of Virginia* (n.p., 1912), 60–61.
42. Smith, *Managing White Supremacy*, 3–4.
43. Brooks, *The Uplift Generation*.
44. Smith, *Managing White Supremacy*, 46–49; Ellis, *Race Harmony and Black Progress*, 80–112.
45. Shepherd, *Avenues of Faith*, 225–26.
46. August Meier and Elliott Rudwick, "Negro Boycotts of Segregated Streetcars in Virginia, 1904–1907," *Virginia Magazine of History and Biography* 81, no. 4 (October 1973): 479–87.
47. "Need for More Room," *Richmond Times-Dispatch*, January 26, 1912.
48. "Council Votes to Separate Races," *Richmond Times-Dispatch*, March 7, 1911.
49. "Council May Block Use of Church by Negroes," *Richmond Times-Dispatch*, October 5, 1914; "Aldermen Concur in Effort to Block Sale," *Richmond Times-Dispatch*, October 7, 1914; "Congregation Opposed to Sale of Immanuel," *Richmond Times-Dispatch*, October 13, 1914; "Books of Church Opened by Order of Judge Scott," *Richmond Times-Dispatch*, October 18, 1914. Eventually, the Immanuel trustees succeeded in making the sale. "Deed Transfers Church to Negro Congregation," *Richmond Times-Dispatch*, February 23, 1915.
50. "Mayor to Pass on Measure Today," *Richmond Times-Dispatch*, April 19, 1911.
51. "Segregation Law Attacked in Court," *Richmond Times-Dispatch*, May 26, 1915; "Segregation Case is Dismissed from Docket," *Richmond Times-Dispatch*, December 14, 1917. For the impact of the *Warley* decision on the national level, see Richard Rothstein, *The Color of Law: A Forgotten History of How Our Government Segregated America* (New York: Liveright, 2017).
52. "Hold Funeral Services Today of Carrington," *Richmond Times-Dispatch*, January 26, 1933.
53. "Fact-Finding Body is Sought By Negroes As to Segregation," *Richmond Times-Dispatch*, January 14, 1929; "Action Delayed Again on Plan of Segregation," *Richmond Times-Dispatch*, January 15, 1929.
54. "Tucker Urges Better Streets Sewers, New Suburban Districts," *Richmond News-Leader*, January 28, 1929.

55. "Fact-Finding Body is Sought by Negroes as to Segregation," *Richmond Times-Dispatch*, January 14, 1929; "Action Delayed Again on Plan of Segregation," *Richmond Times-Dispatch*, January 15, 1929.
56. "'Ku Klux' Menace Peace of South Dr. Bowie Charges," *Richmond Times-Dispatch*, December 6, 1920; "Let It Prove Its Americanism," *Richmond Times-Dispatch*, December 7, 1920; "Bowie Would Stop Ku Kluxers from Parading Streets," *Richmond Times-Dispatch*, September 19, 1921; "Dr. Bowie Charges Ku Klux Klan is Menace to Peace of the South," *Richmond Planet*, December 11, 1920. *Fisk University News* 11, no. 5 (February 1921): 27–28. Mary-Cooke Munford was on the Fisk board of trustees and likely forwarded Bowie's sermon.
57. "Fight Over Klan at Old St. Paul's," *Richmond Times-Dispatch*, September 22, 1924. See also the *Southern Churchman* editorial, "The Poison of Mob Lawlessness," likely written by Bowie, July 30, 1921.
58. "Many Changes in the Church Music of Richmond this Season," *Times*, September 15, 1901, 16; "St. Paul's Church Honors Memory of Jacob Reinhardt," *Times*, November 20, 1921, 23; "Anglo-Saxon Club Starts National Organization," *Richmond Times-Dispatch*, October 24, 1923, 4.
59. Smith, *Managing White Supremacy*, 76–129.
60. Brendan Wolfe, "Racial Integrity Laws (1924–1930)," *Encyclopedia Virginia*, Virginia Foundation for the Humanities, https://encyclopediavirginia.org/entries/racial-integrity-laws-1924-1930/, accessed May 9, 2018.
61. "Anglo-Saxon Club May Take Appeal in Sorrells Case," *Richmond Times-Dispatch*, December 10, 1924.
62. "Noted Citizens Sign for Racial Integrity Bill," *Richmond Times-Dispatch*, March 5, 1925; "Anglo-Saxon Club Starts National Organization," *Richmond Times-Dispatch*, October 24, 1923, 4.
63. John Powell to Mrs. B. B. Munford, March 5, 1926, Papers of John Powell, Special Collections, University of Virginia Library, Charlottesville, VA.
64. Richard B. Sherman, "The 'Teachings at Hampton Institute': Social Equality, Racial Integrity, and the Virginia Public Assemblage Act of 1926," *Virginia Magazine of History and Biography* 95, no. 3 (July 1987): 275–300.
65. "Race Separation Advocates Win," *Richmond Times-Dispatch*, January 27, 1926.
66. Gordon Blaine Hancock, "'Good Will'" (May 16, 1931); "Interracial Committees" (April 29, 1933); "Wence?" (October 14, 1933); "Another Conference" (May 26, 1934); "The Interracial Luncheon" (June 23, 1934); "Interracialism" (April 10, 1937); "Religion Fails" (December 4, 1937), *Norfolk Journal and Guide*.
67. "Graham Hails 'New South' at Racial Meeting," *Richmond Times-Dispatch*, December 9, 1931. Smith, *Managing White Supremacy*, 136–37.
68. "Report of the Tenth Annual Meeting, Virginia Commission on Interracial Cooperation, St. Paul's Parish House, Richmond, April 30, 1930," Adele Goodman Clark Papers, 1849–1978, Special Collections and Archives, James Branch Cabell Library, Virginia Commonwealth University, Richmond, VA.
69. "Better Racial Feeling Urged at Big Meeting," *Richmond Times-Dispatch*, January 23, 1934; "Negro in State to Be Topic at Session Here," *Richmond Times-Dispatch*, January 23, 1934. See also *Parish Register*, 1934.

180 | NOTES TO PAGES 89–94

70. "Rabbi Mendoza Will Address Racial Group," *Richmond Times-Dispatch*, April 23, 1933.
71. *Richmond Times-Dispatch*, February 11, 1929, 9; "1,000 Present for Talks on Racial Question," *Richmond Times-Dispatch*, February 9, 1931, 9.
72. *Richmond Planet*, November 15, 1930.
73. Plans for Moton as speaker were made for the 1929 annual conference, but because he couldn't make it, the meeting was actually held in 1930. St. Paul's Vestry Book, October 29, 1929, January 13, 1930, St. Paul's Church (Richmond, VA) Records, 1828–1963; Virginia Museum of History & Culture, Richmond, VA; *Parish Register*, Fall 1930; "Negro Leader Says Race Well Treated in U.S.," *Richmond Times-Dispatch*, October 29, 1930.
74. Benjamin Brawley, *A Social History of the American Negro* (New York: Macmillan, 1921), 263; Carter G. Woodson, "Finding A New Way for Cooperation," *Negro History Bulletin* 1, no. 7 (April 1938): 1.
75. "U. of Virginia to Bar Colored Ex-Smith Girl," *Chicago Tribune*, September 20, 1935, 14; "U.VA. Board of Visitors Directs That Negro Girl Be Refused Admittance," *Staunton News-Leader*, September 20, 1935, 1
76. *Parish Register*, Pre-Lent, 1939.
77. *Fourteenth Annual State-Wide Conference, Virginia Commission on Interracial Co-operation, April 24, 1933, Richmond, Virginia, St. Paul's Episcopal Church*, Adele Goodman Clark Papers, 1849–1978, Special Collections and Archives, James Branch Cabell Library, Virginia Commonwealth University, Richmond, VA.
78. "Dean Houston Tells Problem Faced by Negro," *Richmond Times-Dispatch*, January 30, 1934.
79. Smith, *Managing White Supremacy*, 136–39.
80. Smith, *Managing White Supremacy*, 241. Brooks, *The Uplift Generation*, 177.
81. J. Douglas Smith, "'The Ordeal of Virginius Dabney': A Southern Liberal, the Southern Regional Council, and the Limits of Managed Race Relations," paper delivered at the Southern Regional Council & the Civil Rights Movement Conference, University of Florida, October 2003.
82. "Hackett Soon to Issue FHA Plan for City," *Richmond Times-Dispatch*, August 19, 1934; "Slum Project to Take Time, Mayor Warns," *Richmond Times-Dispatch*, October 14, 1934; "PWA to Seek 12 Billion on 5-Year Plans," *Richmond Times-Dispatch*, October 31, 1934; "City Slum Project Planned by PWA, Fear Speculation," *Richmond Times-Dispatch*, November 24, 1934; "Negro Housing Project Up To Mayor's Group," *Richmond Times-Dispatch*, June 19, 1935.
83. "Property Owners Halt Slum Project," *Richmond Times-Dispatch*, August 11, 1935; "Negro Housing Decision Due by U.S. Soon," *Richmond Times-Dispatch*, August 28, 1935.

4. St. Paul's in Reaction

1. "Sacred Shrine of the Confederacy Rounding Out Century of Life," *Richmond Times-Dispatch*, March 3, 1943.
2. See, for instance, *Richmond Times-Dispatch*, April 16, 1960.

3. See, for instance, "Rev. D.B. Cordes Joins St. Paul's," *Richmond Times-Dispatch*, April 2, 1948.
4. *Parish Register*, 1951.
5. Vincent Chesley Franks, *Our Great Triumvirate: A sermon preached at St. Paul's Episcopal Church, Richmond, Virginia, January 16, 1944* (Richmond, VA: n.p., 1944).
6. Vincent Chesley Franks, *Noblesse Oblige! An Encomium to General Robert E. Lee Preached at St. Paul's Episcopal Church, Richmond, Virginia, January 20, 1946* (Richmond, VA: n.p., 1946).
7. Bishop Robert R. Brown, *"And One Was a Soldier": The Spiritual Pilgrimage of Robert E. Lee* (Shippensburg, PA: White Mane Books, 1998).
8. Arthur P. Davis, "With a Grain of Salt: Times Change—Even in Virginia," *New Journal and Guide*, June 30, 1945.
9. "Who Has God's Word on Integration?" *Staunton News-Leader*, December 18, 1955.
10. "Mr. Davis and St. Paul's," *Richmond Dispatch*, April 17, 1898. "Hospital Richmond," *Richmond Times-Dispatch*, December 7, 1942, 12; "The Service Center at Old St. Paul's," *Richmond Times-Dispatch*, July 23, 1956, 11.
11. *Parish Register* for Lent, 1948, 1951, and 1952.
12. "Bids Extended to Assemblymen," *Richmond Times-Dispatch*, January 17, 1950, 2; "R. E. Lee Committee Will Meet Tomorrow," *Richmond Times-Dispatch*, January 7, 1960.
13. "Capital Ceremony Will Dedicate Bust of Jefferson Davis Today," *Richmond Times-Dispatch*, June 25, 1952.
14. *Parish Register*, 1958.
15. "UDC Delegates Arrive in City for Convention," *Richmond Times-Dispatch*, November 12, 1950; "Jefferson Davis Birthday Will Be Observed Here Today," *Richmond Times-Dispatch*, June 3, 1943; "Local UDC will honor Davis' Birthday," *Richmond Times-Dispatch*, June 6, 1945; "Jefferson Davis' Birthday will be Observed Here Monday," *Richmond Times-Dispatch*, June 2, 1946; "UDC Chapter Plans Service to Honor Davis," *Richmond Times-Dispatch*, May 28, 1952; "UDC Members Look to Past and Future," *Richmond Times-Dispatch*, November 12, 1962.
16. "Blues Prepare to Celebrate Birthday," *Richmond Times-Dispatch*, May 2, 1948; "Richmond Blues Wind Up 163rd Anniversary Rites," *Richmond Times-Dispatch*, May 11, 1952; "Blues Parade," *Richmond Times-Dispatch*, May 8, 1961, 2.
17. "President Given Warm Welcome on Visit to City," *Richmond Times-Dispatch*, May 10, 1954. The visit had been arranged by St. Paul's junior warden, Major General William Tompkins, a United States Military Academy classmate of Eisenhower's. "Eisenhower to Attend Church Here," *Richmond Times-Dispatch*, March 3, 1954.
18. Letter, Rev. Robert Brown to Dwight D. Eisenhower, February 16, 1954, St. Paul's Church Papers St. Paul's Church (Richmond, VA) Records, 1828–1963, Virginia Museum of History & Culture, Richmond, VA.
19. Robert J. Cook, *Troubled Commemoration: The American Civil War Centennial, 1961–1965* (Baton Rouge: Louisiana State University Press, 2011).
20. "Ceremony Marks Start of Visitor Center," *Richmond Times-Dispatch*, October 15, 1960.

21. "Ceremony Marks Start of Visitor Center"; "Walking Tour Slated of Civil War Sites," *Richmond Times-Dispatch*, March 26, 1962.
22. St. Paul's Vestry Book, June 5, 1916, 120, St. Paul's Church (Richmond, VA) Records, 1828–1963, Virginia Museum of History & Culture, Richmond, VA; *Parish Register*, Summer, 1930.
23. *Parish Report*, 1967, 11.
24. *Parish Register*, 1951.
25. St. Paul's Vestry Book, January 8, 1950, St. Paul's Church (Richmond, VA) Records, 1828–1963, Virginia Museum of History & Culture, Richmond, VA.
26. Hunter "Mac" McGuire, interview by Geoffrey Switz and Christopher Graham, Richmond, VA, May 5, 2017.
27. "Sailor's Action At St. Paul's Laid to Drink," *Richmond Times-Dispatch*, May 6, 1948; Anne Hobson Freeman, "Lee," *Commonwealth Magazine*, January 1979.
28. John M. Coski, *The Confederate Battle Flag: America's Most Embattled Emblem* (Cambridge, MA: Belknap, 2006), 98–109.
29. Kevin M. Schultz, *Tri-Faith America: How Catholics and Jews Held Postwar America to its Protestant Promise* (New York: Oxford University Press, 2011), 52–53.
30. Mary L. Dudziak, *Cold War Civil Rights: Race and the Image of American Democracy* (Princeton, NJ: Princeton University Press, 2011).
31. Shattuck, *Episcopalians and Race*, 93.
32. Shattuck, *Episcopalians and Race*, 89. The quote is Shattuck's.
33. Schultz, *Tri-Faith America*, 180–83.
34. Shattuck, *Episcopalians and Race*, 93–94.
35. Turner Arrington to The Rt. Rev. F. D. Godwin, D.D., January 17, 1956. Copy of letter in possession of St. Paul's Episcopal Church.
36. John T. Kneebone, "George MacLaren Brydon (1875–1963)," *Dictionary of Virginia Biography*, Library of Virginia, https://www.lva.virginia.gov/public/dvb/bio.asp?b=Brydon_George_MacLaren, accessed May 27, 2019.
37. "Voice of the People," *Richmond Times-Dispatch*, November 8, 1957.
38. "Voice of the People," *Richmond Times-Dispatch*, February 2, 1957; "Voice of the People," *Richmond Times-Dispatch*, March 17, 1957; "Voice of the People," *Richmond Times-Dispatch*, April 7, 1957.
39. Turner Arrington to The Rt. Rev. F. D. Godwin, D.D., January 17, 1956. Copy of letter in possession of St. Paul's Episcopal Church, Richmond, VA.
40. Richmond City Planning Commission, *A Master Plan for the Physical Development of the City* (Richmond, VA: City Planning Commission, 1946), 110, 112, 115.
41. "Bright Rises to Disagree with Strauss: Slum Clearance is Debated Here," *Richmond Times-Dispatch*, April 25, 1939, 3.
42. "Gilpin Court Dedication Set for 5 P.M.," *Richmond Times-Dispatch*, April 28, 1943, 8; Julian Maxwell Hayter, *The Dream is Lost: Voting Rights and the Politics of Race in Richmond, Virginia* (Lexington: University Press of Kentucky, 2017), 52–53.
43. "T. C. Boushall to Lead Talks on Education," *Richmond Times-Dispatch*, November 27, 1946.

44. "Readiness for Postwar Boom in Construction is Stressed at Housing Leaders' Meeting," *Richmond Times-Dispatch*, February 24, 1943.
45. "Richmond's Proposed Housing Faces Hurdles Before Approval," *Richmond Times-Dispatch*, September 25, 1949, 1; "Housing Body Noncommittal on U.S. Loan," *Richmond Times-Dispatch*, November 27, 1949, 1; "Slum Work is Endorsed by Council," *Richmond Times-Dispatch*, February 28, 1950, 1; "Study Due This Week on Housing Ordinance," *Richmond Times-Dispatch*, October 1, 1950, 1. Historian Julian Hayter notes that "in clearing so-called slums, local authorities not only honored segregation patterns by relocating blacks to segregated public housing but also often razed areas that segregationist leadership had done the bare minimum to maintain in the first place." Hayter, *The Dream Is Lost*, 52.
46. "Highway Department Approves Expressway Plan but Opponents Protest Strongly to Councilman," *Richmond Times-Dispatch*, May 22, 1951; "Expressway Referendum Is Scheduled November 6," *Richmond Times-Dispatch*, October 2, 1951.
47. "Four Incumbents Elected Here to Council as Five Newcomers in Richmond Politics Win Seats," *Richmond Times-Dispatch*, June 11, 1952; "Anderson Invites Property-Owner Plan for Pike Job," *Richmond Times-Dispatch*, December 31, 1952; "'Tentative' Toll Route Plan Given Councilmen," *Richmond Times-Dispatch*, January 8, 1953; "Toll Road Through City to Point South of Petersburg Advocated," *Richmond Times-Dispatch*, July 21, 1953; "Expressway Committee Keeps Silent," *Richmond Times-Dispatch*, January 14, 1953.
48. "Toll Road Authority Endorsed: City Route Is Strongly Supported," *Richmond Times-Dispatch*, July 29, 1953; "Toll Road Idea Backed By Legislator's Group," *Richmond Times-Dispatch*, August 13, 1953; "City Council Votes 7 to 1 For Toll Road Authority," *Richmond Times-Dispatch*, January 7, 1954.
49. "Route Is Fixed For Intercity Superhighway," *Richmond Times-Dispatch*, August 2, 1955; "New Problems On Pike Route Face Authority," *Richmond Times-Dispatch*, August 3, 1955; "New Group Begins Task of Relocating Families Toll Road Will Displace," *Richmond Times-Dispatch*, August 25, 1955; "City Studies Joint Federal, Private Plan for Slum Clearance and Rehabilitation," *Richmond Times-Dispatch*, February 20, 1955; "Pike Will Change Many of Richmond's Old Traffic Patterns," *Richmond Times-Dispatch*, August 7, 1955; "Carver Slum Clearing Project Squeaks By in Council, 5 to 4," *Richmond Times-Dispatch*, October 25, 1955; "New Housing Units Made Two Projects," *Richmond Times-Dispatch*, January 12, 1956; "Fairfield Court Low Bid Given," *Richmond Times-Dispatch*, May 10, 1957. See also Harry Kollatz Jr., "The Distressway," *Richmond Magazine* (December 2016), 36, 37.
50. Mary Wingfield Scott, *Old Richmond Neighborhoods* (Richmond, VA: Whittet & Shepperson, 1950), 301; Mary Wingfield Scott, *Houses of Old Richmond* (Richmond, VA: Valentine Museum, 1941); "Old Neighborhoods of Richmond: A Wig-Maker and His 'Garden,'" *Richmond Times-Dispatch*, November 1, 1952, 53.
51. On the NAACP campaign, see Marvin T. Chiles, "'A Period of Misunderstanding': Reforming Jim Crow in Richmond, Virginia, 1930–1954," *Virginia Magazine of History and Biography* 129, no. 3 (2021): 244–79; Margaret Edds, *We Face the Dawn:*

Oliver Hill, Spottswood Robinson, and the Legal Team that Dismantled Jim Crow (Charlottesville: University of Virginia Press, 2018).

52. "Lancaster Sees Need for Negro School Busses," *Richmond Times-Dispatch*, May 21, 1942.
53. "Gap in Pay of Teachers Being Closed in South," *Richmond Times-Dispatch*, October 17, 1943.
54. "Schools Will 'Collapse' if Integrated at Once, Virginians Tell Court," *Richmond Times-Dispatch*, April 10, 1955.
55. "Continued Segregation Declared as State Policy," *Richmond Times-Dispatch*, June 24, 1955.
56. Buford Scott (1896–1973) is the son of Frederic W. Scott, mentioned earlier as the Rector of the Board of Visitors at the University of Virginia deciding against admitting Black students in 1935. In this book, he is distinguished from his son Sidney Buford Scott (1933–2019), commonly known as Buford but to be differentiated in subsequent pages as "S. Buford Scott."
57. "Historic 1954 Court Decision Echoes Still in State's Life," *Richmond Times-Dispatch*, May 18, 1969; "Supporters of Gray Plan Encouraged by Reports," *Richmond Times-Dispatch*, January 1, 1956; "Prompt Call of Assembly Advocated," *Richmond Times-Dispatch*, July 15, 1956.
58. Matthew D. Lassiter and Andrew B. Lewis, "Massive Resistance Revisited: Virginia's White Moderates and the Byrd Organization," in Matthew D. Lassiter and Andrew B. Lewis, eds., *The Moderates' Dilemma: Massive Resistance to School Desegregation in Virginia* (Charlottesville: University of Virginia Press, 1998), 6–8.
59. "Local Group Hits Stanley School Plan," *Richmond Times-Dispatch*, September 12, 1956.
60. "Boushall is Opposed for Education Post," *Richmond Times-Dispatch*, May 6, 1958; "South Norfolk Man Gets Boushall Education Post," *Richmond Times-Dispatch*, May 14, 1958.
61. Anne Hobson Freeman, interview by Christopher Graham, Richmond, VA, April 25, 2017.
62. "Lancaster Stresses Need for Schools," *Richmond Times-Dispatch*, September 1, 1959.
63. "Baptists Will Lead Session at St. Paul's Parish House," *Richmond Times-Dispatch*, December 5, 1943.
64. Virginia Council of Churches, https://vacouncilofchurches.org/about-vcc/history/, accessed June 10, 2019.
65. "Miller Declares Fellowship Barred by 'Iron Curtain' Minds," *Richmond Times-Dispatch*, December 13, 1948, St. Paul's Vestry Book, February 14, 1949, St. Paul's Church (Richmond, VA) Records, 1828–1963, Virginia Museum of History & Culture, Richmond, VA.
66. St. Paul's Vestry Book, October 9, 1950, St. Paul's Church (Richmond, VA) Records, 1828–1963, Virginia Museum of History & Culture, Richmond, VA.
67. "Four Supreme Court Justices Deny Waller Stay of Execution," *Richmond Times-Dispatch*, June 28, 1942. The failed campaign for clemency attracted high-profile

supporters including First Lady Eleanor Roosevelt and H. St. George Tucker, the Episcopal Church's Presiding Bishop and Bishop of Virginia.
68. "2 Policemen Found Guilt in Rape Case," *Richmond Times-Dispatch*, January 18, 1947; "Judge Upholds Jury Verdict Against Davis," *Richmond Times-Dispatch*, March 22, 1947.
69. "Segregation Held Matter For Assembly," *Richmond Times-Dispatch*, February 18, 1954.
70. Social Service Committee minute book, St. Paul's Church (Richmond, VA)
71. St. Paul's Vestry Book, May 12, 1941, December 14, 1942, and April 9, 1945, St. Paul's Church (Richmond, VA) Records, 1828–1963, Virginia Museum of History & Culture, Richmond, VA.
72. St. Paul's Vestry Book, April 13, 1953, St. Paul's Church (Richmond, VA) Records, 1828–1963, Virginia Museum of History & Culture, Richmond, VA.
73. *Parish Register*, 1951.
74. Douglas E. Thompson, *Richmond's Priests and Prophets: Race, Religion, and Social Change in the Civil Rights Era* (Tuscaloosa: University of Alabama Press, 2017), 33–34.
75. Thompson, *Richmond's Priests and Prophets*, 33–34.
76. "Ministers Rap State's Move in Race Issue," *Richmond Times-Dispatch*, January 29, 1957.
77. St. Paul's Vestry Book, February 11, 1957, St. Paul's Church (Richmond, VA) Records, 1828–1963, Virginia Museum of History & Culture, Richmond, VA.
78. "152 in Survey Favor RMA's Stand on Race," *Richmond Times-Dispatch*, February 4, 1957.
79. "Dr. Franks Cites Responsibilities of Christians Here," *Richmond Times-Dispatch*, March 5, 1953.
80. St. Paul's Vestry Book, November 14, 1949, St. Paul's Church (Richmond, VA) Records, 1828–1963, Virginia Museum of History & Culture, Richmond, VA.
81. St. Paul's Vestry Book, November 14, 1949, St. Paul's Church (Richmond, VA) Records, 1828–1963, Virginia Museum of History & Culture, Richmond, VA.
82. St. Paul's Vestry Book, March 12, 1951, St. Paul's Church (Richmond, VA) Records, 1828–1963, Virginia Museum of History & Culture, Richmond, VA.
83. Edward L. Bond and Joan R. Gunderson, "The Episcopal Church in Virginia, 1607–2007," *Virginia Magazine of History and Biography*, 115, no. 2 (2007): 310; "Episcopalians Vote to End Segregation," *Richmond Times-Dispatch*, May 21, 1949.
84. "Church Asks Interracial Commission," *Richmond Times-Dispatch*, May 21, 1954.
85. "Diocesan Stand Challenged," *Richmond Times-Dispatch*, July 10, 1958.
86. Undated resolution, St. Paul's Archives.
87. Bond and Gunderson, "The Episcopal Church in Virginia, 1607–2007," 314–315, "Diocesan Stand Challenged," *Richmond Times-Dispatch*, January 29, 1959; "Bishop Proposes Racial Study Group," *Richmond Times-Dispatch*, January 29, 1959.
88. Mary Tyler Cheek, "A Brief Statement on the Supreme Court Decision," Racial Study Commission papers, ca. 1959, p. 3. Mary Tyler Freeman Cheek McClenahan

Papers, Special Collections and Archives, James Branch Cabell Library, Virginia Commonwealth University, Richmond, VA.

89. Eppa Hunton IV, Racial Study Commission papers, ca. 1959, Mary Tyler Freeman Cheek McClenahan Papers, Special Collections and Archives, James Branch Cabell Library, Virginia Commonwealth University, Richmond, VA. Raymond Brown later found himself at the center of the integration crisis at Little Rock's Central High School in 1957. See Elizabeth Jacoway, *Turn Away Thy Son: Little Rock, The Crisis that Shocked the Nation* (New York: Free Press, 2007), 195–213.

90. *The Race Problem and the Church: The Report of the Racial Study Commission of the Diocese of Virginia* (Richmond, VA: Protestant Episcopal Church in the Diocese of Virginia, 1960); "Race Policy Offered for Episcopal Group," *Richmond Times-Dispatch*, January 28, 1960.

91. "St. Catherine's Places Negro on Waiting List," *Richmond Times-Dispatch*, May 28, 1963; Marcellus Wright Jr., to Robert L. Gordon Jr., June 21, 1963; Mrs. Leslie Cheek Jr., to The Rt. Rev. R. F. Gibson, D.D., April 14, 1964, both in Mary Tyler Freeman Cheek McClanahan Papers, Special Collections and Archives, James Branch Cabell Library, Virginia Commonwealth University, Richmond, VA.

92. "Robert E. Lee Racial Story Is Called 'Myth,'" *Richmond Times-Dispatch*, October 23, 1949, 2; Virginius Dabney, "Lee and the Lee-gends," *Richmond Times-Dispatch*, December 30, 1966, p. 16.

93. Benjamin Muse, "Clergymen Taunted for Upholding Law," *Washington Post*, December 5, 1954, B2, Isidor F. Stone, "A Story about General Robert E. Lee with a Moral for Today's South," *I. F. Stone's Weekly*, March 26, 1956, 4, Billy Graham, "Billy Graham Makes Plea for an End to Intolerance," *Life*, October 1, 1956, 138–15; Billy Graham, "Why Don't Our Churches Practice the Brotherhood They Preach?" *Reader's Digest*, August 1960, 52–54, Ralph McGill, "Lee's Example to Bigots," *Evening Sun* (Baltimore), December 5. 1963, 47.

94. Shattuck, *Episcopalians and Race*, 87–107; "Our Neo-Abolitionists," *Richmond Times-Dispatch*, January 2, 1960.

95. Hayter, *The Dream is Lost*, 19–62, 70–71, "Abolition of State Poll Tax Urged to Reinforce Vote Act," *Richmond Times-Dispatch*, January 26, 1966.

96. Harry Kollatz Jr., "Irreconcilable Differences," *Richmond Magazine*, November 19, 2012.

97. Hayter, *The Dream is Lost*, 61; "Group Set Up Here to Seek New Council," *Richmond Times-Dispatch*, November 13, 1963.

98. "White Group Backs Reid's Candidacy," *Richmond Times-Dispatch*, July 10, 1965.

99. Anne Hobson Freeman, interview by Christopher Graham, Richmond, VA, April 25, 2017.

100. "Racial Balance Held Key Issue in Annexation," *Richmond Times-Dispatch*, February 17, 1969. See also Hayter, *The Dream is Lost*, 95–96.

101. "Chesterfield Annexation Order," *Richmond Times-Dispatch*, December 20, 1969.

102. Benjamin Campbell, *Richmond's Unhealed History* (Richmond, VA: Brandylane, 2012), 162–67. For a detailed study of the lawsuit and subsequent election, see

John V. Moeser and Rutledge M. Dennis, *The Politics of Annexation: Oligarchic Power in a Southern City* (Cambridge, MA: Schenkman, 1982).
103. Black Economic Development Conference, "Black Manifesto," *The Church Awakens: African Americans and the Struggle for Justice,* https://episcopalarchives.org/church-awakens/items/show/202/, accessed December 27, 2020.
104. Shattuck, *Episcopalians and Race,* 178–213.
105. Bowie, *Learning to Live,* 254, 256.
106. Bowie, *Learning to Live,* 260–61; "'Tone' of Editorial Page on Race Issue Criticized," *Richmond Times-Dispatch,* January 4, 1957, 12.
107. Bowie, *Learning to Live,* 259–60.

5. Effective Witness

1. Shelley Rolfe, "Clergy in Area Will Consider Negro Demand," *Richmond Times-Dispatch,* May 27, 1969; Shelley Rolfe, "Demand is Repeated for 'Reparations,'" *Richmond Times-Dispatch,* May 29, 1969; Bob Brickhouse, "Clergymen to Study Needs of Negroes," *Richmond Times-Dispatch,* June 3, 1969; Web DeHoff, Jr., "Area Clergy Readying Reply to Negro Demands," *Richmond Times-Dispatch,* June 6, 1969; Shelley Rolfe, "Clergy Group Accepts Reports on Negro Needs," *Richmond Times-Dispatch,* June 24, 1964.
2. Walter Russell Bowie, *Learning to Live: An Autobiography* (New York: Abingdon, 1969), 261.
3. John S. Spong, "A Statement on THE BLACK MANIFESTO," delivered at St. John's Church, Lynchburg, VA, June 1, 1969, Mary Tyler Freeman Cheek McClenahan Papers, 1930–1999, Special Collections and Archives, James Branch Cabell Library, Virginia Commonwealth University, Richmond, VA.
4. Jason Sokol, *There Goes My Everything: White Southerners in the Age of Civil Rights, 1945–1975* (New York: Alfred A. Knopf, 2006).
5. Spong, "A Statement on THE BLACK MANIFESTO."
6. John Shelby Spong, *Here I Stand: My Struggle for A Christianity of Integrity, Love & Equality* (New York: HarperCollins, 2000), 103–8, 179–80. See also St. Paul's Vestry Book, December 15, 1969, 192.
7. "A Message to All Episcopalians," *Richmond Times-Dispatch,* October 22, 1969, A7. The St. Paul's signatories included individuals that Spong later remembered as a political spectrum from "liberal" to "John Bircher." John Shelby Spong, interview by Elizabeth O'Leary and Christopher Graham, Richmond, VA, April 30, 2019.
8. Spong, *Here I Stand,* 173.
9. "Four Churches Will Sponsor Forum Series," *Richmond Times-Dispatch,* October 4, 1968. See also *Parish Report,* 1968.
10. *Parish Report,* 1970, 1973, and 1976.
11. *Parish Report,* 1970. In late 1970, the Benevolent Fund donated $250 to the restoration of Coburn Hall at Virginia Union University. St. Paul's Vestry Book, June 15, 1970, 217–19.

12. St. Paul's Vestry Book, February 8, 1928; Judge Brockenbrough Lamb, Chancery Court opinion, February 26, 1959; *Parish Report*, 1980.
13. *Parish Report*, 1970, 1973, and 1976.
14. The cover of the 1969 *Parish Report* pictures a Black and White child together in the Oral School.
15. John Shelby Spong, "Be Witnesses in Jerusalem, Samaria, and the World," June 4, 1972, Hobson Family Papers, Sally Archer Anderson Hobson, Virginia Museum of History & Culture, Richmond, VA.
16. St. Paul's Vestry Book, March 16, 1970, 205, 207–8; April 20, 1970, 209–10.
17. Spong, *Here I Stand*, 184–85, 188–89.
18. St. Paul's Vestry Book, January 11, 1971, 234.
19. St. Paul's Vestry Book, February 8, 1971, 237–39.
20. St. Paul's Vestry Book, May 17, 1972, June 19, 1972, October 9, 1972, and November 13, 1972. The Isaiah committee put the $3,000 balance into an exploratory visit to New York City to investigate strategies for the subsequent years' project. *Parish Report*, 1973.
21. St. Paul's Vestry Book, February 15, 1973; April 9, 1973; July 9, 1973; "St. Paul's Gives $50,000 for Street Academy Budget," *Richmond Times-Dispatch*, July 14, 1973.
22. St. Paul's Vestry Book, February 11, 1974.
23. St. Paul's Vestry Book, February 9, 1976; October 11, 1976.
24. *Parish Report*, 1978.
25. St. Paul's Vestry Book, February 12, 1979.
26. *Parish Report*, 1971–72.
27. St. Paul's Vestry Book, January 11, 1971, 234; February 14, 1972.
28. *Parish Report*, 1971; *Parish Report*, 1972. St. Paul's Vestry Book, April 19, 1971, 243, 245; May 17, 1971, 246, 247. The Peter Paul Center, now operating as an independent agency, remains a vibrant nonprofit providing children and youth in the East End and Church Hill with services and activities. See https://peterpauldevdenter.org/about-us/, accessed June 18, 2019.
29. St. Paul's Vestry Book, February 14, 1972.
30. St. Paul's Vestry Book, March 20, 1972; April 17, 1972; February 15, 1973; April 9, 1973.
31. "Our History," Housing Opportunities Made Equal of Virginia, Inc., https://homeofva.org/about-us/history/, accessed June 18, 2019.
32. HOME continues today as one of the leading fair housing organizations in the country. Spong, *Here I Stand*, 212–13. Patricia S. Morris, "Promises Kept: A Study in Organizational Evolution," 9–11, https://homeofva.org/wp-content/uploads/2019/01/HOME-HISTORY.pdf, accessed June 18, 2019.
33. *Parish Profile*, 1976, St. Paul's Episcopal Church.
34. John Shelby Spong 125th anniversary address, Hobson Family Papers, Sally Archer Anderson Hobson, Virginia Museum of History & Culture, Richmond, VA.
35. Lyons Burke, Susie Scott, S. Buford Scott, Mary Ann Ready, Rob Corcoran, and Susan Corcoran, interview by Elizabeth O'Leary and Christopher Graham, Richmond, VA, December 3, 2017.

36. Rev. Rodney Rice, phone interview by Elizabeth O'Leary, Richmond, VA, January 5, 2018.
37. Spong, *Here I Stand*, 174–81.
38. Adrian Luxmoore, Scott Sirles, Louisa Sirles, and Lee Switz, interview by Elizabeth O'Leary, Anne Hayes, and Christopher Graham, Richmond, VA, December 7, 2017
39. Adrian Luxmoore, Scott Sirles, Louisa Sirles, and Lee Switz, interview by Elizabeth O'Leary, Anne Hayes, and Christopher Graham, Richmond, VA, December 7, 2017
40. Adrian Luxmoore, Scott Sirles, Louisa Sirles, and Lee Switz, interview by Elizabeth O'Leary, Anne Hayes, and Christopher Graham, Richmond, VA, December 7, 2017
41. Lyons Burke, Susie Scott, S. Buford Scott, Mary Ann Ready, Rob Corcoran, and Susan Corcoran, interview by Elizabeth O'Leary and Christopher Graham, Richmond, VA, December 3, 2017.
42. The 1976 *Parish Profile* indicated that of the 1800 present members, "forty percent have joined the congregation in the last 7 years."
43. *Parish Profile*, 1976, 8, St. Paul's Episcopal Church.
44. St. Paul's called the first woman priest regularly ordained in the Diocese of Virginia, Patricia Merchant Park, as assistant rector in 1977.
45. "New Haven Rector Due at St. Paul's," *Richmond Times-Dispatch*, April 12, 1977; "Florida Meeting Brought Understanding, Bishop Says," *Richmond Times-Dispatch*, October 21, 1977, F1; "'Vast Possibilities' Are Seen at St. Paul's," *Richmond Times-Dispatch*, April 13, 1977.
46. Hayter, *The Dream is Lost*; 159–194; Bill Miller, "Richmond's Silent Decision Makers," *Richmond Times-Dispatch*, February 26, 1978, B1; Shelley Rolfe, "A New Crusade," *Richmond Times-Dispatch*, April 25, 1979, B1.
47. "Downtown Churches Join Hands," *Richmond Times-Dispatch*, October 28, 1978; St. Paul's Vestry Book, November 12, 1979; February 11, 1980; *Parish Report*, 1981, 13.
48. "St. Paul's Ecumenical Program Set," *Richmond Times-Dispatch*, January 29, 1979.
49. *Parish Report*, 1979.
50. *Parish Report*, 1980.
51. St. Paul's Vestry Book, November 10, 1980.
52. *Parish Report*, 1982.
53. Rev. Benjamin P. Campbell, communication with author, June 12, 2019.
54. *Parish Report*, 1981; *Parish Report*, 1982; *Parish Report*, 1983; *Parish Report*, 1984; *Parish Report*, 1985; *Parish Report*, 1986.
55. Semi-Annual Meeting, Verbal Report, B. P. Campbell, January 1981; Richmond Urban Institute Evaluation Feedback, ca. 1981; "Analysis," Minutes of the Council of the Richmond Urban Institute, June 30, 1982; Report of Retreat, October 16–17, 1982, in Richmond Urban Institute Archives, 1979–1986 (M 258), Special Collections and Archives, James Branch Cabell Library, Richmond, VA.
56. "Mixing Tentative for Many," *Richmond Times-Dispatch*, September 23, 1981, 1, 5.
57. Brooke Taylor, "Valentine Race Relations Exhibit to 'Generate Some Light . . . Heat,'" *Richmond Times-Dispatch*, February 2, 1986, H1.
58. *Parish Report*, 1982; "Vestiges of racism remain, psychologist says," *Richmond Times-Dispatch*, February 23, 1983.

59. Brandon Walters and Deveron Timberlake, "To the Manner Born," *Style Weekly*, November 5, 2003.
60. Mary Tyler Cheek McClenahan, "Eyes on Richmond," October 22, 1999; St. Paul's Vestry Book, September 21, 1993.
61. *Parish Report, 1982; Parish Report, 1984; Parish Report, 1986*; St. Paul's Vestry Book, January 21, 1986; September 19, 1989.
62. *Parish Report, 1982; Parish Report, 1983; Parish Report, 1984; Parish Report, 1985; Parish Report, 1986.*
63. Reverend Canon Robert Hetherington, interview by Elizabeth O'Leary and Christopher Graham, Richmond, VA, May 31, 2019.
64. St. Paul's Vestry Book, July 26, 1983. Biddle's resignation was unrelated to church outreach programming and budgets.
65. "A Parish Profile of St. Paul's Episcopal Church, Richmond, Virginia, June 1976," St. Paul's Church, Richmond, VA.
66. *The 188th Annual Council of the Protestant Episcopal Church in the Diocese of Virginia* (1983), 160–61.
67. *The 189th Annual Council of the Protestant Episcopal Church in the Diocese of Virginia* (1984), 145–46.
68. *The 191st Annual Council of the Protestant Episcopal Church in the Diocese of Virginia* (1986), 173–76.
69. *The 193rd Annual Council of the Protestant Episcopal Church in the Diocese of Virginia* (1988), 343.
70. General Convention, *Journal of the General Convention of... The Episcopal Church, Phoenix, 1991* (New York: General Convention, 1992), 249, 278, 301, 371, 382, 768, 844.
71. "House of Bishops Pastoral Letter on Sin of Racism," *Episcopal News Service*, April 21, 1994, 25–31.
72. Rob Corcoran, *Trustbuilding: An Honest Conversation on Race, Reconciliation, and Responsibility* (Charlottesville: University of Virginia Press, 2010), 193–195; Alberta Lindsey, "Thirty Years a Priest, Never in a Rut," *Richmond Times-Dispatch*, November 30, 1996.
73. "I'm for trying to work as hard as you can from the inside," said Hetherington. Thomas Mullen, "Private Club Membership Delicate Issue for Many Clergy," *Richmond Times-Dispatch*, February 22, 1991, 2.
74. Ed Briggs, "Pastors to Crusade Against Crime: Debate Stirs Long-Smoldering Racial Feelings," *Richmond Times-Dispatch*, September 28, 1991, B8; Thomas Mullen, "More Clergy Sought at Meeting," *Richmond Times-Dispatch*, October 8, 1991, 4; Ed Briggs, "Black, White Churches Unite in Crusade Against Area Crime," *Richmond Times-Dispatch*, November 2, 1991.
75. St. Paul's Vestry Book, April 28, 1992.
76. St. Paul's Vestry Book, May 18, 1993.
77. "Ruby Martin Dies at 70—Served in Wilder Cabinet," *Richmond Times-Dispatch*, May 9, 2003, B1.
78. Lyons Burke, Susie Scott, S. Buford Scott, Mary Ann Ready, Rob Corcoran, and

Susan Corcoran, interview by Elizabeth O'Leary and Christopher Graham, Richmond, VA, December 3, 2017.
79. Corcoran, *Trustbuilding*, 47–50, 52, 59–63; "Race Relations Dialogue Puts Focus on Women," *Richmond Times-Dispatch*, June 12, 1993, B3; Michael Paul Williams, "Unity Walk to Take Positive Steps," *Richmond Times-Dispatch*, June 14, 1993, B1.
80. Mike Allen, "Social Exclusion Is Topic At Class: Lawyer Contends Diversity at Work Not Seen at Play," *Richmond Times-Dispatch*, February 28, 1994, B1.
81. Carlos Santos, "Resigning Was Move For Peace at U.Va.," *Richmond Times-Dispatch*, March 23, 1994, B1.
82. Gordon Hickey, "Historic Problem Seen in Historical Panel Discussion," *Richmond Times-Dispatch*, September 20, 1997, B6.
83. St. Paul's Vestry Book, October 17, 1995.
84. St. Paul's Vestry Book, November 12, 1995.
85. St. Paul's Vestry Book, October 15, 1996; February 18, 1997.
86. *Parish Report*, 1997–98.
87. St. Paul's Vestry Book, February 18, 1997.
88. St. Paul's Vestry Book, December 16, 1997.
89. Memorandum, *St. Paul's Case Study*; St. Paul's Vestry Book, December 15, 1998.
90. See, for instance, *Richmond Times-Dispatch*, February 7, 1978.
91. Ed Briggs, "Choosing a Church: Comfort Counts," *Richmond Times-Dispatch*, May 30, 1986, A1.
92. *Parish Report*, 1994–95.
93. *Parish Report*, 1998–99.
94. *Parish Report*, 2000–2001.
95. St. Paul's Vestry Book, December 17, 2002. See also Mary Kay Huss, interview by Christopher Graham, Richmond, VA, May 6, 2019.
96. Liz Whitehurst, "History: Micah Ministry," unpublished paper, St. Paul's Episcopal Church; Lyons Burke, Susie Scott, S. Buford Scott, Mary Ann Ready, Rob Corcoran, and Susan Corcoran, interview by Elizabeth O'Leary and Christopher Graham, Richmond, VA, December 3, 2017.
97. St. Paul's Vestry Book, June 16, 1998; Alberta Lindsey, "Church to Start Micah Initiative," *Richmond Times-Dispatch*, November 14, 1998, B10; In addition to Martin and Carr, S. Buford Scott was instrumental in the founding of the Micah Initiative. The founding strategic team included parishioners Don Cowles, Nan Ellen Ritsch, David White, and Larry French. Liz Whitehurst, "History: Micah Ministry."
98. St. Paul's Vestry Book, July 16, 2002, April 2003, September 16, 2003, and October 21, 2003.
99. St. Paul's Vestry Book, October 21, 2003, December 16, 2003, and April 20, 2004. In addition to the recession, St. Paul's Endowment Fund had greater restrictions on the use of its revenue than it does at the present time, limiting its availability.
100. St. Paul's Vestry Book, October 19, 2004.
101. St. Paul's Episcopal Church Strategic Plan, St. Paul's Vestry Book, July 16, 2002.
102. St. Paul's Vestry Book, June 19, 2001.
103. St. Paul's Vestry Book, December 18, 2001.

104. St. Paul's Vestry Book, June 17, 2008, February 17, 2009, August 4, 2009, and September 15, 2009.
105. St. Paul's Vestry Book, December 18, 2012, February 13, 2013, January 23, 2015, March 18, 2014, September 9, 2014, November 18, 2014, December 16, 2014, and January 20, 2015.
106. Jason S. Lantzer, *Mainline Christianity: The Past and Future of America's Majority Faith* (New York: New York University Press, 2012), 49–119. *The 175th Annual Council of the Protestant Episcopal Church in the Diocese of Virginia* (1970) and *The 211th Annual Council of the Protestant Episcopal Church in the Diocese of Virginia* (2006).
107. St. Paul's Vestry Book, March 20, 2012; Kevin M. Levin, "Why Doesn't Anyone Think It's Cool to Dress Up Like a Confederate Soldier Anymore?" *The Atlantic*, February 28, 2018, https://www.theatlantic.com/national/archive/2012/02/why-doesnt-anyone-think-its-cool-to-dress-up-like-a-confederate-soldier-anymore/253716/, accessed June 19, 2019; Reverend Melanie Mullen, "Sermon, 9.27.20," YouTube video, 19:15, September 29, 2020, https://www.youtube.com/watch?v=HmmZlDx3pQ4.
108. St. Paul's Vestry Book, February 18, 2014, and March 18, 2014.
109. St. Paul's Vestry Book, April 20, 2010.
110. John M. Coski, *The Confederate Battle Flag: America's Most Embattled Emblem* (Cambridge, MA: Belknap, 2006), 184–291.
111. General Convention, *Journal of the General Convention of . . . The Episcopal Church, Columbus, 2006* (New York: General Convention, 2007), 665–66.
112. Nathan D. B. Connolly, *We Live Here*, podcast audio, September 22, 2017, https://news.stlpublicradio.org/podcast/we-live-here/2017-07-11/removing-confederate-monuments-why-now-and-whats-next/, accessed May 13, 2019.
113. Jemar Tisby, "What the Church Can Learn from Taking Down Confederate Monuments," *The Witness*, May 18, 2017, https://thewitnessbcc.com/what-the-church-can-learn-from-taking-down-confederate-monuments/, accessed June 1, 2019. Some public historians, sure that St. Paul's intended to remove its memorials, including windows, charged it with "Whitewashing not only our history but also of our collective memory." Ashley Luskey, "No Mere Morality Play: Why We Need Confederate Memorials Now More Than Ever," *History@Work*, September 29, 2015, https://ncph.org/history-at-work/ashley-luskey-civil-war-memory-post/, accessed June 1, 2019.
114. "St. Paul's Episcopal Church Congregational Conversations Summary Report and Raw Data," *Richmond Times-Dispatch*, November 24, 2015; "St. Paul's lives up to its name," *Richmond Times-Dispatch*, November 24, 2015, A8.

Epilogue: Our Sacred Obligation Now

1. St. Paul's Vestry resolution, November 10, 2015.
2. Elizabeth L. O'Leary, "'A Memorial to Those Who Made Her History': Material Acts of Remembrance at St. Paul's, 1845–2020," unpublished paper, 2020, St. Paul's archives.
3. The research has also produced Elizabeth L. O'Leary, "'A Memorial to Those Who

Made Her History': Material Acts of Remembrance at St. Pauls, 1845–2020'"; Anne S. Hayes, "Rediscovering the Past: Memorial Plaques at St. Paul's Church, 1887–2000," unpublished manuscript in author's possession; Anne S. Hayes, "The Lee Communion Story: A Monumental Myth Examined," all three unpublished manuscripts in St. Paul's archives.

4. The Memorials Committee began its work based on museum professional Gretchen Jennings's idea of "institutional body language." Gretchen Jennings, "The Empathetic Museum: Institutional Body Language," *Museum Commons*, June 29, 2013, https://museumcommons.com/2013/06/the-empathetic-museum-institutional.html, accessed November 1, 2020

5. The vestry accepted, but then tabled this dramatic decision during a new rector search.

6. *Traces of the Trade: A Story from the Deep North*, produced and directed by Katrina Browne, 2008.

7. St. Paul's Episcopal Church, "Bending Toward Truth: Presiding Bishop Michael Curry Speaks," YouTube video, 28:37, November 28, 2018, https://www.youtube.com/watch?v=TErcaBquwGw&t=1151s.

8. My thinking on the historical imagination is informed by Priya Satia, *Time's Monster: How History Makes History* (Cambridge, MA: Belknap, 2020).

9. Christopher A. Graham, "The Lost Cause Myth," in *The Inclusive Historian's Handbook*, American Association for State and Local History and National Council for Public History, May 12, 2020 (Accessed November 1, 2020), https://inclusivehistorian.com/lost-cause-myth/, Chris Graham, "Myths & Misunderstandings: Stonewall Jackson's Sunday School," *American Civil War Museum* blog, October 12, 2017, https://acwm.org/blog/myths-misunderstandings-stonewall-jacksons-sunday-school/, accessed November 1, 2020; Allen C. Guelzo, "Lee, Robert E., and Slavery," *Encyclopedia Virginia*, Virginia Humanities, February 13, 2019, https://www.encyclopediavirginia.org/lee-robert-e-and-slavery/, accessed November 1, 2020. So, too, is the Lee Communion story frequently employed by conservatives to deny historical racism. See for instance Jay Winik, "What John Kelly Got Right About Robert E. Lee," *Wall Street Journal*, November 3, 2017, https://www.wsj.com/articles/what-john-kelly-got-right-about-robert-e-lee-1509745645/, accessed July 5, 2020.

10. *Richmond Times-Dispatch*, June 6, 2020, and July 12, 2020.

11. Emily Guskin, Scott Clement, and Joe Heim, "Americans show spotty knowledge about the history of slavery but acknowledge its enduring effects," *Washington Post*, August 28, 2019.

12. Sam Wineburg, *Historical Thinking and Other Unnatural Acts: Charting the Future of Teaching the Past* (Philadelphia: Temple University Press, 2001), 3–27.

13. I distinguish between "history" and "the past" based on Roy Rosenzweig and David Thelen, *The Presence of the Past: Popular Uses of History in American Life* (New York: Columbia University Press, 2000)

14. Historian Priya Satia writes, "We have to take the ethical claims of historical actors seriously to understand how ordinary people acting in particular institutional and

cultural frameworks can, despite good intentions, author appalling chapters of human history." Satia, *Time's Monster*, 5.

15. Jennifer Harvey, *Dear White Christians: For Those Still Longing for Racial Reconciliation* (Grand Rapids, MI: Eerdmans, 2014); Austin Channing Brown, *I'm Still Here: Black Dignity in a World Made for Whiteness* (New York: Convergent, 2018), 165–74; Jemar Tisby, "Reconciliation and Justice, Are They Friends or Enemies?" Pass the Mic, podcast audio, December 16, 2019, https://podcasts.apple.com/us/podcast/reconciliation-and-justice-are-they-friends-or-enemies/id1435500798?i=1000459820066.

16. Bob Brown, "Downtown Richmond houses of worship vandalized during weekend destruction. Some will keep graffiti as a reminder," *Richmond Times-Dispatch*, June 1, 2020.

17. The Stations and the accompanying booklet can be viewed at https://www.stpaulsrva.org/stations-of-st-pauls/.

BIBLIOGRAPHY

Archival Sources

The Archives of the Episcopal Church
Acts of Convention
The Church Awakens: African Americans and the Struggle for Justice, http://episcopalarchives.org/church-awakens/

Library of Virginia, Archives Research Services, Richmond, VA
First African Baptist Church, Richmond, Minute Book, 1841–1859

St. Paul's Archives, Richmond, VA

Special Collections and Archives, James Branch Cabell Library, Virginia Commonwealth University, Richmond, VA
Adele Goodman Clark Papers, 1849–1978
Mary Tyler Freeman Cheek McClenahan Papers
Richmond Urban Institute Archives, 1979–1986

Special Collections, University of Virginia Library, Charlottesville, VA
Papers of John Powell

The Valentine, Richmond, VA
Valentine Family Papers, 1786–1920

Virginia Museum of History & Culture, Richmond, VA
Powhatan Ellis Papers, 1856–1890
Bolling Walker Haxall Account Book, 1851–1883
Hobson Family Papers
Hollywood Memorial Association Papers
St. Paul's Church (Richmond, VA) Records, 1828–1963
Rutherfoord Family Papers

NARA Microfilm Accessed via Ancestry.com

Sixth Census of the United States, 1840. (NARA microfilm publication M704, 580 rolls). Records of the Bureau of the Census, Record Group 29. National Archives, Washington, DC.

Seventh Census of the United States, 1850. (NARA microfilm publication M432, 1009 rolls). Records of the Bureau of the Census, Record Group 29; National Archives, Washington, DC.

Seventh Census of the United States, 1850—Slave Schedule. (NARA microfilm publication M432, 1,009 rolls). Records of the Bureau of the Census, Record Group 29; National Archives, Washington, DC.

Eighth Census of the United States, 1860. (NARA microfilm publication M653, 1,438 rolls). Records of the Bureau of the Census, Record Group 29; National Archives, Washington, DC.

Eighth Census of the United States, 1860—Slave Schedule. (NARA microfilm publication, M653, 1,438 rolls). Records of the Bureau of the Census, Record Group 29; National Archives, Washington, DC.

Ninth Census of the United States, 1870. (NARA microfilm publication, M593, 1,761 rolls). Records of the Bureau of the Census, Record Group 29; National Archives, Washington, DC.

Tenth Census of the United States, 1880. (NARA microfilm publication T9, 1,454 rolls). Records of the Bureau of the Census, Record Group 29. National Archives, Washington, DC.

Selected Online Databases

Encyclopedia Virginia, Virginia Foundation for the Humanities.
Students of the University of Virginia, https://uvastudents.wordpress.com.
Virginia Untold: The African American Narrative, Library of Virginia.

Other Primary Sources

"Address of the Democratic State Committee to the People of Virginia." *Alexandria Gazette.* December 1, 1883.

"An Address to Christians throughout the World, by a Convention of Ministers, assembled at Richmond, Va., April, 1863." Philadelphia: n.p., 1863.

Anderson, Archer. "Robert Edward Lee. An address delivered at the Dedication of the Monument to Robert Edward Lee at Richmond, Va., May 19, 1890." Richmond, VA: Lee Monument Association, 1890.

Avary, Myrta Lockett. *Dixie after the War.* New York: Doubleday, Page, 1906.

Blassingame, John, et al., eds. *The Frederick Douglass Papers: Series One—Speeches, Debates, and Interviews.* New Haven: Yale University Press, 1979.

Brown, Henry. *Narrative of the Life of Henry Box Brown, Written by Himself.* Manchester: Lee and Glynn, 1851.

Castleman, T. T., ed. *Plain Sermons for Servants.* 2nd ed. New York: Stanford & Delisser, 1858.

Chesterman, W. D. *The James River Tourist.* Richmond, VA: Dispatch Steam Print House, 1879.

Davis, Arthur P. "With a Grain of Salt: Times Change—Even in Virginia." *New Journal and Guide* (June 30, 1945).

Hancock, Gordon B. "Between the Lines" column, (Norfolk). *New Journal & Guide.*

Johns, Rt. Rev. J. *A Memoir of the Life of the Rt. Rev. William Meade, D.D.* Baltimore: Innes, 1867.

Journals of the Annual Convention of the Protestant Episcopal Church in Virginia (1840–2016). Various publishers.

Minnigerode, Charles. *Power: A Sermon Preached at St. Paul's Church, Richmond.* Richmond, VA: W. H. Clemmitt, 1864.

———. *"He That Believeth Shall Not Make Haste": A Sermon Preached on the First of January, 1865, in St. Paul's Church, Richmond.* Richmond, VA: Chas. H. Wynne, 1865.

Moore, Annie C. "Saint Mary's Memorial Church: In Memory of the Beloved Colored 'Mammies' of the South." *The Spirit of Missions* 82 (1917).

McCarthy, Carlton. *Walks about Richmond: A story for boys, and a guide for persons visiting the city desiring to see the principal points of interest, with an index showing the exact location of each point mentioned.* Richmond, VA: McCarthy & Ellyson, 1870.

McGuire, Judith. *Diary of A Southern Refugee During the War, by a Lady of Virginia.* New York: E.J. Hale, 1868.

Page, Thomas Nelson. "The Lynching of Negroes: Its Causes and Its Prevention" *North American Review* 173, no. 566 (January 1904): 34–38.

The Race Problem and the Church: The Report of the Racial Study Commission of the Diocese of Virginia (Richmond, VA: Protestant Episcopal Church in the Diocese of Virginia, 1960).

Reese, George H. ed. *Proceedings of the Virginia State Convention of 1861, February 13-May 1.* Richmond: Virginia State Library, 1965.

Richmond Virginia, A Guide to and Description of its Principal Places (Richmond, VA: J. W. Randolph & English, 1881).

Rutherfoord, John C. *Speech of John C. Rutherfoord, of Goochland, in the House of Delegates of Virginia, on the removal from the commonwealth of the free colored population, delivered February 18, 1853.* Richmond, VA: Ritchies & Dunnavant, 1853.

Stowe, Harriet Beecher. *The Key to Uncle Tom's Cabin; Presenting the Original Facts and Documents Upon Which the Story Is Founded [. . .].* Boston: John P. Jewett, 1854.

Terrell, Mary Church. "Lynching from a Negro's Point of View." *North American Review* 178, no. 571 (June 1904): 853–68.

Tucker, Hon. John Randolph. *The Southern Church Justified in its support of the South in the Present War.* Richmond, VA: Wm. H. Clemmitt, 1863.

Winik, Jay. "What John Kelly Got Right About Robert E. Lee." *Wall Street Journal,* November 3, 2017, https://www.wsj.com/articles/what-john-kelly-got-right-about-robert-e-lee-1509745645/ (accessed July 5, 2020).

Woodson, Carter G. "Finding A New Way for Cooperation." *Negro History Bulletin* 1, no. 7 (April 1938): 1–2.

Newspapers and Magazines

Afro-American Churchman (Petersburg, VA)
Carolina Churchman
Chicago Tribune
Churchman

Confederate Veteran
Daily Press (Newport News, VA)
Daily Progress (Raleigh, NC)
Daily State Journal (Richmond)
Evening Sun (Baltimore)
Fisk University News
Harrisburg Telegraph (Harrisburg, PA)
I. F. Stone's Weekly
Lexington Gazette
Life
New Journal and Guide (Norfolk)
New York Times
Parish Register
Reader's Digest
Richmond Daily Dispatch
Richmond Dispatch
Richmond Enquirer
Richmond Examiner
Richmond Magazine
Richmond News-Leader
Richmond Planet
Richmond Times-Dispatch
Southern Churchman
Staunton News-Leader
Staunton Spectator
Style Weekly (Richmond)
Times (Richmond)
Washington Post

Oral Histories

Burke, Lyons, Susie Scott, S. Buford Scott, Mary Ann Ready, Rob Corcoran, and Susan Corcoran. Interview by Elizabeth O'Leary and Christopher Graham, Richmond, VA, December 3, 2017.

Freeman, Anne Hobson. Interview by Christopher Graham, Richmond, VA, April 25, 2017.

Hetherington, Reverend Canon Robert. Interview by Elizabeth O'Leary and Christopher Graham, Richmond, VA, May 31, 2019.

Luxmoore, Adrian, Scott Sirles, Louisa Sirles, and Lee Switz. Interview by Elizabeth O'Leary, Anne Hayes, and Christopher Graham, Richmond, VA, December 7, 2017

McGuire, Hunter "Mac". Interview by Geoffrey Switz and Christopher Graham, Richmond, VA, May 5, 2017.

Rice, Rev. Rodney. Phone interview by Elizabeth O'Leary, Richmond, VA, January 5, 2018.

Spong, John Shelby. Interview by Elizabeth O'Leary and Christopher Graham, Richmond, VA, April 30, 2019.

Secondary Sources

Alexander, Michelle. *The New Jim Crow: Mass Incarceration in the Age of Colorblindness.* New York: New Press, 2010.

Baker, Meredith Henne. *The Richmond Theater Fire: Early America's First Great Disaster.* Baton Rouge: Louisiana State University Press, 2012.

Barnes, Diane. *Artisan Workers in the Upper South: Petersburg, Virginia, 1820–1865.* Baton Rouge: Louisiana State University Press, 1996.

Becoming Beloved Community. https://episcopalchurch.org/beloved-community/.

Blair, William. *Cities of the Dead: Contesting the Memory of the Civil War in the South, 1865–1914.* Chapel Hill: University of North Carolina Press, 2004.

Block, Susan Taylor. *Temple of Our Fathers: St. James Church, 1729–2004.* Wilmington, NC: Artspeaks, 2004.

Brawley, Benjamin. *A Social History of the American Negro.* New York: Macmillan, 1921.

Brown, Robert R. *"And One Was a Soldier": The Spiritual Pilgrimage of Robert E. Lee.* Shippensburg, PA: White Mane Books, 1998.

Bond, Edward L., and Joan R. Gunderson. "The Episcopal Church in Virginia, 1607–2007." *Virginia Magazine of History and Biography* 115, no. 2 (2007).

Bowie, Walter Russell. *Learning To Live: An Autobiography.* New York: Abingdon, 1969.

———. *Sunrise in the South: The Life of Mary-Cooke Branch Munford.* Richmond, VA: William Byrd Press, 1942.

Brooks, Clayton McClure. *The Uplift Generation: Cooperation Across the Color Line in Early Twentieth-Century Virginia.* Charlottesville: University of Virginia Press, 2017.

Brown, Austin Channing. *I'm Still Here: Black Dignity in a World Made for Whiteness.* New York: Convergent, 2018.

Browne, Katrina, dir. *Traces of the Trade: A Story from the Deep North.* San Francisco, CA: California Newsreel, 2008.

Bruce, Kathleen. *Virginia Iron Manufacture in the Slave Era.* New York: Century, 1931.

Campbell, Benjamin. *Richmond's Unhealed History.* Richmond, VA: Brandylane, 2012.

Chesson, Michael B. *Richmond After the War.* Richmond: Virginia State Library, 1981.

Chiles, Marvin. "Down Where the South Begins: Black Richmond Activism Before the Modern Civil Rights Movement, 1899–1930." *Journal of African American History* 105 (2020): 56–82.

———. "'A Period of Misunderstanding': Reforming Jim Crow in Richmond, Virginia, 1930–1954." *Virginia Magazine of History and Biography* 129, no. 3 (2021): 244–79.

Christian, William Asbury. *Richmond, Her Past and Present.* Richmond, VA: L. H. Jenkins, 1912.

Clark, Erskine. *Wrestlin' Jacob: A Portrait of Religion in Antebellum Georgia and the Carolina Low Country.* Tuscaloosa: University of Alabama Press, 1999.

Coates, Ta-Nehisi. "Why Do So Few Blacks Study the Civil War?" *The Atlantic*, special commemorative issue (February 2012).

Connolly, Nathan D. B. *We Live Here.* Podcast audio. September 22, 2017.

Cook, Robert J. *Troubled Commemoration: The American Civil War Centennial, 1961–1965.* Baton Rouge: Louisiana State University Press, 2011.

Cooper, William J. *Jefferson Davis, American*. New York: Vintage, 2000.
Corcoran, Rob. *Trustbuilding: An Honest Conversation on Race, Reconciliation, and Responsibility*. Charlottesville: University of Virginia Press, 2010.
Coski, John M. *The Confederate Battle Flag: America's Most Embattled Emblem*. Cambridge, MA: Harvard University Press, 2009.
Cox, Karen L. *Dixie's Daughters: The United Daughters of the Confederacy and the Preservation of Confederate Culture*. Tallahassee: University Press of Florida, 2003.
Dabney, Virginius. *Richmond: The Story of a City*. Rev. ed. Charlottesville: University Press of Virginia, 1990.
Dailey, Jane. *Before Jim Crow: The Politics of Race in Postemancipation Virginia*. Chapel Hill: University of North Carolina Press, 2000.
Daly, John Patrick. *When Slavery Was Called Freedom: Evangelicalism, Proslavery, and the Causes of the Civil War*. Lexington: University Press of Kentucky, 2004.
"Davenport and Allen Auction Co." *Style Weekly*. May 10, 2011.
Dew, Charles B. *Ironmaker to the Confederacy: Joseph R. Anderson and the Tredegar Iron Works*. Richmond: Virginia State Library, 1999.
Dooley, Mrs. James H. *Dem Good Ole Times*. New York: Doubleday, Page, 1906.
Dorn, T. Felder. *Challenges on the Emmaus Road: Episcopal Bishops Confront Slavery, Civil War, and Emancipation*. Columbia: University of South Carolina Press, 2013.
Dudziak, Mary L. *Cold War Civil Rights: Race and the Image of American Democracy*. Princeton, NJ: Princeton University Press, 2011.
Edds, Margaret. *We Face the Dawn: Oliver Hill, Spottswood Robinson, and the Legal Team that Dismantled Jim Crow*. Charlottesville: University of Virginia Press, 2018.
Egerton, John. *Speak Now Against the Day: The Generation Before the Civil Rights Movement in the South*. Chapel Hill: University of North Carolina Press, 1994.
Ellis, Mark. *Race Harmony and Black Progress: Jack Woofter and the Interracial Cooperation Movement*. Bloomington: Indiana University Press, 2013.
Faust, Drew Gilpin. *This Republic of Suffering: Death and the American Civil War*. New York: Vintage, 2009.
Foster, Gaines M. *Ghosts of the Confederacy: Defeat, the Lost Cause, and the Emergence of the New South, 1865–1913*. New York: Oxford University Press, 1987.
———. "Today's Battle Over the Confederate Flag Has Nothing to Do with the Civil War." *Zocalo Public Square*. October 23, 2018.
Franks, Vincent Chesley. *Noblesse Oblige! An Encomium to General Robert E. Lee Preached at St. Paul's Episcopal Church, Richmond, Virginia, January 20, 1946*. Richmond, VA: n.p., 1946.
———. *Our Great Triumvirate: A Sermon Preached at St. Paul's Episcopal Church, Richmond, Virginia, January 16, 1944*. Richmond, n.p., 1944.
Frederickson, George M. *The Black Image in the White Mind: The Debate on Afro-American Character and Destiny, 1817–1914*. Middletown, CT: Wesleyan University Press, 1971.
Freeman, Anne Hobson "Lee." *Commonwealth Magazine*. January 1979.
Genovese, Eugene D. *A Consuming Fire: The Fall of the Confederacy and the Mind of the White Christian South*. Athens: University of Georgia Press, 1998.

———. *Roll, Jordan, Roll: The World the Slaves Made.* New York: Vintage, 1976.
Gilmore, Glenda Elizabeth. *Defying Dixie: The Radical Roots of Civil Rights, 1919–1950.* New York: W. W. Norton, 2009.
Glasgow, Ellen Anderson Gholson. *The Woman Within: An Autobiography.* New York: Harcourt Brace, 1954.
Glymph, Thavolia. *Out of the House of Bondage: The Transformation of the Plantation Household.* New York: Cambridge University Press, 2008.
Graham, Christopher Alan. "Evangelicals and 'Domestic Felicity' in the Non-Elite South." *Journal of Southern Religion* 15 (2013).
———. "Faith and Family in the Antebellum Piedmont South." PhD diss., University of North Carolina at Greensboro, 2013.
———. "The Lost Cause Myth." *The Inclusive Historian's Handbook.* American Association for State and Local History and National Council for Public History, May 12, 2020.
———. "Myths & Misunderstandings: Stonewall Jackson's Sunday School." *American Civil War Museum* (blog). October 12, 2017 (Accessed November 1, 2020). https://acwm.org/blog/myths-misunderstandings-stonewall-jacksons-sunday-school/.
Gryborski, Michael. "Episcopal Church Calls for Removal of All Confederate Flags; Says It's a Symbol 'at Odds with the Love of Jesus Christ.'" *Christian Post.* July 3, 2015.
Hale, Grace Elizabeth. *Making Whiteness: The Culture of Segregation in the South, 1890–1940.* New York: Vintage, 1998.
Hansen, Scott Britton. "Education for All: The Freedmen's Bureau Schools in Richmond and Petersburg, 1865–1870." MA thesis, Virginia Commonwealth University, 2008.
Harlow, Luke. "The Long Life of Proslavery Religion." In *The World the Civil War Made,* edited by Gregory Downs and Kate Masur. Chapel Hill: University of North Carolina Press, 2015.
Harris, Odell Greenleaf. *Bishop Payne Divinity School, Petersburg, Virginia, 1878–1949.* Alexandria, VA: Protestant Episcopal Theological Seminary, 1980.
Harvey, Jennifer. *Dear White Christians: For Those Still Longing for Racial Reconciliation.* Grand Rapids, MI: Eerdmans, 2014.
Hayes, Anne S. "The Lee Communion Story: A Monumental Myth Examined." Unpublished manuscript in author's possession.
———. "Rediscovering the Past: Memorial Plaques at St. Paul's Church, 1887–2000." Unpublished manuscript in author's possession.
Hayter, Julian Maxwell. *The Dream is Lost: Voting Rights and the Politics of Race in Richmond, Virginia.* Lexington: University Press of Kentucky, 2017.
Hillyer, Reiko. "Relics of Reconstruction: The Confederate Museum and Civil War Memory in the New South." *Public Historian* 33, no. 4 (November 2011): 35–62.
Housing Opportunities Made Equal of Virginia, Inc., History, http://homeofva.org/about-us/history/, accessed June 18, 2019.
Irons, Charles F. "And All These Things Shall Be Added unto You: The First African Baptist Church, Richmond, 1841–1865." *Virginia Cavalcade* 47, no. 1 (Winter 1998): 26–35.
———. *The Origins of Proslavery Christianity: White and Black Evangelicals in Colonial and Antebellum Virginia.* Chapel Hill: University of North Carolina Press, 2008.

———. "Urban Black Protestants and the Predicament of Emancipation." Paper presented at Reconstruction and the Arc of Racial (In)Justice, Jepson School of Leadership, University of Richmond, September 16, 2016.

Jacoway, Elizabeth. *Turn Away Thy Son: Little Rock, The Crisis that Shocked the Nation.* New York: Free Press, 2007.

Janney, Caroline E. *Burying the Dead But Not The Past: Ladies' Memorial Associations & the Lost Cause.* Chapel Hill: University of North Carolina Press, 2008.

Jemison, Elizabeth L. *Christian Citizens: Reading the Bible in Black and White in the Postemancipation South.* Chapel Hill: University of North Carolina Press, 2020.

Jennings, Gretchen. "The Empathetic Museum: Institutional Body Language." *Museum Commons*, June 29, 2013, https://museumcommons.com/2013/06/the-empathetic-museum-institutional.html, accessed November 1, 2020.

Johnson, Corey G. "Bryan Stevenson on Charleston and Our Real Problem with Race." *The Marshall Project.* June 24, 2015, accessed November 3, 2020.

Johnson, Walter. *River of Dark Dreams: Slavery and Empire in the Cotton Kingdom.* Cambridge, MA: Belknap, 2017.

Karp, Matthew. *This Vast Southern Empire: Slaveholders at the Helm of American Foreign Policy.* Cambridge, MA: Harvard University Press, 2018.

Kelley, Blair L. M. *Right to Ride: Streetcar Boycotts and African American Citizenship in the Era of Plessy v. Ferguson.* Chapel Hill: University of North Carolina Press, 2010.

Kimball, Gregg D. *American City, Southern Place: A Cultural History of Antebellum Richmond.* Athens: University of Georgia Press, 2000.

Kneebone, John T. *Robert Stiles' Civil Wars.* Unpublished manuscript.

Lankford, Nelson. *Richmond Burning: The Last Days of the Confederate Capital.* New York: Penguin Books, 2003.

Lassiter, Matthew D., and Andrew B. Lewis. "Massive Resistance Revisited: Virginia's White Moderates and the Byrd Organization." In *The Moderates' Dilemma: Massive Resistance to School Desegregation in Virginia*, edited by Matthew D. Lassiter and Andrew B. Lewis, 1–21. Charlottesville: University of Virginia Press, 1998.

Lee, Heath Hardage. *Winnie Davis: Daughter of the Lost Cause.* Lincoln, NE: Potomac Books, 2014.

Levin, Kevin M. "Why Doesn't Anyone Think It's Cool to Dress Up Like a Confederate Soldier Anymore?" *The Atlantic*, February 28, 2018.

Lindgren, James M. *Preserving the Old Dominion: Historic Preservation and Virginia Traditionalism.* Charlottesville: University of Virginia Press, 1993.

Loth, Calder. *Windows of Grace, A Tribute of Love: The Memorial Windows of St. Paul's Episcopal Church, Richmond, Virginia.* Richmond, VA: St. Paul's Episcopal Church, 2004.

Luker, Ralph E. *The Social Gospel in Black and White: American Racial Reform, 1885–1912.* Chapel Hill: University of North Carolina Press, second edition, 2000.

Luskey, Ashley. "No Mere Morality Play: Why We Need Confederate Memorials Now More Than Ever." *History@Work*, September 29, 2015, https://ncph.org/history-at-work/ashley-luskey-civil-war-memory-post/.

Marty, Martin E. *Righteous Empire: The Protestant Experience in America.* New York: Harper & Row, 1977.
Meier, August, and Elliott Rudwick. "Negro Boycotts of Segregated Streetcars in Virginia, 1904–1907." *Virginia Magazine of History and Biography* 81, no. 4 (October 1973).
Mitchell, Mary H. *Hollywood Cemetery: The History of a Southern Shrine.* Richmond: Virginia State Library, 1985.
McElya, Micki. *Clinging to Mammy: The Faithful Slave in Twentieth-Century America.* Cambridge, MA: Harvard University Press, 2007.
Moeser, John V., and Rutledge M. Dennis. *The Politics of Annexation: Oligarchic Power in a Southern City.* Cambridge, MA: Schenkman, 1982.
Moore, Christopher C. "Apostle of the Confederacy: J. William Jones and the Question of Ecumenism and Denominational Identity in the Development of Lost Cause Mythology." PhD diss., Baylor University, 2016.
Norman Jr., Worth Earlwood. *James Solomon Russell: Former Slave, Pioneering Educator, and Episcopal Evangelist.* Jefferson, NC: Macfarland, 2012.
O'Leary, Elizabeth L. *From Morning to Night: Domestic Service in Maymont House and the Gilded Age South.* Charlottesville: University of Virginia Press, 2004.
———. "'A Memorial to Those Who Made Her History': Material Acts of Remembrance at St. Paul's, 1845–2020." Unpublished paper, 2020, St. Paul's archives.
Orsi, Robert. "Everyday Miracles: The Study of Lived Religion." In *Lived Religion in America: Toward a History of Practice*, edited by David D. Hall. Princeton, NJ: Princeton University Press, 1997.
Page, Anne Rose. *Sketches of Old Virginia Family Servants.* Philadelphia: Isaac Ashmead, 1847.
Pryor, Mrs. Roger A., et al., *Gen. Robert Edward Lee: Soldier, Citizen, and Christian Patriot.* Richmond, VA: Royal, 1897.
Reed, John Shelton. *Glorious Battle: The Cultural Politics of Victorian Anglo-Catholicism.* Nashville: Vanderbilt University Press, 2000.
Richmond City Planning Commission. *A Master Plan for the Physical Development of the City.* Richmond, VA: City Planning Commission, 1946.
Rosenzweig, Roy, and David Thelen. *The Presence of the Past: Popular Uses of History in American Life.* New York: Columbia University Press, 2000.
Rothman, Joshua D. *Notorious in the Neighborhood: Sex and Families Across the Color Line in Virginia, 1787–1861.* Chapel Hill: University of North Carolina Press, 2003.
Rothstein, Richard. *The Color of Law: A Forgotten History of How Our Government Segregated America.* New York: Liveright, 2017.
Satia, Priya. *Time's Monster: How History Makes History.* Cambridge, MA: Belknap, 2020.
Schultz, Kevin M. *Tri-Faith America: How Catholics and Jews Held Postwar America to its Protestant Promise.* New York: Oxford University Press, 2011.
Schwarz, Philip J. "General Lee and Visibility." Paper delivered to the Stratford Hall Plantation Seminar on Slavery, August 4, 2000.
———. *St. Paul's Episcopal Church: 150 Years, 1845–1995.* Richmond, VA: St. Paul's Episcopal Church, 1995.

Scott, Mary Wingfield. *Houses of Old Richmond.* Richmond, VA: Valentine Museum, 1941.
———. *Old Richmond Neighborhoods.* Richmond, VA: Whittet & Shepperson, 1950.
———. *Winkie.* N.p., ca. 2011.
Shattuck, Gardiner H., Jr. *Episcopalians & Race: Civil War to Civil Rights.* Lexington: University Press of Kentucky, 2000.
Shepherd, Samuel C., Jr. *Avenues of Faith: Shaping the Urban Religious Culture of Richmond, Virginia, 1900–1929.* Tuscaloosa: University of Alabama Press, 2001.
———. "South and North: The Exceptional Seminary Education of Walter Russell Bowie." *Anglican and Episcopal History,* 87, no. 1 (March 2018): 1–33.
Sherman, Richard B. "The 'Teachings at Hampton Institute': Social Equality, Racial Integrity, and the Virginia Public Assemblages Act of 1926." *Virginia Magazine of History and Biography* 95, no. 3 (July 1987).
Smith, J. Douglas. *Managing White Supremacy: Race, Politics, and Citizenship in Jim Crow Virginia.* Chapel Hill: University of North Carolina Press, 2002.
———. "'The Ordeal of Virginius Dabney': A Southern Liberal, the Southern Regional Council, and the Limits of Managed Race Relations." Paper delivered at The Southern Regional Council & the Civil Rights Movement Conference, University of Florida, October 2003.
Snay, Mitchell. *Gospel of Disunion: Religion and Separatism in the Antebellum South.* Chapel Hill: University of North Carolina Press, 1997.
Stowell, Daniel W. *Rebuilding Zion: The Religious Reconstruction of the South, 1863–1877.* New York: Oxford University Press, 1998.
Takagi, Midori. *"Rearing Wolves to Our Own Destruction": Slavery in Richmond, Virginia, 1782–1865.* Charlottesville: University Press of Virginia, 1999.
Tarter, Brent, et al., *The Campaign for Woman Suffrage in Virginia.* Charleston, SC: History Press, 2020.
Thompson, Douglas E. *Richmond's Priests and Prophets: Race, Religion, and Social Change in the Civil Rights Era.* Tuscaloosa: University of Alabama Press, 2017.
Tisby, Jemar. "Reconciliation and Justice, Are They Friends or Enemies?" *Pass the Mic.* Podcast audio, December 16, 2019. https://podcasts.apple.com/us/podcast/reconciliation-and-justice-are-they-friends-or-enemies/id1435500798?i=1000459820066
———. "What the Church Can Learn from Taking Down Confederate Monuments." *The Witness,* May 18, 2017, https://thewitnessbcc.com/what-the-church-can-learn-from-taking-down-confederate-monuments/.
Turner, Elizabeth Hayes. "Mollie Ragan Macgill Rosenberg." Texas State Historical Association. https://tshaonline.org/handbook/online/articles/froaw/.
Turner, Nicole Myers. *Soul Liberty: The Evolution of Black Religious Politics in Postemancipation Virginia.* Chapel Hill: University of North Carolina Press, 2020.
Savage, Kirk. *Standing Soldiers, Kneeling Slaves: Race, War, and Monument in Nineteenth-Century America.* 2nd ed. Princeton, NJ: Princeton University Press, 2018.
Sokol, Jason. *There Goes My Everything: White Southerners in the Age of Civil Rights, 1945–1975.* New York: Alfred A. Knopf, 2006.

Spong, John Shelby. *Here I Stand: My Struggle for A Christianity of Integrity, Love & Equality.* New York: HarperCollins, 2000.
Stiles, Robert. *Four Years Under Marse Robert.* New York: Neale, 1904.
Still, William. *The Underground Rail Road.* Philadelphia: Porter & Coates, 1872.
Tarter, Brent. "William Barret." In *Dictionary of Virginia Biography,* edited by John T. Kneebone, 1:353–54. Richmond: Library of Virginia, 1998.
Tyler, Lyon G. ed. *Men of Mark in Virginia* 5. Washington, DC: Men of Mark, 1909.
Tyler-McGraw, Marie. *An African Republic: Black & White Virginians in the Making of Liberia.* Chapel Hill: University of North Carolina Press, 2007.
Valley of the Shadow: Two Communities in the American Civil War. Virginia Center for Digital History, University of Virginia Library.
Weber, Gustavus A. *Report on Housing and Living Conditions in the Neglected Sections of Richmond, Virginia.* Richmond, VA: Whittet & Shepperson, 1913.
Wineburg, Sam. *Historical Thinking and Other Unnatural Acts: Charting the Future of Teaching the Past.* Philadelphia: Temple University Press, 2001.
Weddell, Elizabeth Wright. *St. Paul's Church: Its Historic Years and Memorials.* Richmond, VA: William Byrd Press, 1931.
White, Ronald C., Jr. *Liberty and Justice for All: Racial Reform and the Social Gospel, 1877–1925.* New York: Harper & Row, 1990.
Wilson, Charles Reagan. *Baptized in Blood: The Religion of the Lost Cause, 1865–1920.* Athens: University of Georgia Press, 1980.

INDEX

Abraham (enslaved man), 36
Adams-Riley, Rev. Wallace, 1, 2, 5, 145, 147, 149, 151
"Address to Christians throughout the World," 32–33
Afro-American Churchman, 49
Alabama (band), 4
Alexander, Michelle, 6
Allen, James, 14
Allen, Otway, 52, 66, 79
Allen, William C., 18, 40
Allman Brothers, 4
All Saints Episcopal Church, 177n29
American Civil War, 32–37; centennial, 98; sesquicentennial, 1, 147
American Colonization Society, 19
Ancarrow's Landing, ix
Anderson, Archer, 43–44, 51, 66, 73, 80
Anderson, Dones, 109
Anderson, George Wayne, 85
Anderson, Joseph Reid, 12, 15, 17, 19, 24, 31, 36, 40, 52, 54, 59, 61, 66, 73
Anderson, Sally Archer, 63
Anderson, William A., 66, 67
Anglo-Saxon Clubs, 87
Antrim, Nora Lee, 97, 123
Archer, Rosalie, 75, 83
Arrington, Turner, 101–2, 103, 114–15
Atterholt, Mary, 143
Ayer, Alton, 141–42

Bacon, John L., 34
Bainbridge Richmond Community Action Program Center, 126
Barney, Charles, 15
Barney, Mary, 15

Barret, William, 12
Barrett, Janie Porter, 70
Bartholomew, Harland, 103–4
Belle Island Iron Works, 15
Biddle, Rev. Craig, III, 130–31, 136
Bishop Payne School, 45
Black Education Teams, 128
Black Lives Matter, 6, 148, 154
Black Manifesto, 119, 122
Black religious lives, 11, 38, 48–49, 58
Blair, Adolphus, 59
Bolton, James, 41, 45, 51
Bonhoeffer, Dietrich, 101
Book of Common Prayer, 28
Boushall, Thomas C., 96, 104–5, 105–6, 107, 109, 110, 117, 125, 127
Bowen, W., 18
Bowie, Rev. Walter Russell, 3, 9, 71–72, 74–75, 79, 80, 81, 83, 86, 119–20, 121, 123, 126, 129, 158
Bowler, Antoinette, 106
Boyle, Sarah Patton, 117
Bozeman, Edward, 11
Branch, John Kerr, 79, 82, 154
Bragg, Caroline, 45
Bragg, Rev. George Freeman, Jr., 45, 49, 50
Brasfield, Evans, 124, 126, 127
Brawley, Benjamin, 91, 116
Bright, J. Fulmer, 89, 92, 104
Brooks, James, 14
Broun, Thomas L., 63–66
Brown, Austin Channing, 159
Brown, Henry "Box," 12, 167n54
Brown, Rev. Robert, 94, 97, 98, 109–10, 114
Brown, Stepney, 16, 39

208 | INDEX

Browne, Katrina, 152
Brown v. Board of Education, 95, 101, 106–8, 110, 112, 113, 120
Bruton Parish Church, 22
Bryan, Thomas P., Jr., 105, 109
Brydon, Rev. G. Maclaren, 102–3
Buchannan v. Warley, 85
Bultmann, Rudolph, 101
Byrd, Harry F., 87, 107, 120

Campbell, Hannah, 11
Campbell, Rev. Benjamin P., 132–33, 144
Carlton, Ambrose, 31
Carmichael, Rev. Hartley, 53, 54, 55, 56
Carmichael, Stokely, 121
Carpenter's Kids, 145
Carr, Betsy, 144
Carrington, Richard, 79, 85, 87–88, 89–90, 126, 158
Cary, Rev. Hundson, 136
Castleman, Rev. Thomas, 24; Plain Sermons for Servants, 23
Catton, Bruce, 1
Centenary Methodist Church, 13, 124
Center on Aging of the Presbyterian School of Christian Education, 127
Central Virginia Food Bank, 135
Cephas, B. A. "Sonny," 117
Chesnut, Mary, 35
Chiles, James A., 94–95, 96
Chiles, Richard, 37, 94–95
Church Hill Area Revitalization Team, 127
Christian, A. H., Jr., 81
Christian, Andrew D., 81, 86
Christian, William, 11
Church's Teachings, The, 101
Civil Rights Act (1964), 117
Civil Rights Movement, 93, 96, 98, 101, 106–8, 116, 121, 124, 131, 137, 146, 148
Civil War, The (Time-Life), 4
Civil War reenacting, 4–5
Clark, Kenneth B., 134
Clark Springs, 74

Coates, Ta-Nehisi, 5–6
Coleman, James, 109
Coleman, John, 132
Colonization Society of Virginia, 19
Commission on Interracial Cooperation, 82–83, 85–86, 88–89, 91, 92, 93, 108, 110
Community House for Negro People, 70
Community Reinvestment Act (1977), 133
Confederate flag, 3
Confederate Museum, 53, 63, 70
Confederate Soldiers & Sailors Memorial, 53
Connolly, Nathan, 148
Cooper, Samuel, 35
Corbett, Rev. Linwood, 121, 126
Corcoran, Rob, 140, 141
Corcoran, Susan, 140
Country Club of Virginia, 123, 130, 131
COVID-19, 159
Cowles, Don, 140, 142
Cox, Rev. Harvey, 139
Craigie, Walter W., Sr., 123
Creighton Court, 106
Crutchfield, E. Mulford, 76
Curry, Rt. Rev. Michael B., 152

Dabney, Robert Lewis, 21
Dabney, Virginius, 116
Daily Planet, The, 135
Dame, Rev. William Meade, 56, 58
Damell, Robert, 1, 76–78, 91, 108, 140, 155, 157, 161
Daniel, William V., 117
Daniels, Jonathan, 139
Danville riot, 43–44
Dashiell, Rev. T. Grayson, 39
Davenport, Frank B., 74
Davenport, Griffin, 14
Davenport, Isaac, 14
Davis, Arthur, 94–95
Davis family memorials, 54
Davis, Jefferson, 35, 37, 40, 51, 52, 53, 58, 61, 68, 73, 91, 95, 97, 98, 129, 154, 155;

memorial window, 53, 55–56, 58–59, 61, 73; monument, 73
Davis, John, 27
Davis, Varina Anne "Winnie," 60, 73
Davis, Varina Howell, 54, 55, 60, 73
Davis v. County School Board of Prince Edward County, 107
Deas, Joe, 76
Dew, Thomas Roderick, 21
Dick (enslaved man), 11
dignity/integrity, 135
domestic service, 75–76
Dooley, Sallie May, 62, 63, 65, 80
Douglass, Frederick, 21, 26, 91, 166n54
Dovell Act (1936), 92
Dowdey, Clifford, 97
Downtown Cooperative Ministry, 124, 131
Dukes of Hazzard, 3, 4
Dungee, John, 18, 39
Dunlop, James, 12, 14, 18, 31
Dupree, Rev. Charles, 160
Duval, Rev. William, 24

East End Fuel Program, 133
Ebenezer Baptist Church, 26, 78
Edwards, Don, 151
Eisenhower, Dwight David, 98
Ellis, Thomas, 19, 30, 31, 42
Ellison, J.M., 89
emancipation, 32, 37, 41
Emanuel A. M. E. Church (Charleston, SC), 1, 6, 147, 149
Emmanuel Church, 30
Empie, Rev. Adam, 22, 24
Episcopal Church, 6, 7, 23, 27, 66, 118–19, 137, 138–39, 148; 1907 Convention, 67; Becoming Beloved Community, xi, 7; Commission on Colored Work, 67–68; Committee on Racism, 137; Department of Christian Education, 101; Freedman's Commission, 38, 170n28; General Convention Special Program, 119, 122–23, 126, 127, 129; House of Bishops, 68, 137, 138; House of Deputies, 50; Sewanee Plan, 50; Union of Black Clergy and Laymen, 119
Episcopal Diocese of South Carolina, 23, 30, 112
Episcopal Diocese of Virginia, 14, 19, 21, 23, 24, 28, 37, 39, 43, 44, 49, 66, 77, 82, 116, 117, 123, 143; 1859 Richmond Committee, 30–31; 1860 Committee, 27–29, 113; Colored Missionary Jurisdiction, 49, 50, 112; Committee on Race, 137–38, 141; Committee on the Religious Instruction of Colored People, 38; Department of Christian Education, 114; Department of Christian Social Relations, 114, 127; Desegregation, 112–16; Missionary Society, 33, 39, 45, 102, 110; Racial Study Commission, 113–15, 116; Standing Committee on Colored Congregations, 38, 39
Episcopal Society for Cultural and Racial Unity (ECRU), 117
Evans, Richard, 26
Evergreen Cemetery, 78, 79

Fairfield Court, 106
faithful servant, 78–79
Family Crisis Shelter, 127
Federated Council of Churches, 111
Fields, Scott T., 156
First African Baptist Church, 13, 26, 27, 167n54
First Baptist Church, 13, 130
Fishwick, Rev. Jeffrey, 131
Fisk University, 86
Floyd, George, 159–60
Forman, James, 121; *Black Manifesto*, 119, 122
Forsyth, Rev. Robert, 73
Fox, Rev. Charles W., 112
Franks, Rev. Vincent, 94, 108, 110
free Black people, 19
Freedmen's Bureau, 38, 39

Freedom House, 135
Freeman, Anne Hobson, 99, 108, 110, 119
Freeman, Douglas Southall, 82, 113, 116
Fry, J. J., 19
Fulton Medical Clinic, 127

Gallego Mills, 15
Garrett, W. E., 89
Gateway House, 135
George, Miles, 16
German Lutheran Evangelical Church, 13
Gibson, George D., 117
Gibson, Rt. Rev. Robert F., 115
Gilpin Court, 104
Gladden, Washington, 80
Glasgow, Ellen, 75
Gooch, Rev. Uly, 121
Goode, John, 67
Good News Jail Mission, 135
Goodwin, Rt. Rev. Frederick Deane, 101–3, 113
Gordon, Robert, 115
Gordon, Thomas C., Jr., 118
Gorgas, Josiah, 35
Graham, Billy, 116
Graham, Frank Porter, 89
Grandison (enslaved man), 18
Gray, Garland, 107
Gray Plan, 107
Gregory, Edward "Pope," 135
Gwathmey, Robert, 14

Hall, David, 7
Hall, Rt. Rev. Robert, 129
Hall, Wiley, 93
Hampton Institute, 77, 78
Hancock, Gordon Blaine, 88–89
Harper v. Virginia Board of Elections, 117
Harris, Milly, 11
Harris, Nellie T., 97, 99
Harvard University, 71
Harvey, Jennifer, 159
Hatcher, Jordan, 19
Haxall, Anne, 17–18

Haxall, Bolling, 12, 17, 19, 31, 36, 59
Haxall, Clara, 17–18
Haxall, R. B., 31
Haxall, William Henry, 17
Haxall & Brother, 18
Haxall Flour Mills, 15, 17
Hayes, Anne S., 151
Hayter, Julian, 183n45
Heatherington, Rev. Canon Robert, 137, 139–40, 142, 143, 145
Hecht, Jim, 128
Heistand, Rev. Joseph, 98, 101, 110
Hill, Oliver, Sr., 106, 109, 117
Hillside Court, 106
Hilton, John, 27, 161
Hines, Rt. Rev. John, 119
historical imagination, 52, 75, 79, 83, 95, 103, 114, 147, 149, 154, 155–56, 159
Hobson, Graham, 85
Hobson, Rt. Rev. Henry, 100
Holiday, Henry, 54
Hollywood Cemetery, 42, 74
Hollywood Memorial Association. *See* Ladies Hollywood Memorial Association
Holton, Linwood, 127
"Holy City Seen of John," 72
Home Base, Inc., 133–34
Hood Temple AME Zion Church, 85
Housing Act (1949), 105
Housing Act (1954), 106
Housing Act (1968), 128
Housing Opportunities Made Equal, 128
Houston, Charles, 89, 92–93
Hubbard (enslaved man), 16
Hunton, Eppa, 73
Hunton, Eppa IV, 113–15, 125, 126

Immanuel Baptist Church, 85
Ingram, John L, 109
Initiatives of Change/Hope in the Cities, 140–41, 142
Interdenominational Ministerial Alliance of Richmond and Vicinity, 85, 86
Irving, William, 27

Jackson, Alice B., 91–92
Jackson, Thomas "Stonewall," 61, 94, 156
Jackson Ward, 78, 81, 84, 93, 105, 119
James Madison's Montpelier, 152
Joe (enslaved man), 11
Johns, Rt. Rev. John, 27, 35, 37, 38
Johnson, Andrew, 40
Jones, Catesby B., 122
Jones, Fontaine, 79
Jones, Lou Belle, 79
justification for racism, 19–24, 41–42, 44, 45–48, 102, 125

Kilpatrick, James J., 108
King, Rev. Dr. Martin Luther, Jr., 101, 118, 120, 121, 139
Ku Klux Klan, 82, 84, 86–87, 122

Ladies Hollywood Memorial Association, 42, 73, 74
Lancaster, Dabney, 87, 96, 106, 107, 108
Lee, Fitzhugh, 55, 73
Lee, Mary Tabb Bolling, 73
Lee, Robert E., 4, 35, 37, 40, 52, 54, 61, 68, 71, 86, 94, 97, 100, 129, 155, 156; communion story, 1, 4, 6, 63–66, 91, 116–17, 129–30, 155; memorial, 52–53, 56–58, 66
Leigh Street Methodist Episcopal Church, 80, 90
Le Roy, Jean, 123, 129
Lewis, Major, 109
Lightener, John, 109
Lincoln, Abraham, 31
Local Initiatives Support Corporation, 134
Lost Cause, ix, 5, 42–43, 51–53, 56, 60, 61, 62, 63, 64, 70–71, 72–73, 74–75, 116–17, 119, 130, 142, 148, 152
Lowe, Rev. Canon Fletcher, 145
Lumpkin, Robert, 14
Lumpkin's Slave Jail, 141
Luxmoore, Adrian, 130
Luxmoore, Page, 144

Lynchburg Hose and Fire Insurance Company, 18
Lyons, Allen, 12–13

Macfarland, Nancy, 34, 42
Macfarland, William H., 15, 18, 19, 26, 31, 40–41, 44, 52
Macgill, Charles, 60
Maclachlan, Rev. Hugh, 81
Macmurdo, James, 36
Mahone, William, 43
Mann, William H., 123
Marcus-David Peters Circle, 160
Marsh, Henry L., III, 118, 131
Marshall, Gertrude, 15
Marshall, John, 13
Martin, Henry S., Jr., 140
Martin, Ruby Grant, 129, 140, 143, 161
Martin, Trayvon, 160
Massenburg Bill, see Public Assemblages Act (1926)
Massive Resistance, 95, 101, 106–8, 109, 117
Matthews, Charles, 26
Maury, Mathew Fontaine, 94
Maury, Richard L., 74
McCance, Thomas, 15, 31, 41, 44
McCarthy, Carlton, 51
McCaw, James B., 18, 34
McClenahan, Mary Tyler Cheek, 113, 115, 119, 133, 134
McDowell, Carter, 132, 134
McGuire, Hunter Holmes, 99
McGuire, Hunter "Mac," 99, 123
McGuire, Judith, 34, 35
Meade, Rt. Rev. William, 19, 20, 22, 23, 27, 33; *Sermons Addressed to Masters and Servants*, 21; *Sketches of Old Virginia Family Servants*, 27
Miller, Frances Pickens, 108
Minnigerode, Rev. Charles F., 1, 20, 24, 30, 33, 34, 35, 39, 40, 45, 53, 68, 123, 129, 175n106
Minor, E. C., 35
Minor, Kate Pleasants, 63, 79, 83

mission to the slaves/colored people, 22, 33
Mitchell, John, Jr., 84
Mitchell, Julia, 16–17
Mitchell, Samuel P., 16, 26, 30
Moncure, Henry Wood, 14
Monumental Church, 13–14, 26, 30, 87
Monumental Hotel, 18
Moore, Lawrence, 76
Moore, Rev. Howard C., 121, 126
Moore, Rt. Rev. Richard Channing, 14
Moses (enslaved man), 36
Moton, Robert Russa, 91, 108
Mountcastle, Frank, 140
Mullen, Rev. Melanie, ix, 145, 147, 151, 161
Munford, Beverley Bland, 63, 70, 73
Munford, Mary-Cooke Branch, 70–71, 79, 81, 83, 84, 85, 87, 88, 93, 125, 126, 134, 158, 179n56
Muse, Benjamin, 116

National Association for the Advancement of Colored People, 92, 106
National Conference on Religion and Race, 101
National Housewives League, 75–76
National Memorial for Peace and Justice, 151
Negus, Lucy, 129
Nelson, Jane, 135
Niebuhr, Reinhold, 101
Norwood, Rev. William, 14, 24, 45

Offender Aid and Restoration, 128
Old Dominion Iron & Nail Works, 17
O'Leary, Elizabeth, 151
Omohundro, Silas, 14
Orsi, Robert, 7
Oxford Movement, 21

Page, Thomas Nelson, 62–63
Palmer, William, 31
Pascoe, H. Merrill, 105, 123
paternalism, 11, 12, 20, 37, 39, 40, 45–46, 48, 70, 79, 82, 127, 129, 146, 155, 159,

Pegram, John, 1, 35, 61, 98
Pegram, William, 35
Person, Alberta, 144
Peterkin, Rev. Joshua, 24, 32
Peter Paul Center, 132, 135
Pettit, Rev. Walton, 127, 128
Plain Sermons for Servants, 23
Plecker, Walter, 87, 92
Plessy v. Ferguson, 83, 106
Pollard, John, 91
Powell, John, 87
Powhatan Correctional Center, 131
proslavery Christianity, 20–30, 36–37, 48, 51, 71, 156, 165n43
Protestant Episcopal Church. *See* Episcopal Church
Public Assemblages Act (1926), 78, 79, 87

Race Relations Day, 91, 108
Racial Integrity Act (1924), 77, 79, 87, 154
Randolph, Rt. Rev. Alfred, 45–48, 49, 51, 66, 67, 79, 102, 154
Rauschenbusch, Walter, 80
Rawles, James, 122
Readjuster Party, 43, 49, 66
Ready, Mary Ann, 130
Reconstruction Act (1867), 41
Reid, W. Ferguson, 118
Reinhardt, Jacob, 87
religious pluralism, 100–101
reparations, 148, 159
Rice, Rev. Rodney, 129, 140
Richardson, David, 85
Richardson, William H., 24
Richmond (Virginia), 11, 12, 14, 37, 51, 72, 94, 101, 103–6, 161; 1949 Master Plan, 103–6, 105; 2020 protests, 10, 156, 159–60; annexation, 117–18; Black majority council, 118, 131; Chamber of Commerce, 104, 105; churches, 13, 74, 81, 141; Civil War, 34, 36; housing, 80, 93, 103–4, 128, 134, 158; Hustings Court, 36; industry, 12, 14, 15; Jefferson Hotel, 70; Mayor's Court, 36; Memorial Hospital,

70, 79; memorial landscape, 10, 42–43, 63, 74, 94, 160, 175n106; police, 11, 76; political parties, 15, 41, 43, 49, 66, 70; Reconstruction, 40–41, 70; segregation ordnance (1911), 84, 85; slavery, 15, 17–19; slave trade, 14; streetcar boycott, 84; urban renewal, 104–7
Richmond Area Clergy Association, 121, 126
Richmond Better Housing Coalition, 134
Richmond Crusade for Voters, 117–18
Richmonders Involved to Strengthen our Communities (RISC), 145
Richmond Forward, 117–18
Richmond Hill, 142, 144
Richmond Human Rights Commission, 133
Richmond Light Infantry Blues, 97 98
Richmond Minister's Association, 110
Richmond & Petersburg Railroad Company, 17
Richmond-Petersburg Turnpike, 106
Richmond Redevelopment and Housing Authority, 104, 105
Richmond Renaissance, 133
Richmond Urban Forum, 134, 141, 142
Richmond Urban Institute, 132–34, 135, 142; African Art & Cultural Collective, 133; Citizens Transportation Council, 133; Grassroots Economic Development, 133; Richmond United Neighborhoods, 133; Wednesday's Child, 132; Youth Employment Programs, 132
Richmond Urban League, 93
Ritchie, John, 128
Ritchie, Virginia, 128
Riverside Church (New York), 121
Robertson, Archibald G., 107
Robinson, Mary, 26
Robinson, Poiteaux, 26
Rogers, Edythe, 132–33
Rosenberg, Mollie Macgill, 61
Roslyn, 113, 114
Ross, Anne, 54, 56, 58, 79

Ross, George, 79
Russell, Rev. James Solomon, 45
Rutherfoord, John C., 19, 22

Satia, Priya, 193n14
Schwarz, Philip J., 4, 141, 175n105
Scott, Buford, 107, 184n56
Scott, Frederic W., 91, 184n56
Scott, Mary Wingfield, 75, 106f
Scott, Nancy, 27, 161
Scott, R. Carter, 85
Scott, S. Buford, 117, 123, 128, 129, 141, 143, 184n56
Scott, Susie, 129
secession, 31
Second African Baptist Church, 26
Second Baptist Church, 128
Second Presbyterian Church, 13, 121, 124
segregation laws, 83–84, 86, 87
Sermons Addressed to Masters and Servants, 21
Seventh Street Christian Church, 81
Sewanee Plan, 50
Seward, Julia, 132
Shockoe Bottom, 14, 16, 141
Shockoe Hill Cemetery, 79
Shockoe Slip, 14
Shockoe Valley, 13, 84
Shrine Mont, 113, 114
Shuttlesworth, Rev. Fred, 120
Sikorosky, Eugene, 127
Sirles, Scott, 130
Sketches of Old Virginia Family Servants, 27
Smith, H. Laurie, 104
Smith, Junius, 177n29
Social Gospel movement, 71–72, 79, 80–81, 82, 119, 146
Society for the Betterment of Housing and Living Conditions in Richmond, 81
Soldier's Aid Society of Virginia, 34
Sons of Confederate Veterans, 147
Southern Churchman, 20, 21, 22
Spong, Rt. Rev. John Shelby, 2, 121–23, 125, 126–27, 128, 129, 130, 148

Sprigg, Rev. D. F., 33
Spring Hill House, 143, 144
St. Andrew's Episcopal Church (Lawrenceville, Va.), 45
Stanley, Thomas B., 107, 110
State Capitol of Virginia, ix
St. Catherine's School, 116
Steger, John, 19, 30
Stevens, Alexander, 4
Stevenson, Bryan, 164n8
Stewart Family (Annie Carter, Elizabeth Hope, John, Lucy Norma), 53–54
Stewart, Thomas, 13
Stiles, Robert, 61
Still, William, 16
St. James Episcopal Church, 13, 21, 22, 32, 55
St. John's Episcopal Church, 13, 24
St. John's Episcopal Church (Lynchburg), 121
St. Mark's Episcopal Church, 39
St. Monica's Mission, 77
Stone, I. F., 116
Stowe, Harriet Beecher, 165n43
St. Paul's Church Home for Orphans, 12, 35, 73, 85, 124
St. Paul's Episcopal Church, 1, 12, 19, 27, 30, 33, 34, 42, 51, 60, 66, 68, 71, 78, 85, 89, 92, 94, 96, 98, 117, 120, 121, 122, 126, 133, 151–52, 155, 159; Adult Development Center, 124; Benevolent Fund, 124, 126, 187n11; Christian Social Relations Committee, 124, 128; congregation, x, 2, 4, 6, 7, 12, 19, 33, 35, 40, 48, 51, 58, 62, 64, 78, 79, 83, 85, 103, 116, 120, 123, 139, 145, 152, 157, 187n7; Emmaus (walk-in ministry), 131, 135, 145; endowment, 73–74; Episcopal Church Women, 124; History and Reconciliation Initiative, ix, x, 7, 151–53; identity, x, 1, 37, 60–61, 72, 73, 74, 76, 94, 98, 100, 108, 123, 129–30, 137, 142–43, 144, 146, 147, 148, 149, 152, 158; Isaiah 58:12 Program, 126–27, 128; Lenten Lunches, 111; memorials, ix, 1, 2, 53–61, 71, 73, 75, 94, 97, 98–99, 122, 129, 142, 146, 151, 152, 161; Micah Initiative, 143–44, 145, 152; Oral School, 124; Outreach Board, 134, 135, 143, 145; Prison Visitation Project, 135, 143, 144; Racial Reconciliation Task Force, 141–42; Scott Hall, 130; segregation within, 27, 33, 50, 73, 76, 109; slaveholding patterns of members, 15–18, 26–27; Sunday School, 24, 34, 38; Tucker Club, 97; Urban Missioner, 132, 145; vestry, 7, 14, 33, 40, 53, 72, 99, 109, 110, 111, 114, 126, 127, 130, 144, 146, 160, 193n5
St. Paul's Normal and Industrial College, 45
St. Peter's Catholic Church, 13, 124
St. Peter's Episcopal Mission, 127
St. Philip's Episcopal Church, 30, 33, 39, 80, 137, 141, 146, 170n28
Street Academy, 127
St. Stephen's Episcopal Church (Petersburg), 39
St. Stephen's Normal and Theological School, 45 (see also Bishop Payne School)
Student Nonviolent Coordinating Committee, 116
Sunday Schools, 23, 24, 26, 39, 156
Sweatt v. *Painter*, 111
Switz, Don, 132
Switz, Lee, 141, 144, 151

Taff (enslaved man), 36
Taft, William Howard, 87
Taylor, Breonna, 160
Taylor, Lucy, 79
Taylor, Rev. Junius, 80
Taylor, W. G., 109
Terrell, Mary Church, 174n101
Third Street A. M. E. Bethel, 131
31st Street Baptist Church, 141
Thompson, Harry, 109
Tillich, Paul, 101
Tinsley, Jesse, 106
Tisby, Jemar, 149, 159
tourism, 51, 98, 99, 146, 155

Trail of Enslaved Africans, ix, 141
Tredegar Iron Works, 13, 15, 17, 24, 73
Trenholm, George, 35
Trent, Martha Ann, 11
Truman, Harry S., 100
Trump, Donald J., 7
Truth and Reconciliation, 7, 148
Tucker, Elizabeth, 15
Tucker, H. St. George, Jr., 123, 128
Tucker, John Randolph, 168n1
Tucker, Rev. Beverly D., Jr., 79, 82, 83, 85, 86, 87, 89–90, 92, 108, 110, 168n1
Tyler, John, 37
Tyler, Margaret, 27, 161

Union Presbyterian Seminary, 130
Union Theological Seminary, 71, 119
United Confederate Veterans, 55, 73
United Daughters of the Confederacy, 53, 55, 60, 63, 73, 77, 97, 129, 142, 147
United Sons of Ham, 18
University of Virginia, 91, 141

Valentine, Mann S., 18, 25
Valentine, Sarah Benetta, 21–22, 24–26, 31
Virginia Association Opposed to Woman Suffrage, 80
Virginia Constitutional Convention (1902), 66–67, 74, 83
Virginia Council of Churches, 108, 111
Virginia Equal Suffrage League, 79–80
Virginia General Assembly, 19, 43, 66, 77, 80, 87–88, 92, 97, 109, 110, 118
Virginia Industrial School for Colored Girls, 70
Virginia Institute for Pastoral Care, 135
Virginia Interfaith Center for Public Policy, 145
Virginia State College, 92
Virginia Theological Seminary, 71, 114, 119
Virginia Union University, 88, 89, 187n11

Volunteer Emergency Foster Care, 135
voting rights, 79–80
Voting Rights Act (1965), 117

Walker, Annie Rose, 80
Walker, Maggie L., 84
Walker, Michelle, 151
Walker and Harris Tobacco Factory, 20
Waller, Odell, 109
Walton Act (1894), 66
Warwick, Abraham/Abram, 15, 26
Washington Hotel, 18
Washington, Janelle, 161
Weddell, Elizabeth Wright, 68
Weddell, Rev. Alexander, 45
Weeden, Agnes, 79
Wellford, McDonald "Mac," 112, 114–15
Westmoreland Club, 113
Wheat, James, Jr., 118
Whitcomb Court, 106
White, Rev. Robb, 45
Whitfield, C. Roger, 145
Wickham, Williams, 53
Wilder, L. Douglas, 140
William (enslaved man), 18
Williams, E. Randolph, 81, 87, 93, 104, 109
Williams, Mary Mason Anderson, 79–80
Williams, Rev. Robert, 90
Wilmer, Rev. Richard, 30
Wilson, Walker, 27, 161
Wineburg, Sam, 158
Wise, Henry A., Sr., 67
Wise, John S., 67
Woodbridge (Virginia), 4
Woodbridge, Rev. George, 30
Woodson, Carter G., 91, 116
Woodville Elementary School, 143–44, 145

Zion Union Association, 45

www.ingramcontent.com/pod-product-compliance
Lightning Source LLC
LaVergne TN
LVHW090252301225
828761LV00028B/370